BRITISH THEATRE AND THE RED PERIL

British Theatre and the Red Peril examines the portrayal of communism in plays written for the British theatre between 1917 and 1945, when contemporary commentators described the theatre as second only to the press in terms of its significance as a medium of communication. It demonstrates how, at a time when the capitalist system seemed on the verge of collapse, the theatre played a significant part in communicating and manipulating political propaganda in order to influence audiences. The book draws on published and unpublished scripts and archive documents and includes a chronological table of important events and productions between 1917 and 1945. It reveals explicit right-wing propaganda produced within mainstream British theatre and questions the assumption that political theatre is almost always left-wing.

'The author is careful to make the point that he is not in the business of seeking to unearth undiscovered gems. Rather, in six well-constructed chapters, he charts the response to plays dealing with the "Red Peril" from the terrified reaction of the early twenties, through the more inquisitive tone of the "intellectual" thirties to the paradoxical situation of the war years when the "evil empire" became an essential ally. He is equally illuminating on material that is more familiar, and sheds light on the extent to which the business of censorship during this period involved not just the Lord Chamberlain, but the Home Office, the Foreign Office and even the monarch.'
Dominic Shellard, *Department of English Literature, University of Sheffield*

Steve Nicholson is Head of Theatre Studies and Principal Lecturer at the University of Huddersfield. He studied at Exeter and Lancaster and worked with the White Horse Travelling Theatre before beginning his teaching career at the University of Leeds.

D0357972

EXETER PERFORMANCE STUDIES

Exeter Performance Studies aims to publish the best new scholarship from a variety of sources, presenting established authors alongside innovative work from new scholars. The list explores critically the relationship between theatre and history, relating performance studies to broader political, social and cultural contexts. It also includes titles which offer access to previously unavailable material.

Series editors: **Peter Thomson,** Professor of Drama at the University of Exeter; **Graham Ley,** Lecturer in Drama at the University of Exeter; **Steve Nicholson,** Head of Theatre Studies and Principal Lecturer at the University of Huddersfield.

BRITISH THEATRE AND THE RED PERIL

The Portrayal of Communism 1917–1945

Steve Nicholson

UNIVERSITY
of
EXETER
PRESS

First published in 1999 by
University of Exeter Press
Reed Hall, Streatham Drive
Exeter, Devon EX4 4QR
UK
www.ex.ac.uk/uep/

British Library Cataloguing in Publication Data
A catalogue record of this book is available from the British Library

Paperback ISBN 0 85989 637 4
Hardback ISBN 0 85989 636 6

Typeset in 11/13pt Caslon by Kestrel Data, Exeter

Printed and bound in Great Britain by
Short Run Press Ltd, Exeter

Contents

Illustrations

(Front cover)
The Red Light, New Theatre, 1931

(Following page xx)
1. *The Right to Strike*, Duke of York's, 1920

2. *The Silver Lining*, Ambassador's Theatre, 1921

3. *Yellow Sands*, Haymarket, 1926

4. *Yellow Sands*, Haymarket, 1926

5. *The Bear Dances*, Garrick Theatre, 1932

6. *Tovarich*, Lyric Theatre, 1935

7. *Tovarich*, Lyric Theatre, 1935

8. *Trial of a Judge*, Group Theatre, at Unity Theatre, 1938

9. *The Russians*, Old Vic Company, at The Playhouse, 1943

Preface and Acknowledgements

This book is about one particular aspect of political theatre in Britain between 1917 and 1945. It cuts across many possible alternative routes through the period by focusing on plays with a common, broad theme—those which in one way or another represented communism or the Soviet Union to British theatre audiences.

After the first two chapters, the material is treated on a broadly chronological basis. Before that, Chapter One introduces some of the relevant frames and contexts through which the material may be viewed, and Chapter Two examines three detailed examples to show some of the ways in which censorship was applied to plays which contained what the authorities considered to be an unacceptable political dimension. The next two chapters both deal with the period up until the end of the 1920s, the first looking at plays which were set in Britain, and the second at plays where the actual or symbolic setting was intended to stand for Soviet Russia. The fifth chapter spans the whole of the 1930s, and the last substantial chapter examines the very different period of the Second World War, during much of which Britain and the Soviet Union were military allies. Since not only the plays but many of the playwrights written about are likely to be unfamiliar, an appendix provides biographical information about the playwrights and further details about original performances, where these are available.

Identifying the politics of performances means entering into a hugely complex and contentious area of study, and although this book necessarily engages with such issues as audience and critical responses as well as with the formal theatrical constraints within which plays were written, there is much that is beyond its scope. Impossible though it may be to separate form and content—especially when talking about ideology —the main focus of the exploration here is on the written texts themselves, and the political messages which the plays communicated.

One of the reasons why this has seemed appropriate is that so very few of the plays discussed here are likely to be known to many readers. In a sense, the research for this book has been a process of excavation—or perhaps exhumation. It is not that the plays have been especially difficult to locate: while it is true that many of them have never been published, and that their performances were sometimes in private clubs rather than public venues, the fact that new scripts were almost always submitted to the Lord Chamberlain for licensing means that they have been collected. But for whatever reason, almost all of them are long forgotten and unfamiliar to practitioners and academics alike. By reopening some buried caskets and extracting at least fragments of their content, I hope to make it more possible for others to carry out quite different tests on the remains uncovered.

As well as interesting those who are concerned with the history and development of political theatre in Britain, I would suggest the findings must also contribute to our understanding of the social and political history of the period. There is no doubt that between 1917 and 1945, the theatre was one of the principal media for the communication of ideas; in one sense, then, this book is very much about propaganda. Not every playwright mentioned intentionally enlisted in a conspiracy to help defend capitalism and denigrate the alternatives—though some clearly did; but individual writers had only a limited say in what was and was not seen in theatres. The practice of control and management may not always have been effective or rigorous, but manipulation of the theatrical medium by both the exclusion of unwelcome material and the inappropriate definition of certain stories as 'harmless' or 'non-political' was nevertheless part of an important battle waged to retain the social order and the status quo.

Theatre of the 1920s and 1930s is not generally associated with politics—unless it is with the challenge of agit-prop which developed outside the mainstream. For example, in his retrospective commentary *The Turbulent Thirties*, J.C. Trewin asserts that

> To a drama historian of the future the Thirties will mean such diverse things as the plays of J.B. Priestley, James Bridie, Emlyn Williams . . . the Coward of *Private Lives* and *Cavalcade* and *Conversation Piece*; the work of 'Gordon Daviot' and . . . of Dodie Smith; Shaw's conversations . . . the last bitter plays of Maugham; the Gielgud classical seasons, the rise of the Old Vic, the flowering

of Olivier; the flourish of Drury Lane and its Novello musical plays
. . . Eliot's first verse dramas . . . the development of British ballet.[1]

Similarly, Ronald Blythe claims in *The Age of Illusion: England in the Twenties and Thirties* that 'the skies were falling but the attitude of the British theatre was "no comment" '.[2] There is, of course, a perfectly valid argument that the avoidance of political subjects is itself an effective political strategy, and plenty of escapist entertainment went on in theatres throughout the period covered by this book. That, however, we already knew. What I hope to begin to demonstrate here is the rather more surprising fact that there was also a substantial number of plays which engaged quite directly with explicit political narratives, contexts, themes and characters. And of course, this book is concerned only with one particular theme; there are many others which could be explored.

I began working on the material for this book a long time ago—indeed, it sometimes seems as if the span of the writing period matches that of the period under discussion. I am grateful to many people for their assistance, and should like in particular to express my gratitude to staff in the Study Room of the Theatre Museum for their help, and likewise to Kathryn Johnston and Sally Brown in the Manuscripts Department of the British Library. Also to Eric Norris (Master Bookseller) for a series of chases (some of them wild and involving geese), to Peter Ettridge for careful reading and to Richard Willis for his support. Most especially, I should like to thank my wife, Heather, for endless encouragement, patience and emptying of litter trays.

Finally, I should like to dedicate this book to my parents, Roy and Enid Nicholson, for whom this period was not an object of study but where they lived.

Brief Chronology

<table>
<tr><td>PLAYS</td><td>EVENTS</td></tr>
</table>

1918

Annajanska, The Wild Grand Duchess first performed at the Coliseum Theatre in January.

Bolsheviks dissolve Russian Parliament and transfer powers to Moscow; Czar executed.
British troops land in Russia to protect Czarist supplies.

The Russian Monk first submitted for licence in February. Never performed in public.

In November, Britain and Germany sign peace treaty; British War Cabinet decides to support White Army in Russia against the bolsheviks.

Reparation first performed in Lancaster in March.

British General Election won by Lloyd George and coalition government.

1919

The Bolshevik Peril first performed in Tredegar in March.

Russian Civil War continues; Churchill wants Britain to send further troops to help defeat bolsheviks. Policy opposed by Labour Party. The 'Hands off Russia' campaign is launched.

Joan of the Sword first performed in Norwich in June.

The Bolshevik first performed in Reptford in December.

Police and railway workers take strike action over wages and union rights.

1920

British dockers refuse to load ship believed to be supplying the White Army; the TUC threatens to call a General Strike if Britain intervenes to support the White Army.
Red Army defeats the Whites.

In August, the Communist Party of Great Britain is formed.

The Right To Strike opens at the Garrick Theatre in September.

Continuing discontent over wages and conditions leads to industrial action by miners and railway and transport workers; fearing revolution, the government introduces an Emergency Powers Act, and strikes are suspended.

It's All Wrong opens at The Queen's Theatre in London in December.

1921

The Silver Lining, The King's Favourite, and *Dream of a Winter Evening* performed together at the Ambassadors Theatre in March.

In June, the Labour Party Annual Conference rejects affiliation with Communist Party, which continues to apply for affiliation till 1928.

Ambrose Applejohn's Adventure opens at the Criterion Theatre in July (closes August 1922 after 454 performances).

The Terror opens at Liverpool Playhouse in September.

Publication of *The Image Breaker* by Eleanor Gray. No record of production.

1922

Mussolini forms Fascist
government in Italy.

The Beating on the Door opens at St
James's Theatre in November.

Conservatives under Bonar Law
defeat Lloyd George in General
Election.

Unemployed march from Glasgow
to London.

1923

Conservatives under Baldwin hold
power in General Election.

1924

Death of Lenin; Stalin takes power.

In January, first Labour
government elected under Ramsay
Macdonald, and in February Britain
recognises the Soviet Union. In
October, the Labour Party loses
power following the publication of
'Zinoviev Letter'. Baldwin becomes
Prime Minister.

Society for Cultural Relations with
the USSR is founded.

1925

The Grand Duchess first performed
at the Globe Theatre in January.

First Blood first performed in
Stockport.

Labour Party Conference makes
individual members of the
Communist Party ineligible for
Labour Party membership, and
requests Trade Unions not to send
communists as delegates.

1926

The Forcing House first performed at the Little Theatre in February.

A Place in the Shade first performed at the Regent Theatre in February.

Trotsky expelled from Moscow.

Labour On Top first performed at the Hippodrome, Hulme, in May.

Hearts and Diamonds first performed at the Strand in May.

What Might Happen first performed at the Savoy Theatre in June.

Yellow Sands first performed at the Haymarket in November.

Following the strike by British miners, there is a General Strike in May; this is ended in less than a week, though the miners' strike continues. Before and during the strike, members of the British Communist Party are arrested and tried under the Incitement to Mutiny Act, and houses and Party headquarters are raided.

1927

Red Nights of the Tcheka first performed at the Festival Theatre, Cambridge, in May.

In May, Britain breaks off trade relations with the Soviet Union, following police raids on a British company suspected of espionage.

The Volga Boatman (first version) first performed in Mexborough in September.

In September, the British TUC suspends relations with the USSR.

Paul I first performed at the Court Theatre in October.

British Broadcasting Company formed.

First sound film made.

1928

Shadows of Strife first performed in Sheffield in March.

Such Men are Dangerous opens at the Duke of York's in September, following provincial tour.

In Britain, women get the vote on equal basis with men.

xiii

1929

The Volga Boatman (second version) first performed at Carshalton in February.

Red Rust first performed at the Little Theatre in February.

Trotsky expelled from the Soviet Union.

Lenin first performed at the Royalty Theatre in February as part of the trilogy, *Peace, War and Revolution.*

Rasputin first performed by the Stage Society in April.

In May, Ramsay Macdonald forms a minority Labour government after the General Election.

Red Sunday first performed at the Arts Theatre in June.

1930

Daily Worker begins publication.

1931

Britain in grip of Depression; by December, 2.5 million are out of work.

Mosley leaves the British Labour Party and forms the New Party.

Roar China refused a licence for public performance at Cambridge. Performed privately in Manchester by the Unnamed Society in November.

The Red Light first performed at the New Theatre in November.

September Budget imposes pay cuts on ministers, judges, armed forces, teachers and unemployed; in October, the British naval force at Invergorden mutinies; the Labour government collapses and is succeeded by a coalition National Government under Macdonald, which wins large majority in General Election.

1932

World Disarmament Conference opens in Geneva (February).

Unemployment in Britain reaches its highest pre-war level; In July, hunger marchers demonstrate in London.

The Bear Dances first performed at the Garrick Theatre in November.

Mosley founds British Union of Fascists.

1933

When the Crash Comes first performed at the Birmingham Repertory Theatre in March.

Hitler becomes German Chancellor in January, and Reichstag fire is blamed on communists.

The People's Court first performed at the Embassy Theatre in April.

Germany withdraws from League of Nations (October).

Oxford Union passes resolution that 'this House will in no circumstances fight for King and Country'; a Conservative candidate advocating increased military spending defeated by Labour in by-election.

1934

Stalin begins purge of Communist Party.

Mosley speaks at Olympia—extreme violence perpetrated by his followers is debated in Parliament.

British government announces new plans for re-armament, and in December the London Disarmament conference ends without agreement; Peace Pledge

Union is founded, quickly reaching a membership of 100,000.

USSR admitted to League of Nations.

Left Review begins publication.

1935

Tovarich first performed at the Lyric Theatre in April.

Show trials in the Soviet Union.

Silver Jubilee of George V (May).

Land's End first performed at the People's Theatre in Newcastle in May.

Baldwin replaces Macdonald as Prime Minister; Atlee becomes leader of the Labour Party. National Government retains a large majority.

The British Communist Party abandons its policy of attacking all classes other than the workers, in favour of building united platform against Fascism.

Founding of Left Book Club.

1936

Civil War begins in Spain; many people from Britain join the International Brigade to fight against Franco.

Hitler wins 99% of the vote in election.

Bees on the Boat Deck first performed at the Lyric in May.

George V dies; Succession and Abdication of Edward VIII.

Crossroads first performed at Croydon in September.

In October, unemployed march from Jarrow to London.

Mosley tries to lead anti-Jewish march through London, but is prevented by determined resistance.

Where's That Bomb first performed at Unity Theatre in London in November.

Public Order Act passed, prohibiting political uniforms and empowering the police to ban processions.

BBC Television begins broadcasting.

Unity Theatre formed.

1937

Russian Roundabout first performed in Glasgow in January.

Moscow show trials and execution of leaders and generals.

The Fall of the House of Slusher first performed at Unity Theatre in London in March.

George VI crowned.

Chamberlain succeeds Baldwin as Prime Minister.

Tsar Lénine first produced at the Westminster Theatre in June.

Halifax visits Hitler in policy of appeasement.

Distant Point first performed at the Gate Theatre in November.

Britain forbids recruitment of subjects to help Republicans in Spain.

Aristocrats first performed at Unity Theatre in London in December.

London busmen strike (May).

1938

In February, British Foreign Secretary, Eden, resigns in protest against policy of appeasement towards Hitler.

Trial of a Judge first performed by Group Theatre—at Unity Theatre—in March.

In March, German troops invade Austria.

Britain recognises Italian sovereignty in Ethiopia, and negotiations between Hitler and Chamberlain lead to a Munich agreement over Czechoslovakia.

Geneva first performed at Malvern in August.

Trenches for air raid shelters are dug in London parks; gas masks and blackout precautions are distributed.

Demonstration by unemployed people blocks Oxford Street.

1939

Britain recognises Franco's Fascist government in Spain.

German troops enter Czechoslovakia.

Britain gives a guarantee to Poland that it will help defend it if Poland is attacked.

Russia and Germany sign pact of non-aggression; Germany invades Poland; in September, Britain and France declare war on Germany.

In November, the Soviet Union invades Finland.

1940

The Star Turns Red first performed at Unity Theatre in March.

Finland signs a peace treaty with the Soviet Union.

Strike Me Red first performed at the David Lewis Theatre in Liverpool in May.

Launcelot's Dream first produced in 1940/41 by Teeside Unity Theatre.

Jack and the Giant Killer first performed by Unity Theatre.

German forces advance through Europe into France.

Churchill replaces Chamberlain as Prime Minister.

Battle of Britain and the Blitz.

Trotsky assassinated in Mexico.

1941

According to Plan and *Erna Kremer of Ebenstadt* first performed by London's Unity Theatre in March.

The Spectre that Haunts Europe submitted to the Lord Chamberlainin September. Not licensed for public performance.

Alexander Nevsky and *Salute to the New Year* both first broadcast on BBC radio in December.

Dostiageff and the Others first performed by London's Unity Theatre.

Rudolf Hess, Hitler's deputy, lands in Scotland, apparently expecting high-level support for his government.

Germany breaks its pact and invades the Soviet Union.

1942

Salute to the U.S.S.R. first broadcast on radio in April.

An Agreement of the Peoples first performed at Earl's Court in June.

The Cave by Y. Galitzky published in *Our Time* in June. No record of public performance.

In May, Britain and the Soviet Union sign a treaty of friendship.

Membership of the British Communist Party reaches 56,000, from 12,000 in 1941.

Russians desperately resist German forces in the Siege of Leningrad.

House of Regrets first performed at the Arts Theatre in October.

Huge demonstrations in Trafalgar Square to support the opening of a Second Front against Hitler in order to relieve the Russians.

1943

Salute to the Red Army performed at the Royal Albert Hall in February.

The Russians first performed at the Playhouse in June.

Alliance for Victory first performed in June.

The Spirit of Russia first broadcast on radio in November.

Meeting of Churchill, Roosevelt and Stalin (November).

We Are Advancing and *Ring in the New* both first broadcast on radio in December.

1944

Publication of *Soviet One-Act Plays*, edited by Herbert Marshall, in 1944.

In October, Churchill visits Moscow.

Comrade Detective first performed by Unity Theatre in London in December.

1945

Yalta agreement between Britain, USA and USSR (February).

The March Hare Resigns first broadcast on radio in March.

Germans surrender (May).

Landslide Labour victory in British General Election (July).

1946

Salute to All Fools first broadcast on radio in April.

GARRICK THEATRE

DAILY MIRROR MATINEE.

"THE RIGHT TO STRIKE" is not a propaganda play, but it raises a number of vitally important questions. In this play, doctors propose to withhold professional skill needed to succour a striker's wife because the strike, undertaken by workers in an essential national service, inflicts suffering upon people not parties to the dispute.

As the middle classes are restive under threats af national strikes and talk of counter-strikes the audience is invited to say whether such reprisals are justified. The voting papers should be given to the attendants at the exits after the performance, so that the result may be given in to-morrow's DAILY MIRROR. The short expressions of opinion should be posted early, and addressed The Editor, The Daily Mirror, Bouverie Street, London, and endorsed "Matinee.

1) The *Daily Mirror* invited audience members at certain performances of *The Right to Strike* in 1920 to vote for or against the doctors' decision to strike.

2) The programme cover for a trilogy of plays including *The Silver Lining*, performed at the Ambassador's Theatre in 1921. (*Courtesy of the V&A Picture Library.*)

JOE : " You'll help to look after the under-dogs—the best we can, together?"
LYDIA : " No, Joe. You'll look after the under-dogs—and I'll look after you."

3) The final image of *Yellow Sands* as the Bolshevik repents and finds true love. As the stage direction put it: 'For the first time in the play Joe's face breaks into a smile, and they kiss'. Frank Vosper as Joe Varwell and Muriel Hewitt as Lydia. (*Courtesy of the V&A Picture Library.*)

THE BOLSHIE'S WOOING

Lydia Blake . . . . Miss Muriel Hewitt.

4) Haselden's cartoon in *Punch* satirising the communist approach to love-making in *Yellow Sands*. (*Reproduced with permission of* Punch *Ltd.*)

GARRICK THEATRE,
17th October, 1932.

"THE BEAR DANCES"

Prominent publicists are assuring us that Europe is becoming "Russia-minded." It is indisputable that our Western civilisation is watching, with bated breath, the outcome of the experiment of the U.S.S.R. Is Russia in her birth-throes giving life to a torch-bearer in the van of civilisation, or to a monster which, if allowed to flourish, may devastate the world as we know it?

THE ANSWER IS VITAL

to each and all of us, for the problem of Russia to-day is the problem of the civilised world to-morrow.

Knowing the interest which you take in this subject, I venture to draw your attention to this tragi-comedy of Soviet Russia — "THE BEAR DANCES" — which Mr. LEON M. LION is presenting at the GARRICK THEATRE, on October 31st. next.

The Author, Mr. F. L. LUCAS, the novelist and critic, has set out to show Russia as she really is to-day—through the lives of her fanatic youth, of her peasants, and of the doomed "former people." The comedy, the thrill and the glamour of this strange country's stranger turmoils have, for fifteen years, been crying aloud for dramatisation, and in "THE BEAR DANCES" the Author has achieved a play that is, not propaganda, but drama.

ELENA MIRAMOVA and OLGA LINDO

will interpret the two strange sisters, and other principals in the long cast of 40 odd characters will include—

HENRY HEWITT,
HENRY VIBART,
ABRAHAM SOFAER,
GYLES ISHAM,
and
MAURICE BROWNE

The decor and design are being carried out by Robert Lutyens.

Already there is a rush of reservations for the first week. May I suggest that you leave your booking at the Box Office before ten o'clock to-night,

CHARLES LANDSTONE,
Business Manager.

5) Publicity leaflet for F.L. Lucas's *The Bear Dances* at the Garrick Theatre in 1932.

Tovarich, 1935:

6) *above*, Evelyn Roberts as Charles Dupont discovers that his servants are Russian aristocratic emigrés; Eugenie Leontovich as the Archduchess Tatiana and Cedric Hardwicke as Prince Mikail.

7) *left*, Francis L. Sullivan as the Soviet Commissar and Eugenie Leontovich as Tatiana. As the caption put it: 'In the past, and under his hands, the Archduchess was bestially treated by the Commissar before she was allowed to escape from Russia'.

(Both from an unidentifiable periodical. Courtesy of the V&A Picture Library.)

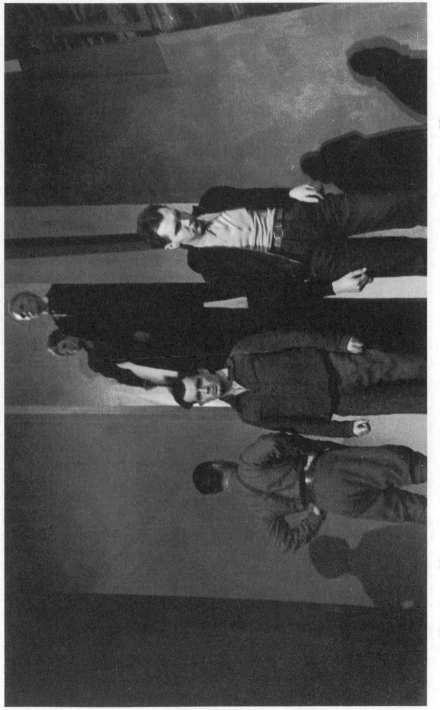

8) The Group Theatre production of Stephen Spender's *Trial of a Judge* performed at Unity Theatre, 1938. (*Courtesy of Humphrey Spender.*)

9) Olga Lindo as Marya and Russell Thorndike as The Quisling Mayor in *The Russians*, 1943. (*Photograph originally published in Picture Post. Courtesy of the V&A Picture Library.*)

1

Not a Political Arena?

EVELINE: I can't think why you go on working, working, working like you do; making more and more money, when we've already got far more than we'll ever know what to do with.
SIR REGINALD: Well, I go on for the simple reason that I can't stop.[1]

In 1892 the Lord Chamberlain's Chief Examiner of Plays claimed that the public would not 'care to have places of amusement turned into political arenas', and in 1909 his successor told the Parliamentary Joint Select Committee investigating theatre censorship that 'the stage is not a political arena', and that it was 'not desirable that specially important political questions' should be discussed there.[2] Given the control exerted by the censorship over what could be publicly performed, these two statements would seem likely to confirm the assumption that what was going on inside theatres in the first half of the twentieth century had little connection to what was going on outside. Shaw, Galsworthy, Granville-Barker and Priestley are among the few British writers whose plays are recognised as contradicting this rule, though the achievements outside the mainstream of such initiatives as the Workers' Theatre Movement, Unity Theatre, the Group Theatre and Theatre of Action have been more recently documented and celebrated.[3]

This book will question the supposed absence of political theatre from mainstream culture, by examining some of the plays and performances written or produced in Britain between 1917 and 1945 which purported to offer audiences a demonstration of left-wing ideology in action. Through focusing on this one strand of political drama, consisting of plays linked by their theme, it becomes clear that politicised narratives had a much stronger presence in the culture of the inter-war period than has previously been recognised. It is also important to say at the outset that many of these plays were far from obscure or unimportant when they were originally presented, even though they have largely failed to survive as performance texts or to feature in recorded accounts of the period.

If it is the case that political plays of this period have been neglected, one must next ask why it might be important to rediscover them. Are unjustly forgotten masterpieces about to re-emerge? A few of the plays considered here are indeed stimulating in their own right and merit greater attention, yet it must be admitted that many others would deserve to remain in dusty obscurity if the sole criteria for selection were aesthetic value and literary or theatrical quality. There are other reasons, I suggest, why they need to be recovered. Writing in 1929, the playwright and theatre critic Hubert Griffith had no doubt that 'theatre, if left alone, is the one institution popular and powerful enough to counteract the influence of the Press'.[4] Certainly there is evidence that performances frequently generated argument and confrontation both within and well beyond the auditorium, and, rightly or wrongly, theatre was perceived by both the Left and the Right, by politicians and by commentators, to be one of the principal avenues through which ideas could be spread and audiences influenced. The very fact that a text could be freely published and read, but had to secure a licence from the Lord Chamberlain before it could be staged in public, indicates the extent to which performance was identified as a force which needed to be managed. Theatre was one of the principal sites for reinforcing or, potentially, for challenging ideological positions masquerading as self-evident truths; that being so, a fuller understanding of the nature and range of political performances may not only add to our knowledge of the history of British theatre in the twentieth century, but also make a contribution to our historical reading of national and world events of these decades.

In reassessing the theatre of the twenties and thirties, we are therefore not only looking at the plays and productions themselves but also at what was and was not permitted in public performances. On the most straightforward level this concerns overt censorship, and it is worth remembering, for example, that throughout the thirties one of the rules of practice for the Lord Chamberlain was to refuse licences to any plays critical of the Nazis. However, outright legal censorship is only the most obvious way of controlling communication. Consent can be manufactured and organised in more subtle ways, and how the boundaries of the 'normal' are established through critical responses becomes equally important. Nevertheless, perhaps nothing shows more clearly the impossibility of defining as a single, coherent entity the period of nearly thirty years covered in this book than the changing policies and actions of the censors. Because what was said and shown in the theatre was seen by governments, by royalty, by newspapers and by other vested interests to matter so much, the changing world outside theatre constantly redefined the possible content and perspectives of the world inside. The sudden change in 1941 when the Soviet Union became Britain's most important ally against the Nazis is only the most extreme example of this, but the attempted control and manipulation of performance content during the Second World War made it worth continuing this study beyond the end of the thirties.

The extent of political censorship in the theatre has been consistently underestimated in written histories. In a book which is perhaps revealingly dedicated 'to the Lord Chamberlains who wielded the blue pencil and to their Examiners of Plays', John Johnston, who worked in the Lord Chamberlain's Office during its last days, argues the opposite of this, suggesting that the case against censorship has been exaggerated. He insists that the Lord Chamberlain saw it as his 'duty to allow all plays submitted to him unless there seemed to be clear and unmistakable reasons to disallow them'. But writers and managers knew the constraints within which they were required to operate, and Johnston explicitly endorses the suppression which took place before plays even reached the Lord Chamberlain:

> Theatre managers were the first link in the censorship chain for they were known to alter some texts themselves, and, in so doing, saved the Examiner quite a lot of work.[5]

It is true that a relatively small number of plays were banned outright, but the real power of censorship is often insidious rather than conspicuous. The fact that relatively few totally unacceptable scripts ever got as far as being submitted—or even written—merely proves the effectiveness of the system. Most writers were not inclined to risk wasting their time working on something which they judged unlikely to be passed for performance, and self-censorship was, as always, an integral part of the method of control.

Victims and critics of the system typically complained that 'plays running counter to any governmental policy' were in effect 'condemned from the very outset'.[6] There is some evidence of writers abandoning the stage and no shortage of playwrights complaining both about the difficulty of airing important issues on the stage at all, and about the censorship of particular opinions. In 1934, Griffith lamented the

> 'unborn children'—the plays that a generation of intelligent young dramatists might have liked to have written but had been warned that they must not write.[7]

The Lord Chamberlain may well have preferred to see himself as a licensor rather than as a censor, as Johnston claims, but this is no more than the usual conceit, conscious or unconscious, of all who impose rules that others must obey. The fact is that plays were freely passed only if they endorsed rather than challenged a certain view of the world, and successive Lord Chamberlains, Examiners and Advisers had few qualms or reservations about acting as the nation's conscience, conveniently confident that what served the interests of the ruling class of society served the interests of the whole country.

It can be argued that theatre censorship was not primarily 'political' in a narrow sense, but was rooted in moral beliefs and certainties. But it was also inevitably and crucially informed by the assumption that the main function of theatre was to entertain. Hubert Griffith argued that censorship was invariably directed against 'the subjects about which intelligent people most readily talk', and that

> every dramatic author who has anything new or vital to say about them has been politely (or peremptorily) warned by the Censor that he had better not say it.[8]

Other writers claimed that the Lord Chamberlain was quite deliberately engaged in 'isolating as far as possible the theatre from the intellectual and imaginative life of the time', and that censorship set out to prevent the expression of

> opinions and reflections which may disturb the status quo of current morality against which sincere modern thought incessantly inveighs.[9]

4

George Bernard Shaw blamed him for the lack of intelligent thought in theatre, and in a telling phrase described British drama as 'shallow-hearted propaganda of gaiety'.[10]

Distracting people from injustice and oppression by entertaining them is, of course, a routine strategy employed by those who hold power. No performance can be neutral in the view it expresses of the world, and to avoid political issues is to act politically. This is perhaps especially true in a society on the verge of cataclysmic upheavals. Meanwhile, the absolute demonising of the Soviet Union and the bolsheviks by much of the media meant that they could be represented in fictions as touchstones of depravity, and used as easy reference points without any need for writers or audiences to engage with real political issues. For most people in Britain, bolshevism was not seen to embody a plausible political alternative, but as evil incarnate, and just as nineteenth-century melodramas had often depended on villains whose malevolent and ruthless actions sprang from a perverse enjoyment of evil for its own sake, so the emergence of the Soviet Union allowed the perpetuation and the revival of a theatrical genre which was already old-fashioned. Politics—of a certain kind—became a proper subject for entertainment, and while it is not the intention of this book to defend or to rewrite the history of the Soviet Union, there is, I think, a value in seeing what is revealed by excavating the undocumented British theatre of propaganda from the 1920s and 1930s. As Vic Allen put it in *The Russians are Coming*, an analysis of western culture's depictions of communism over sixty years, anti-Sovietism became 'an essential element of capitalist ideology'.[11]

As the title suggests, the majority of texts considered in this book aimed broadly to confirm rather than confront the basic structures of a capitalist society, and there were three basic narrative frames through which such plays supposedly exposed the dangers of left-wing ideology. The first focused on the possibility (though the inevitable failure) of a revolutionary uprising within Britain; the second dramatised an actual or imaginary revolution which had taken place elsewhere, often presenting the corruption and terror which resulted, but occasionally acknowledging an element of impractical idealism; the last lamented the problems of the former Russian aristocracy, forced since 1917 to live in anonymous exile elsewhere in Europe. The variations of plot, character, tone, emphasis and sympathy were no doubt partly due to the differing views of individual playwrights, but they can also be seen to relate to

5

broader and changing perspectives within British society. For example, most plays of the early twenties treated the possibility of bolshevik rule as virtually indistinguishable from Armageddon itself; by the thirties, a number of plays were questioning whether it would really make much difference to anything if Britain were ruled by a communist government.

It is probably no coincidence that plays which asserted the inevitability and unalterability of society's structures also failed to challenge or extend theatrical conventions. Believing its values and existence in danger, the writers who defended the status quo in the early twenties attacked its enemies through a theatre of abuse rather than one of argument. Labels such as 'Communist', 'Bolshevik', 'Left-wing' and 'Red' were frequently bandied about and assigned in ways which those who acknowledged those identities would hardly have recognised. Even Somerset Maugham's plays could be denounced as 'Bolshevistic' while a thriller about burglary and blackmail, with no recognisably political dimension at all, used the title of *The Bolshevik* simply to signify, in the words of one character, 'a human monster . . . without heart, pity, or conscience'.[12] Such definition through usage not only reflected but also shaped the way in which left-wing positions could be perceived.

Typically, the language of extreme melodrama was employed to caricature the Left as sadistic and bloodthirsty enemies of all virtue and civilisation. Consider the theatrical language of the first Act climax of *Red Nights of the Tcheka*, a drama in the 'Grand Guignol' style about the savage persecution of White Russians by Reds:

> LEADER: You are Serge Nicolaievitch, Prince Bologdine, one-time officer of the Tzar. [*Giving him a cut, full in the face, with the cane which he holds in his hand*] Take that! You know what awaits you now?
> PRINCE: [*throwing back his bleeding head and defying him*] Yes. That which you have done to hundreds of thousands of Russians who have committed no other crime than that of loving their country; the honour of being tortured by rabble! . . .
> LEADER: All! To suppress them all! Until there is not one left in Russia, nor on the whole Earth.
> *END OF ACT I*[13]

Yet perhaps of equal importance is the way in which those playwrights credited with having constructed a more 'balanced' argument between Left and Right were constrained by the form and conventions available to them. In reviewing *The Right to Strike* in 1920, one of the more perceptive critics comments on how an intelligent play of debate about the rights and wrongs of withholding one's labour if this inflicts suffering on others has ultimately felt the need to trivialise itself and provide a closed ending, because an audience inevitably requires 'the feather pillow of sentiment as a rest for its too suddenly active head'.[14] In the thirties, when some left-wing writers and practitioners did recognise the need to develop new ways of speaking, most reviewers persisted in their suspicion and antagonism towards any theatrical form which dared to challenge the dominant mode of superficial naturalism.

How audiences responded to the frequently crude and didactic messages which were thrust at them by anti-communist theatrical propaganda is harder to gauge, but they were not always silently respectful, or uniformly willing to accept them at face value. Indeed, the terms in which audience behaviour was discussed in newspapers is sometimes more reminiscent for us of descriptions of football supporters than of theatre-goers:

> The majority of gallery frequenters are estimable people, second to none in their enthusiastic support of the drama. There is, unfortun-ately, a hysterical and unbalanced minority that brings the rest of the gallery into disrepute.[15]

In 1920, *The Right to Strike* provoked fighting in the auditorium, a series of articles in *The Times*, a poll conducted through the *Daily Mirror* about whether doctors should be allowed to strike, and the interrogation of the play's producer by the King.[16]

Today, it may seem hard to believe that the theatre could have been seen as so influential in forming public opinion and perceptions. But if we doubt how vital it was it is only necessary to look at how seriously its control was taken by those in power, and the high political levels at which it was discussed. In 1929, for example, Hubert Griffith wrote a historical drama about the Russian Revolution which was produced at the Arts Theatre by Fyodor Komisarjevsky; *Red Sunday* received only four private performances, yet it provoked both a member of the exiled Russian royal family and the former Russian Finance Minister to complain to Buckingham Palace; *The Times* wrote a long leader denouncing the play, the King discussed it with the Lord Chamberlain, and the licence which would have allowed the play to be more widely performed was refused for reasons which were never revealed to the playwright.

I began this chapter with an extract from *Reparation*, an unextra-ordinary and apparently domestic play written in 1918 to tour provincial theatres on a 'twice nightly' basis. The text exemplifies several significant issues which will recur in this book. First, although *Reparation* is ostensibly a crime thriller, there is a strong, if crude, ideological undercurrent to the narrative; while it would not have been billed as a political play, politics is nonetheless woven through the dialogue and the narrative. Second, it is immediately apparent on reading it today how the theatrical vocabulary and form restrict the potential of the ideological debate; while other European theatres experimented with new theatre forms and techniques and with actor/audience relationships, most British theatre clung desperately to antiquated methods and assumptions rooted in the previous century. Since the politics of performance reside in the form and process of construction as well as in the content, this inevitably limited what could be considered and communicated. Third, the stance adopted by *Reparation* is broadly typical of a number of the plays to be discussed, in that though far from demanding a radical upheaval of economic and political structures, it argues not, as might be expected, for things to remain unchanged, but that some tinkering through social and especially economic reform is essential if Britain is to remain as a united nation, at peace with itself.

It is true that Sir Reginald, the successful business man in the play, sees the structures of society as both unalterable and without need of alteration:

> Now the world lives by what is called commerce and this is like the flywheel of an engine. The hub of the wheel is the money market—the spokes represent the capitalists and the financiers. And the millions of workers who toil for the wages they earn are the outer rim of the wheel. The whole goes round and round in one endless whirl. The power of the engine is transmitted from the hub of the wheel, by the spokes, to the rim; but it is the weight of the rim which keeps the engine running. It is a perfectly balanced piece of machinery, but the moment any part gives way the balance of the wheel is destroyed, and the engine runs badly.

To him, any attempts to alleviate the inequalities and the sufferings of the poor are part of the 'cursed system of charity' which is itself the cause of the problem, and which degrades both giver and recipient. Workhouses and prisons are the only necessary provisions for the poor, and Sir Reginald insists he will be 'no party to the forcing of doles upon people'.

Yet the play is not on his side, and the fire blazing in the hearth behind him, as he calmly stands expounding his views in a Victorian sitting-room, may represent a more dangerous possibility than warmth and security. It is his daughter's views, based on instinct rather than on logical argument, which are clearly intended to be much more sympathetic, in a play which was produced in the year in which some British women first obtained the vote:

> Ah! but it seems so wrong to me that we should have so much when there are other poor people with nothing in the world. Dad, I wish you would let me help them. There are so many charities I would like to do something for.[17]

The playwright's unambiguous moral conclusively endorses the daughter's view as Sir Reginald unwittingly kills his own son, who has become a house burglar because of his father's uncompromising severity and meanness. The implication of what the Lord Chamberlain called 'a rather stupid play of coincidence' is that the wealthy must learn to be charitable to those less fortunate than themselves, since the poor are the children and dependents of the rich. The evolution of a more humane and democratic capitalism is essential if the nation is to survive as a cohesive and 'family' unit. Otherwise, the danger threatening to insert the spanner into Sir Reginald's supposedly perfect system was, felt many, real enough.

2

The Revolution will not be Dramatised

The British Public must be maintained in its delusions, like a lunatic beyond hope of recovery, and shut away from its possibility of arriving one step nearer the truth.[1]

When Geo. DeGray, a prolific playwright and producer, sent *The Russian Monk* to the Lord Chamberlain in 1918, the costumes and scenery were already prepared for an extensive tour of major provincial theatres, and he had no reason to doubt that his play would receive a licence.[2] DeGray had written a jingoistic melodrama, and he probably expected that the combination of topicality, action and patriotism, with a touch of the supernatural, would be the ideal basis for success. Yet though he was to spend several years trying to get permission, the allusions to recent political events and actual historical figures prevented *The Russian Monk* from ever being licensed for public performance. In 1918, the Lord Chamberlain, acting on instructions from the government, decided that to allow this melodrama, harmless though it probably was in itself, would make it harder for him to refuse more challenging and subversive dramas dealing with the same subject matter, and might actually encourage other playwrights:

It is probably only the first of many we shall get on this unsavoury subject, *raison de plus* to nip the movement in the bud.

Censorship and control of the theatre is a crucial context against and within which all political drama of this period needs to be seen, and it is an issue which will frequently be referred to in later chapters. The limits of what could and could not be said may have varied greatly at different times, but boundaries always existed. Thus, for example, in reviewing Austin Page's *The Beating on the Door* in 1922, a play which showed at least some understanding of the ideals of the communists, even though it ended by depicting them as the epitome of evil, the *Observer* commented that

> a pro-Bolshevist play would have been interesting and difficult to write, but it might have had trouble with the Censor.[3]

That remark could actually be applied throughout the period covered in this book, and before embarking on a chronological study of the plays it is appropriate to consider some general points about stage censorship, by focusing in detail on three examples of plays which, for explicit political reasons, were never licensed for public performance.

The immediate origins of theatre censorship lay in Walpole's Parliamentary Act of 1737, which had been specifically designed to prevent criticism from the stage of his government and himself. Under this Act, no play was to be performed without first being licensed by the Lord Chamberlain, and since there were no stated rules or guidance as to what he should or should not allow, power was effectively left in the hands of one individual, and subsequently with his Examiners of Plays and those members of the Establishment whose opinions he might choose to consult. The suppression of unwelcome views drove dissident writers such as Henry Fielding out of the theatre, and, in the disingenuous words of John Johnston, Walpole's innovation was so efficacious that before long 'little political censorship needed to be exercised'.[4] Censorship is probably at its most successful when it can remain invisible and unperceived, preventing subversive material from even being created.

In 1843, the Theatres Act confirmed and expanded the powers of the Lord Chamberlain, indicating that he should refuse a licence whenever he was 'of opinion that it is fitting for the preservation of good manners, decorum or of the public peace so to do'.[5] Artistic opposition to stage censorship increased towards the end of the nineteenth century, and in 1909 the government set up a Joint Select Committee 'to report any alterations of the law or practice which may appear desirable'.[6] However, with the support of most theatre managers and actors, the 1909 Committee again confirmed the need for censorship, while attempting to categorise the principles more precisely. Of the seven reasons for which they concluded a licence might reasonably be refused, at least three had direct political implications. The Committee agreed that a play should not 'represent on the stage in an invidious manner a living person, or any person recently dead', that it should not 'be calculated to impair friendly relations with any Foreign Power', and that it should not 'be calculated to cause a breach of the peace'.[7] Yet without much tighter and more explicit definitions, the scope for different interpretations remained considerable. Moreover, the Committee's recommendations were neither binding nor inclusive since no legislation was introduced, and the Lord Chamberlain remained free not only to interpret the terms as he chose, but also to ignore them or to refuse a licence on other grounds which he was not required to justify.

There had never been much expectation that those appointed as Lord Chamberlain or as his official Reader should demonstrate particular qualifications or suitability for undertaking their duties, and a newspaper editor, a bank manager and the author of a vulgar farce all held the post of Examiner of Plays. No training was given when an appointment was made, and the process of licensing or refusing plays undoubtedly contained a considerable degree of arbitrariness and personal whim. There was no procedure for appealing against the decisions, and the Lord Chamberlain was not answerable even to Parliament or required to explain his decisions; an anomaly which further irritated serious playwrights and theatre-goers was that music-halls remained outside his authority, and were therefore theoretically free to treat in a frivolous manner issues which could not even be mentioned within the 'legitimate theatre'.

Perhaps surprisingly, the 1909 Report recommended that submission of a play for licence should be optional, and that unlicensed plays could be legally performed; in practice, however, theatre managers were certain to continue insisting on licences as security against potential prosecutions under other laws. As George Bernard Shaw understood, a licence provided the manager

> with an effective insurance against the author getting him into trouble, and a complete relief from all conscientious responsibility for the character of the entertainment at his theatre.

It was theatre managers rather than playwrights who were liable for prosecution if performances broke the law, and since most of these were business men without the expertise to understand either legal niceties or the intentions of a writer, it was the manager who was sheltered by the Lord Chamberlain's decision:

> The granting of the licence practically places him above the law . . . the Lord Chamberlain could not be put into the dock; and the manager could not decently be convicted when he could produce in his defence a certificate from the chief officer of the King's Household that the play was a proper one.[8]

The standard procedure when a new play was to be produced was for a script to be submitted for licensing by the manager of the theatre where it was to be performed. Providing the Reader's Report indicated nothing contentious, the Lord Chamberlain licensed the script without reading it himself, though cuts or substitutions were frequently demanded. As Johnston tactfully puts it, managers generally found themselves 'able to adapt their work to meet the Lord Chamberlain's requirements', irrespective of the sensibilities of the writer. Indeed, the lack of respect paid to the playwright can be gauged from Johnston's unironic observation, based on his personal experience, that when requests for changes in a submitted text were made

> it was open to the manager of the theatre, or the producer or director of the play, to come and discuss these points with us, *and often the author would come too*.[9] [my emphasis]

According to DeGray, *The Russian Monk* was not a political play but simply presented what his publicity called 'astounding incidents in the life of the Infamous Rasputin'.[10] However, the play's background was the overthrowing of an aristocratic regime—related, of course, to the British royal family—by the Russian Revolution, and it was this which made it unacceptable. Considering when the play was written, it is not surprising to find that it is actually Germany rather than Russia which represents evil, with Rasputin turning out to be a German secret agent; but the political setting is merely the backdrop against which the villainous and evil Rasputin seeks

> WEALTH, and the power it gives to squeeze mankind in the hollow of my hand, and one day sway the destinies of Europe.

Rasputin is shown from childhood onwards to be self-consciously evil in the most exaggerated nineteenth-century tradition:

> FATHER ANSOLEM: Have you no conscience?
> RASPUTIN: No.
> FATHER ANSOLEM: Have you no sense of gratitude?
> RASPUTIN: None.
> FATHER ANSOLEM: Have you no soul?
> RASPUTIN: No.

Fanatically committed to destroying the better world which is un-equivocally represented by Britain, Rasputin goes on to use drugs to manipulate the Czar into signing a secret peace agreement with the Germans. The wish to oppose Britain is seen by the play as the wish to challenge civilisation itself:

> RASPUTIN: The country I serve is all-powerful and will yet be master of the world
> GENERAL: WE are fighting for FREEDOM, and will never own a master.
> RASPUTIN: Aye, THAT is Britain's teaching—and that's why I hate England . . . because she is the great civilizer of the globe—because she's fighting for Freedom. Of all Nations who are linked against us, I hate England most. I hate her—I hate her—I hate her. (*both fists on table*)

The play includes typical war-time propaganda of the most extreme kind, in which the tone is absurdly pro-British throughout. In one highly emotive scene, the Czar is on the point of signing the peace treaty with the Germans when he is reminded of his true duty by the sound of 'Rule, Britannia' being sung off-stage, and in the end, it is entirely thanks to a heroic British officer, that Rasputin is defeated:

> CHARTERIS: He may hypnotise your Empress, he may hypnotise the dupes and fools around him, but he won't hypnotise Great Britain.

Yet DeGray carefully exonerates the Czar from blame, and the final curtain falls as he bemoans his trials and tribulations:

Cheated by my friends, and deceived by those I trusted . . . condemned to be the shuttlecock of man's passion for wealth and power, till I am weary of the world and its vanities. Oh, what would I not give to be a humble peasant labouring in the field . . . but DESTINY forces me on—my path is thick with shadows, and I cannot see my way. Where will it all end? Where will it all end?[11]

Sadly, where it all ended for DeGray was at St James's Palace in the Lord Chamberlain's Office. The 1909 Select Committee had ruled that no play must 'represent on the stage in an invidious manner a living person, or any person recently dead', and the Lord Chamberlain's rejection of *The Russian Monk* was ostensibly because its characters included the Russian Emperor and Empress. In fact, however, the censorship of plays dealing with contemporary events in Russia had been secretly instigated before DeGray's play had even been submitted for licence. In October 1917, the British War Office had sent a polite letter to the Lord Chamberlain, stating that the Russian military had warned them of a forthcoming play about Rasputin:

They have asked us to prevent its representation if possible, because it can only give offence to Russians. Would you be so very kind as to ask the officials who read plays for the Lord Chamberlain to look out for this play when it comes along, and could you arrange that it shall not be passed for representation unless it is innocuous from the point of view of our Allies?[12]

In other words, although licensing was supposedly a matter for the Lord Chamberlain's Office alone, the right was being given to another country's government to determine what could and could not be staged in the British theatre. Sir Douglas Dawson, the Comptroller of the Lord Chamberlain's office, promised that 'special attention' would be given to any such play, and when *The Russian Monk* was submitted, the script was promptly sent to the War Office. By then the former Russian government had been overthrown, but the loyalties of the British Establishment remained unchanged, and Dawson suggested that the Russian General Staff be allowed to read and comment on *The Russian Monk*, even though, as he himself acknowledged, such consultation was quite improper:

Kindly treat this matter as private and confidential as I have no right to part with the scrip [*sic*]

Meanwhile, the Lord Chamberlain's two official Readers, Bednall and Street, recommended that the play be refused a licence, judging the play from the hypothetical perspective of the old Russian order, and discounting entirely the changed circumstances:

> If there were any Russian Government with regular representatives they would be affronted. I do not think advantage should be taken of their non-existence.

Bednall was especially concerned about the dangers of presenting an ineffective leader to British audiences:

> There is no intrinsic harm in this unpleasant farrago; but at this critical moment the personal introduction upon our stage of mis-guided Royalties like those of Russia (closely related as they are to our own King) seems most undesirable.

Street agreed, adding that he found 'something indecent in the exhibition of the weakness and misfortunes of the Russian Royalties so soon after their deposition'.

Ironically, the War Office found it hard to accept that licensing such an old-fashioned and badly written melodrama represented a serious threat to society:

> It is hard to believe that any manager can be found to produce this play and any audience gathered to witness its performance . . . but it is hard to believe that a performance of this weak nonsense can do any harm here or abroad.

Indeed, given the current crisis and uncertainty in Europe, they thought that licensing the play might well be a safer strategy than banning it:

> Were it prohibited, certain people would be sure to say that attempts were being made to support and protect the late Czar . . . and this would be far more dangerous than any mischief that would result if no prohibition.

One official suggested that the dispute could be resolved by fictionalising the names of the Czar and Rasputin, but others were wary of the danger of establishing a precedent:

> I had no idea that Sovereigns were allowed on the stage in such an unfavourable light . . . If we pass this twaddle who will believe us if later we have to refuse something serious.

Acting on instructions from Brigadier General Cockerill, the Lord Chamberlain obediently informed DeGray that he was unable to grant a licence, offering no reasons and giving no indication of the level at which discussions had taken place. When DeGray volunteered to make any alterations necessary he was simply informed that 'at the present time and with the characters set forth' a licence could not be granted.

Though he continued to work on a number of other plays, DeGray was reluctant to abandon *The Russian Monk*, and fifteen months later, in July 1919, he appealed to the Lord Chamberlain for the case to be reconsidered, 'now that Peace has been signed'. But Street and Bednall both insisted that the play remained 'an outrage on all decent feeling', and that their earlier objections 'retain their full force and are beyond the possibility of removal by alteration'. In 1921 DeGray made a final and desperate attempt:

> Now that the Political unrest with regard to Russia has subsided it occurred to me that The Lord Chamberlain might be prevailed upon to re-consider his decision with regard to the above drama . . . If you refer to the manuscript you will find that there is nothing of an offensively Political nature in it . . . and, of course, I would be only too happy to make any alterations or eliminations . . . which may be considered necessary.

The Lord Chamberlain replied only that he saw 'no reason for altering the decision' he had previously made.

The significance of the refusal to license *The Russian Monk* does not lie in the loss to British theatre of a valuable play, and it is hard not to sympathise with the judgement expressed by Sir Douglas Dawson when he passed the script on to the War Office:

> This play will give you an idea of the twaddle our erudite and very intelligent 'readers' have to wade through daily.

More important is what the banning reveals about the operation of censorship. The British government was apparently so concerned about the danger of portraying an incompetent potentate related to the British monarchy, and so prepared to pander to an overthrown regime, that no rewriting or even removal of particular characters could make the play acceptable. No account was taken of the play's sympathies, and the fact that it was entirely pro-British and anti-German is nowhere even remarked upon. The censors were determined to prevent the possibility of plays which might develop more political analyses of events in Russia, and the only argument advanced in favour of allowing this one was the highly political suggestion that to prohibit it might create even more trouble.

A later and much more serious attempt to chronicle the events of the Russian Revolution was Hubert Griffith's *Red Sunday*, directed in 1929 by Komisarjevsky, with a cast which included Robert Farquharson as Lenin and John Gielgud as Trotsky. *Red Sunday* actually received four private performances at the Arts Theatre Club, and after several theatre managers became interested in staging the production commercially, the script was submitted to the Lord Chamberlain with the intention of securing a transfer to the West End. Griffith's play is interesting from a number of perspectives, not least because it showed some recognition of the need to develop a new form more suitable for political theatre; long before Brecht's theories and work were known in Britain, *Red Sunday* might have become a stepping stone along the way. But after secret interference from the highest level, Griffith's chronicling of history was refused its licence and not performed again.[13]

On the face of it, theatre clubs such as the Arts represented a loophole in the censorship restrictions. As private venues performing only to paid-up members, they were outside the Lord Chamberlain's power, and plays which could not be licensed for public performance were frequently performed in such clubs. However, the potential influence of an occasional, inadequately resourced and probably under-rehearsed Sunday performance in comparison to a production running for weeks or months in the commercial sector was slight. Moreover—a wonderfully British paradox this—managers of clubs accepted that their apparent freedom was dependent on the fact that they would not actually use it. Griffith himself caricatured this position through the words of an imaginary manager:

> We are outside the Censor's jurisdiction here, and for that very reason we have to be careful of the plays we do. If it got about that we were using our privilege to do improper plays, our membership would go down immediately.[14]

Similarly, when *Red Sunday* was presented at the Arts, *The Times* published a weighty and disapproving editorial under the heading 'A Dramatic Indiscretion', which contrived to affirm the principle of the artist's right to freedom of expression, while implying that to exercise it in practice is to take unfair advantage because 'a man of honour and independence is no betrayer of his right to speak freely'. Griffith was rebuked for his lack of courtesy, though patronisingly excused as 'probably unconscious of offence', as *The Times* condescendingly allowed that

> we must presume him to have earnestly supposed that he might still serve some purpose by emphasizing the errors of the old government of Russia, and by passing over the errors of the new with a tolerance made easy by inexperience.

Nevertheless, the editorial condemned the play for its sympathy towards the revolution, its criticisms of pre-revolutionary Russia, and the fact that it had dared to depict Czar Nicholas II at all. While freely admitting that the playwright's 'accuracy or inaccuracy is not for the moment in question', they criticised what they called 'the bias of the dramatist's mind'. As always, the powerful perceived their own views and assumptions as the natural position of balance from which all other views necessarily deviated:

> There must be many Russian exiles (and many English are profoundly in sympathy with them) to whom the Bolshevist rule represents the loss of nearly all, material and personal, that made life dear to them . . . A dramatist is entitled to disagree with their politics, but not, in a public show, to assault their private memories.[15]

Predictably, the newspaper's high profile coverage had the effect of drawing *Red Sunday* to the attention of many who might otherwise have known nothing about it, including Peter Bark, the former Russian Finance Minister, now exiled in London as managing director of the Anglo-International Bank. He wrote to Buckingham Palace to complain that 'all persons of Russian nationality were very indignant' to find that such a play had been produced. Not satisfied by the Palace's explanation that the Arts Theatre Club was outside the Lord Chamberlain's jurisdiction, Bark sought an assurance that the play would never be performed again, and the Keeper of the Privy Purse was persuaded to write to the Lord Chamberlain to ask

> whether some pressure could not be brought on the Manager of this theatre to discontinue a performance which was giving so much pain to Russians in London.[16]

The Lord Chamberlain, Lord Cromer, was also contacted directly by the King, who had already received similar complaints from a member of the former Russian aristocracy. Cromer explained that the performance had been 'of a private character within the walls of a club in which I had no jurisdiction', and knowing that the ostensible freedom of private clubs served as a safety valve which helped defuse potential confrontations, he carefully explained that it would not be 'possible *or politic* for there to be any official interference in plays so produced'. [*my emphasis*]

Cromer felt that anyway the matter could be allowed to drop since in his view *Red Sunday* was unlikely to be heard of again, but in fact the script was submitted for licence almost immediately by a theatre manager who offered, somewhat implausibly, to remove completely the characters of the Czar, Czarina and Czarevitch. The Lord Chamberlain's official Reader's Report cautiously acknowledged the merits and factual basis of the play, and even concluded that there was 'nothing in the play of the ordinary causes of banning'; in spite of this recommendation, Cromer not only refused the licence, but in doing so made no reference to the pressure which had already been exerted on him. Instead, he simply and vaguely claimed that decisions as to what could and could not be portrayed on stage were 'governed by circumstances and public taste'. He also took care to spell out to any future prospective manager that *Red Sunday* was beyond the possibility of alteration:

> I do not think it to be in keeping with the general trend of sympathies and feelings in this country to have such a play staged for public performance now or in the near future. It could not fail to cause resentment in the minds of too many people to show the tragedy of the Russian Revolution which has already meant great anguish and suffering.

No authority could prevent the text of *Red Sunday* from being published, and, inevitably, the Lord Chamberlain's ban was employed as a selling point. Griffith also added a lengthy introduction in which he bitterly attacked censorship in general and his experience with this play in particular. In a fictitious letter, supposedly sent to him by the bemused inhabitant of a remote desert island, Griffith significantly pointed out that he had already imposed a considerable degree of self-censorship on his writing. In the characterisation of the Czar, for example, he had

> strained every endeavour to make the portrait as sympathetic as was conceivably consistent with the truth . . . where there was good to be said, you said it. Where there was bad, you left it out.

Griffith was particularly incensed that no account had been taken of historical accuracy or research:

> The question of whether you had treated the facts fairly or unfairly, whether your account was impartial or prejudiced, biassed or unbiassed, was never for a moment under discussion.[17]

He argues that having deliberately manipulated the public into believing Lenin to have been nothing but 'a murderer, a maniac, a deluded fanatic', the authorities in Britain could not allow other views even to be expressed. In one of the strongest claims of the period concerning the extent and influence of theatrical censorship, Griffith subsequently identified a concerted conspiracy:

> The play contained no new fact that was not well known to anyone who had read fifty pages of any official and impartial history. But it had come up against a certain side of British susceptibility. The truth—or even a part of the truth—must not be told on the stage.[18]

The manager who clashed most regularly with the Lord Chamberlain during the late twenties and early thirties was Terence Gray, a producer who was committed to introducing some of the more innovative European and American plays and performance styles and techniques to audiences at Cambridge's Festival Theatre. Gray's choice of material was not generally based on the politics of a text, but experiments in form quite frequently accompanied non-orthodox ideas and explorations of contemporary issues. For example, his production of Toller's *Hoppla!* incorporated cinematic sequences with the dramatic action, but was, as Gray put it, 'mutilated' by the ruling imposed on him by the Lord Chamberlain, who decided that scenes showing 'soldiers firing on the unarmed populace, including women and girls, who are seen falling, and afterwards lying dead', were 'unsuitable for exhibition in this country'.[19]

The conflict in 1931 over Gray's doomed attempt to stage *Roar China* is especially revealing. This would have been the first British production of Tretiakov's play, which had already been staged in Germany, the Soviet Union and America by the time Gray submitted it for licence. The play was based on a historical incident in which British gunboats had threatened to destroy an entire Chinese town in revenge for a single British death, and it amounted to a forceful indictment of British and American colonial imperialism, racism and exploitation. Gray acknowledged that the play contained anti-English propaganda, and in an attempt to pre-empt a possible banning he insisted, perhaps with tongue in cheek, that the effect of seeing propaganda directed against one's own country could only be amusing. 'Needless to say', he wrote, 'it is entirely inoffensive since we know the reality.' He compared producing Tretiakov's play to 'holding a wasp up by its sting' in order to make it visible.[20]

The Reader's Report found *Roar China* 'dubious in its bias against or libel on this country', and particularly objected to the fact that 'our naval officers are stupidly brutal throughout'.[21] Again the issue was raised of whether granting the play a licence might draw less attention than banning it:

> My personal opinion is that as no harm could be done by its production in Cambridge, where no one could believe the picture, and as it is extremely unlikely to be done elsewhere, having no prospect of popularity and except for the Chinese local colour being uninteresting, the Festival Theatre might be allowed to do it with the necessary cuts.

Cromer himself was similarly undecided, and sent the script to the Home Office with an accompanying letter which weighed up the political advantages and disadvantages of permitting the performance:

There is little doubt that if this play is refused a Licence there would be the usual paragraphs in the papers, but if it were licensed we should certainly have further endeavours made for the production of Soviet Propaganda Plays, which I cannot help thinking the Government would consider most undesirable.

The Home Office was also unable or unwilling to make a decision and passed it on to the Foreign Office who, by chance, already possessed a report by a civil servant of a production he had witnessed in Germany. Outraged by its criticism of Britain, he had described Tretiakov's play as

a peculiarly venomous piece of Bolchevist [sic] propaganda—directed chiefly against the British . . . Needless to say the British characters are depicted in the worst possible light, callous and brutal, whilst the Chinese are portrayed as innocent and helpless beings groaning under the yoke of foreign oppression.

Particularly worrying had been the play's impact on its audience:

The theatre was packed, and the impression created in the audience was one of mingled pity, disgust and rage. Whilst some left the building before the performance was over, others shouted 'pfui England' 'pfui Europe' 'Nieder mit England', and other choice things.

Nevertheless, the Foreign Office informed the Lord Chamberlain that they had chosen not to complain about the German production

on the grounds that however unfair and detrimental to British prestige the play may be any such protest abroad would give it greater prominence and do more harm than good.[22]

The implication seemed to be that to license the play for Cambridge would probably cause less publicity and aggravation than to refuse it, but the Foreign Office also suggested that the Lord Chamberlain might care to consult the Admiralty for their view. Cromer not only followed this advice, but openly encouraged the Admiralty to provide the justification he needed to ban Tretiakov's play:

I cannot but think that the Royal Navy, and indeed large sections of the British public and the Press would strongly resent the presentation.

At last Cromer got the support he had been seeking. Rear-Admiral G.K. Chetwode was horrified by the text and categorically insisted that in no circumstances should it be staged. Again, the power attributed to theatre to influence its audiences is striking—as is the assumption of the absolute right of the authorities to prevent the airing of alternative interpretations of events:

> I am authorised to inform you officially that the Admiralty strongly object to this play being licensed to Cambridge or anywhere else under British control. We consider it especially undesirable that young and inexperienced undergraduates should be subjected at their age to this kind of malicious anti-British propaganda.

The licence was refused, and Tretiakov's play was never seen in Cambridge, and barely in Britain.

Gray subsequently mocked the paranoia of the Lord Chamberlain, accusing Cromer's department of having 'struck bottom in its long career of fatuity', and it is indeed easy to laugh at the antics of the censors and the government.[23] Yet the power wielded was not only considerable but also had a sinister aspect. After a private performance of *Roar China* had been given in Manchester by the Unnamed Society in 1931, a member of the public wrote a letter of complaint to the Lord Chamberlain, enclosing a local newspaper review which described the play as 'virulent', 'pure Soviet propaganda' and 'anti-British', and complaining that the performance was an insult to British audiences. Lord Cromer responded by contacting Salford's Chief Constable, who sent a spy to investigate the Unnamed Society, and compile secret reports and dossiers on its members. The completed file sent to the Lord Chamberlain betrays the classist assumptions and prejudices of the authorities, as it explains that the membership of the society was 'most select and includes a number of University Professors', and that only 'persons of considerable ability and influence' were encouraged to join:

> Any suggestion that the Society is a Communistic organization would appear to be wholly refuted by the influencial [sic] public positions and social standing of the majority of its members.

However, the Chief Constable noted the possibility that the society had been infiltrated by 'undesirables . . . holding communistic views' and promised to continue making 'discreet enquiries'. He also enclosed a list of the names of all those involved with the production of *Roar China*, and suggested that the Lord Chamberlain contact the head of the British Secret Services 'in order that the accusations of their being Communists may be confirmed or refuted'.[24] Tretiakov's play was not performed again, and Terence Gray, exhausted by his clashes with the authorities, was soon to retreat into permanent exile from both theatre and Britain.[25]

The three plays considered in this chapter give a striking indication of the role official censorship played and the forms it took throughout the twenties and thirties. While it is an issue which will inevitably surface again, there are particular insights to be gained from considering the wholesale banning of these plays. First, though it was nominally the Lord Chamberlain who made decisions, scripts were unofficially and unhesitatingly passed to other Ministries and beyond in order to ensure that no-one 'important' in society was offended. In effect, the Lord Chamberlain was an unseen instrument of government, the front man for a political Establishment operating like a gentlemen's club, whose members were offered the right to veto anything to which they had objections. Second, 'truthfulness' and 'accuracy' were no guarantee of securing a licence. In 1928, the Lord Chamberlain rejected an adaptation of a Soviet play on the following grounds:

> The objection, I think fatal, is the presentation of the Czar and Czarina in the lights indicated above, *whatever truth there may be in the picture*. It would obviously be deeply offensive to the King.[26] [*my emphasis*]

Since those in authority always define their views as the norm, any plays which contradict their assumptions necessarily demonstrate 'bias'. Third, while there may be no inherent link between political and aesthetic challenges to the status quo, the Lord Chamberlain's political sensitivities undoubtedly hindered artistic developments; *Red Sunday* could have sparked the development of a new form in British theatre, while the banning of *Roar China* was seen to have prevented the British theatre-going public from becoming familiar with a new conception of drama born of an attempt to represent the masses.[27]

Fourth, deliberate and probably successful attempts were made to discourage future plays about unwelcome subjects by preventing the presentation of a precedent. Of equal significance is the related debate within government circles over whether licensing an unwelcome text would cause less trouble than refusing it.

Yet perhaps the most remarkable and intriguing point to emerge from the evidence considered here is just how seriously the issue of censorship was taken at the highest levels of government. Playwrights might have been surprised to know the extent to which their plays were discussed, and the dangers which were perceived in them. It may be that censors exaggerated the importance of the theatre as an influence on society, but senior ministers, foreign leaders, newspaper editors and the royal family were amongst those unwilling to take chances with its power. The threat represented by the existence of the Soviet Union was enormous, and at all costs, people must be prevented from looking at the face of the God which had not yet failed. As Griffith put it in 1929:

> The Russian Revolution, in a sense, is historic. Were it completely so, had it been long petrified into history books, in the dead form of all finished and completed things, it would matter to no one—and could be performed on the stage with impunity. Because, however, its consequences are not yet exhausted, because its after-effects are still living, breathing realities, still an imminently near lesson to every civilised community (either in the sense of what to do, or what to avoid)—because, in a word, almost any aspect of this fantastically interesting phenomenon is of weight and importance and exactly the sort of thing that modern drama should make it its duty to deal with—therefore it must be snubbed officially and the right to perform it unconditionally witheld.[28]

Or as Gray dryly and surely correctly observed two years later when the licence for *Roar China* was refused, 'the feeling of panic and insecurity in high places must be acute'.[29]

3

No More than a Bad Smell
from the North East

DOGNOVITCH: As Russia is crumbling 'neath the iron heel of
the Bolshevist so will England meet the same fate.[1]

In the years immediately following 1917, the British Establishment was
terrified that the revolution which had swept away the Russian
aristocracy would spread through Europe and into Britain. The tech-
nique of propaganda by rhetoric, exaggeration and lies which had been
employed against Germany was therefore increasingly redirected against
the bolsheviks. Churchill described Lenin as a 'monster, crawling down
from his pyramid of skulls', while newspapers spread rumours of
bolshevik plans to murder all capitalists over the age of eight and to
nationalise women, and the British parliament discussed a bolshevist
marriage contract published in *The Times* which abolished 'the right to
possess women of the ages of 17 to 32' and granted male citizens 'the
right to use one woman not oftener than three times a week for three
hours', with a dispensation that 'former owners may retain the right of
using their wives without waiting their turns'.[2]

Sections of the British media set out to convince people that
the bolsheviks were nothing but 'a gang of murderers, thieves, and
blasphemers whom it was almost a sacred duty to destroy as vermin'.[3]
A typically racist attack published in 1920 accused Lenin of 'personal
viciousness bordering on moral perversion', and bolshevik leaders in
general:

> Some of them are Jews . . . taking a revengful toll for their centuries
> of oppression . . . others are Letts, Poles, Armenians, or members
> of the other conquered races.[4]

The imminent downfall of the Soviet government was constantly and perhaps desperately predicted in the press, along with the assertion that the old, traditional order was not gone for ever but could be restored. *The Times* argued that the current regime was 'assuredly not the authentic voice of Russia' and, declaring that 'the remedy for Bolshevism is bullets', led a campaign for armed British intervention to restore what it called the 'real Russia'. According to one recent analysis of anti-Soviet propaganda:

> By the middle of the 1920s, the distortions had already become so commonplace that they were being passed off for truth without any attempt at verification.[5]

Even *The Times* later conceded that, owing in large part to its own propaganda, 'no one had heard of the forces of the Left except in terms that indicated them to be madmen'.[6] This often ill-informed and malicious onslaught against the Soviet Union may have been motivated primarily by fear, but it also acted as a distraction from the huge social problems created at home by five years of European slaughter, at a time when it was especially important that any alternative to the capitalist system could be comprehensively damned. The Communist Party of Great Britain was formed in 1920, and to those in power, every threat of industrial action or dissent seemed a possible harbinger of a violent overturning of the social order.

In order to avoid acknowledging the injustices of British society, extremists and foreigners were habitually blamed with having instigated such threats of trouble, while the ordinary British worker was exonerated of blame and, to secure his allegiance, simultaneously reminded that he was not in sympathy with bolshevik ideas. In 1919, for example, *The Times* told its readers that

> the British working man seldom makes a mistake when he knows the facts, and . . . he does understand the facts about Bolshevism in practice.[7]

Much of the press constantly reiterated the message that the revolutionary movement in Britain was controlled by foreigners, and that it was they who organised any action taken or threatened by workers against their employers. A typical report in *The Times* in February 1919 noted that the police were taking 'active measures against the dangerous political aliens who have been engaged in propaganda in this country', and cited the arrest of two Russians who had been 'preaching Bolshevism' in Manchester.[8] A Conservative MP claimed to have identified a large group in Britain under the control of Germans, whose aim was to weaken Britain by spreading social and sexual depravities and so allow bolsheviks to 'foment anarchy and propagate vice throughout the land'.[9] When the blame could not be pinned on foreigners, it was outsiders and intellectuals who were found guilty of manipulating and duping a naturally loyal working class into acting against their own instincts and interests:

> The real meaning of the present disorders is that, under cover of an ordinary dispute between employers and employed, an attempt is being made to start the 'class war' and to translate into action what has hitherto been merely a phrase. The men on strike . . . are the unconscious instruments of a planned campaign, drawn up by 'intellectuals' in the background, who desire to emulate Lenin and Trotsky.[10]

Several novelists exploited the fear of a British revolution with stories which illustrated the nightmare scenario of Britain subjected to violent communist take-over and rule. In 1919 a novel dealing with the threat of socialism, which had originally been published in 1907 as *The Master Beast*, was reissued as *The Red Fury: Britain under Bolshevism*. The following year the Russian Liberation Committee published *London under the Bolsheviks*, and 1921 saw the production of *Fly-by-Nights*, another tale of bolshevism in post-war Britain, and *A Prince in Petrograd*, which shows a British hero capturing Lenin. In John Buchan's *Huntingtower* of 1922, the Reds are narrowly prevented from establishing control in Scotland, and in *Konyetz* in 1924, plague and the end of the world follow a bolshevik attack on Europe.[11] No play of the period went quite this far, perhaps because the greater power attributed to performance would have made this seem too dangerous.

The lesson that anyone who dares to complain about society or injustice is being perversely and unnecessarily critical is the explicit moral of *It's All Wrong*, a popular and frequently witty allegory performed in 1920. The cast for this widely acclaimed musical revue, which attracted royal audiences for its opening night, featured well-known stars such as Stanley Lupino and Elsie Janis while the cast of characters could almost have been drawn from a medieval morality play. These include King Discontent, whose servants, Jealousy, Pessimism and Bolshevism, imprison the fair maiden Content in order to secure their power, and then dedicate themselves to causing as much misery and discord in the country as possible:

> BOLSHEVISM: I have told your Majesty that with Bolshevism by your side you can rule the world . . . Content must be done away with . . .
> DISCONTENT: Beware, Oh World! I am coming, and I shall rule you. Bolshevism, I depend a great deal on you to help me . . . All the world shall be ruled by Discontent.

Bolshevism is defined through his very name as negative, but it is sometimes the ordinariness of his actions which seems to imply the pervasive threat he embodies, comic though this may sometimes be, as when he seeks to cause unhappiness by disguising himself as a magazine seller and distributing copies of *The Undertaker's Gazette* to customers requesting *Punch*. However, Bolshevism's particular talent is to provoke political dissent, not by offering positive alternatives, but by continually telling people how bad things are at the moment. To further his ends, Bolshevism organises a rail strike, only to find, to his intense disappointment, that the dogged British character is resistant to his wiles:

> DISCONTENT: How's everything—still as bad as ever?
> BOLSHEVISM: No, worse luck! A railway strike, or a rise in fares doesn't seem to faze these Britishers. This country is not going to be so easy for us as Russia or Germany.

A later scene satirises the trade union movement's attempts to organise workers by showing Bolshevism trying to unionise babies and persuade them to complain about the quality of their lullabies, and he even attempts to infiltrate Heaven in order to persuade the Angels to 'down wings'. Meanwhile, the hero, imaginatively named 'English' to make sure there is no mistaking the message, has been set the task of finding one contented person. Unlike Brecht's Gods in *The Good Person of Sichuan*, English does not have to turn a blind eye to reality in order to achieve his goal, for after searching throughout the country he eventually discovers that his own wife is perfectly happy. The very clear message is that dissatisfaction results from the pointless tendency of wanting what you haven't got, and from listening to troublemakers; as one review put it, 'happiness is most often sought after while we have it in our possession all the time', and all would be well if only we would appreciate our homes and families instead of bothering our heads about the world outside.[12] In the final song, even Bolshevism repents and leads the chorus in acknowledging there is nothing really wrong with the economic situation in the country:

> BOLSHEVISM: All the papers say things will come down with a bump,
> Have you really encountered that much talked of slump?
> ALL: No![13]

Where the propaganda of *It's All Wrong* relied on music, light comedy and the excitement caused by seeing star performers, a desperate melodrama from 1919, *The Bolshevik Peril*, depended for its impact more on shock and on a nationalistic racism. Here, the humour is presumably unintentional, though unfortunately there is no way of knowing to what extent audiences took seriously the messages of this lurid melodrama, in which an evil Russian disguises himself as a Belgian, in order to infiltrate the work-force in a Lancashire mill and start the British revolution. The real motivation for Michael Dognovitch, however, seems to be an obsession with seducing beautiful and innocent women.[14] 'In Russia', he claims when accused of fathering an illegitimate child, 'these little affairs are matters of daily occurrence', and after kidnapping the hero's wife, he announces that the marriage laws have been abolished and that 'women are the property of the state'. On capturing his opponents he gleefully commands his guards to 'take the women first', and when the prisoners abscond his response is 'never mind the man, the women must not escape me'. No wonder the play's hero—'touch those women at your peril'—warns the audience of what will be in store for them if the communists ever take power in Britain:

> No honest man's life will be safe—and as far as the women are concerned death would be preferable than the fate that is in store for them.

Dognovitch's second-in-command, an English socialist agitator called Bradshaw, eventually turns against him and appeals to his followers not to let a foreigner murder an innocent woman; but as Dognovitch tells him, it is 'useless appealing to them' since 'they are not Englishmen but countrymen of mine'. As well as starting a British revolution, Dognovitch finds time to destroy the hero's marriage, make the heroine's sister pregnant and then desert her, and murder his own child. Even his feelings towards the heroine vacillate between a desire to seduce her and a wish to burn her alive.

The sexual depravity of the revolutionaries signifies, of course, an equal violence against a natural order which is at the root of their political philosophy. Dognovitch has to seduce the workers into taking direct action against the management, overcoming their wish to trust traditional English methods to solve disagreements:

> DOGNOVITCH: How do you Englishmen propose to get your just rights then?
> SAM: As we always have done, by honest and straightforward means, not like the Bolshevists who murder old men and innocent children.
> NED: You're right Sammy—not to listen to the vile doctrine of the Bolshevists, they are doing their best to disseminate their foul propaganda in this country and I for one will have none of them.

Indeed, the workers and management actually resolve their dispute amicably, as all such disputes would presumably be resolved if it were not for the intrusions of agitators pursuing their own ends. However, Dognovitch then deliberately sabotages the agreement by murdering the owner of the mill—'the first crime of the Bolshevists in England'— simply because he cannot bear to see society at peace. He then makes his plans for total revolution:

> DOGNOVITCH: First we commandeer the banks, we place every wealthy person under arrest—force them to purchase their liberty at our price . . . England will be powerless to help herself—she will be in the throes of revolution this time next week. Britain as you know it will exist no more . . . As Russia is crumbling 'neath the iron heel of the Bolshevist so will England meet the same fate.

Bradshaw realises the true nature of bolshevism only just in time, and that to follow such a doctrine would make him a traitor to his own country:

Destroy England will he—the man's a madman—his dreams are those of a fanatic—as he spoke just now I could read the gleam of madness in his eyes.

Fortunately, the sanity of the working class eventually reasserts itself —'our chaps, disgusted wi' thee, threw up sponge and are helping other side'—and the strength of the British way of life is finally too much for Dognovitch's destructive dreams:

> NED: You are not in bloodstained Russia now but in peaceful England.
> DOGNOVITCH: Peaceful England no longer, the rebellion has started and this town is the first to fall, before the week has passed the whole country will have surrendered to the Bolshevists.
> NED: That it never will . . . do you think your puny efforts will ever overcome the mighty power of the British Empire?

In an action-packed and happy ending, British troops arrive from Manchester, Dognovitch is shot dead, Bradshaw gives up politics to fall in love with Ned's sister-in-law, and Ned's wife is rescued from the burning mill and reunited with her husband, who announces that 'the terror has passed' and that henceforth 'England will never have cause to fear the Bolshevik Peril'.

The excessive propaganda and heightened rhetoric of *The Bolshevik Peril* may now appear risible, but to the Lord Chamberlain in 1919 it seemed a reasonable play. He noted that it was directly inspired by

> newspaper reports of the hoodwinking of British Radicals and Socialists by paid foreign agitators, who for their own purposes lure them on towards Revolution.

He suggested that while the play was 'not perhaps very desirable in choice of subject', it was nevertheless 'inoffensive in treatment', and even that the 'personal and political are blended with some skill'. [15]

A rather better play about industrial conflict was Ernest Hutchinson's *The Right to Strike*, which provoked considerable controversy and became the focal point of a public political debate.[16] The opening night of the production was conspicuously attended by important union leaders and politicians, including Winston Churchill, and special performances were arranged for doctors, Harley Street specialists, MPs, business men, trade unionists, mayors and clergy. *The Times* carried reflections on the play by its medical correspondent, a clergyman in Covent Garden performed extracts of it during his sermon, and the *Daily Mirror* organised ballots during performances, inviting audiences to vote on the principle of whether the medical profession should be allowed to take strike action. On three occasions the King was due to see the production, and each time the Royal Box was cancelled. The play's producer, Leon Lion, noted the monarch's 'avid interest' when they discussed the play privately, and deduced that he had been advised against attending the theatre because of the 'undeniable danger' which would have resulted from audiences watching his reactions to the events on stage. According to Lion, the play's run was shortened at the direct intervention of the Queen, and it is hard to tell how close his tongue is to his cheek when he patriotically salutes this as 'a shining example of diplomacy'.[17]

The Right to Strike is again set in a small Lancashire town, and opens in a comfortable room with a 'cheerful fire burning'. Everything seems homely and reassuring, though the presence of a large map of the Western Front ironically establishes the connection between the recent international war abroad and the coming class war at home. Eric, a young doctor, returns from the war to find that the mood has changed from the peaceful, co-operative way of life he remembers to one of friction and discord; the town is on the verge of suffering a rail strike, and the threat of similar industrial disputes and even civil war hangs over the whole country. Eric is told that the strike has been stirred up by Montague, one of a new breed of professional agitators who 'thrive on other folks' troubles', and who, according to a senior local doctor, has come especially from London to make a name for himself:

> He's one of those middle-class sympathetic intellectuals that the Socialists have got hold of in their cradles. Now they've grown up and are beginning to make mischief.

Montague has apparently already succeeded in manipulating the local union representative into supporting him, and the tragic plot unfolds as Eric joins a group organising a taxi service to break the strike but is killed in a clash with the strikers. In response, the local doctors refuse to treat the families of the railway workers, and the wife of Ben, the essentially decent local union leader, then dies in childbirth. The play ends with remorse all round and the realisation that conflict and confrontations produce suffering rather than solutions.

The Right to Strike was subtitled 'A Play of To-day', and was undoubtedly intended as a serious contribution to an important debate. Written in a broadly naturalistic style, the visual settings also allow a metaphorical level of meaning; the last Act, for example, opens with an oxygen cylinder being carried across the stage which, in a literal sense relates to the need of the dying mother, but perhaps also represents the desperate struggle for survival of a society under threat. The production itself was nearly cancelled before it had opened because of actual strikes, as the government debated whether it was 'in the interests of the nation that all places of entertainment should be closed forthwith', and the *Stage* suggested that it might indeed be 'highly inexpedient and dangerous to produce Strike plays at the present juncture'.[18] Even if a strike by doctors seemed unlikely in real life, reviewers had little doubt that a middle-class revolt was only too liable to occur in one of the professions in the near future. One reviewer claimed that

> there has never been a play more directly topical in its appeal . . . the debates which occur upon the stage are echoes of the debates which members of the audience have for weeks been enjoying among themselves.[19]

According to the play's producer and star, Leon Lion, every performance resulted in

> factional outbursts of applause or derision, according to the political complexion of the audience. These, though mostly good-humoured, could sometimes seem turbulent.[20]

Several reviews suggest that audiences reacted with a fervour more normally associated for us with melodrama and pantomime than with serious political plays, and confirm that they were by no means unified in their response. Different sections and social groups clashed vocally and sometimes even physically during performances:

> It is a long time since I have seen an audience so keenly excited and divided into hostile camps by any play. The hisses at certain passages from gallery and pit were met by counter boos, shouts and cheers.[21]

Some newspapers devoted more column inches to discussing what happened in the auditorium than reviewing the production:

The way in which the play is received is a striking commentary on present social conditions. The points made for the men are received with savage cheers by the gallery, and the strike of the doctors is welcomed with warlike enthusiasm in the better furnished parts of the house. One notes how easily angry passions are let loose on both sides, and realises the intensity of the bad feeling now ruling between the aggressive manual workers and the oppressed middle classes. One feels that the author, if he had liked to do so, might quite easily have provoked a riot.[22]

This level of direct engagement by spectators was welcomed by some reviewers, but others moralised in despairing tones about the dangerous implications of such commitment and belief:

One would have thought that the vast European upheaval and the death of millions would have satisfied any appetite for combat; but no, it was quite obvious that the audience, whether pro- or anti-proletarian, were all most cheerfully, most joyfully out to hit somebody and were revelling in this spectacle of a 'scrap'. Let the pacifist with his theory of millions of obedient working men driven unwillingly to slaughter observe the curious phenomena which take place at the Garrick Theatre.[23]

By contrast with a play like *The Bolshevik Peril*, Hutchinson makes an attempt to dramatise a genuine political debate, and to allow arguments and counter-arguments to be forcefully and effectively expressed. Only the ending, desperate to resolve the situation, is disappointingly sentimental, as Eric's young widow tells the bereaved Ben the solution to creating a better society:

Haven't we all rather lost sight of something this past fortnight —these past six years? Haven't we all rather forgotten that we're only God's children? We've been so busy fighting each other —fighting each other to kill, and fighting each other for our own selfish ends . . . Wasn't it shown us in Galilee two thousand years ago!

Until this final scene, one of the play's strengths has been its repeated contradicting and questioning of statements which at first seem intended to carry the author's voice. In the first scene, for example, Eric's father offers a familiar explanation of why the dispute has needlessly arisen:

Left to ourselves we'd have settled everything; but we've not been. Both the directors and the men have been got at by outsiders —outsiders who are trying to make Valleyhead the fighting ground for a big capital and labour battle.

Yet the play undercuts such simplistic views, allowing us to feel cynical towards the arrogance of a doctor who contemptuously dismisses the workers' desire to improve the world:

It's . . . the desire to have things better than they found them that's the driving force behind. That's why it's so dangerous.

Montague himself can be viewed as an articulate and principled politician whose role is to give strength and policy to the aspirations of local workers, and even if we have reservations about *his* motives, we cannot doubt the sincerity of Ben, the earnest and straightforward local union leader. Ben insists that Montague 'says what we feel', and his own motivation clearly comes from an altrusitic wish to make a better future for his children:

When we all went soldiering we were promised a lot about a better country and a land fit for heroes when we came home. Some of us have been living on these promises for six years. Now we've come back and we've a sort of notion we'd like to see them come true.

To be effective against politicians and managers who make promises more easily than they deliver them, Ben needs the toughness of Montague to advise him. Montague, for example, persuades him that to accept arbitration and negotiation is to walk into a capitalist trap:

Use your own weapon—action! action!—that's what beats them! . . . Whilst you're on strike they're helpless—once they get talking —you're licked.

By the time the doctors criticise the strikers' use of direct action, Ben is able to justify it by telling them with conviction that 'It's the only way the working man knows that you gentle folks seem to understand'. Even Eric's death is not used by Hutchinson simply to condemn the strikers; when the local MP tells Ben and Montague that their behaviour is 'not English', Montague is allowed a robust reply:

It's as English as starving the strikers' women and children to death,
as capital has claimed the right to do in the past . . . The right to
strike is ours, and by God we'll strike properly.

Again, when a solicitor insists that their action has gone 'beyond what
we are accustomed to in England', Montague points out that 'the
working man is quite used to seeing his wife and children killed in these
disputes'.

In the third Act, the on-stage argument ranges broadly over such
issues as the principles and practice of capitalism, the manipulation of
public opinion, the use of violence to effect change, the willingness of
the ruling class to resort to force when necessary, and the question
of whether Parliament can be effective in reforming society or whether
it actually postpones change. These are debates to which political theatre
has frequently returned.[24] Mellor, a Labour MP, insists on the natural-
ness and inevitability of inequality:

It's no good tilting at the whole economic system of the country,
Mr Montague. It's the law of nature, and a hard law I admit, but
a law parliament can't alter for you.

He insists that his party has the power to influence events and to remove
some of the injustices of society, but his complacency and gradualist
approach are challenged by the socialist:

MELLOR: Labour is playing a very big part in reconstruction.
MONTAGUE: The old Parliamentary catch-words—the drug to
keep the working man quiet! . . . It's reconstruction we want—but
it's reconstruction of ideas. Scrap your old shibboleths and start
afresh. You must smash up before you can build.

Montague declares that peaceful methods have already failed and that
violence is now the only method left to effect change:

MONTAGUE: Yes, if you like—call me a Bolshevist . . . if that's
the only way left to us, we'll turn Bolshevist tomorrow.
WRIGLEY: And shoot down anyone who opposes you?
MONTAGUE: Why not? The end justifies the means.
WRIGLEY: Start Russia in Lancashire?
MONTAGUE: You may joke about it, but every thinking man
knows we're nearer to it than you care to admit.

The Times was disconcerted by the political ambiguity of the play and what it saw as Hutchinson's refusal to take sides. It described *The Right to Strike* as 'bad propaganda' because 'it was quite impossible to discover the author's own views'.[25] To quieten and control audiences, both the writer and the producer were forced to appear on stage after performances to assure them that the play was not intended as propaganda, though in fact the manager of the theatre, who was also acting in the play, had previously insisted to the Lord Chamberlain that any censorship of the text would crucially weaken a play which 'contains some of the finest propaganda the Government could wish for'.[26] Perhaps he was being slightly disingenuous, for the play refuses to put the blame for tragedy only on those seeking to change society, and the potential for violence which is implicit in the entrenched position of the oppressors—the iron fist beneath the velvet glove of capitalism— is just as firmly laid bare. One doctor warns the strikers that 'If it comes to a fight, it's the trained soldier class who'll win, not the civilian rabble', while the railway owner himself expresses the ruling class's determination to use whatever weapons are necessary to resist change even more forcefully:

> You take it for granted that the bloated capitalist stands con-
> demned—that he has no friends and that the working man has only
> to hold a pistol to his head to get all he wants. You're wrong. That
> day may come—it hasn't come yet. The capitalist has still a good
> deal of kick left in him. I don't want to fight, but fight I will if you
> push matters to extremes.

For all its faults, *The Right to Strike* was far removed from the light escapism, the stereotypes, and the right-wing certainty of some of the other contemporary accounts of class conflict.

The best-written strike play of the early twenties was probably *First Blood*, in which the Manchester writer Allan Monkhouse again uses a northern confrontation between management and workers to warn of a seemingly inevitable class war.[27] Monkhouse writes in a credibly authentic dialect set against the backdrop of a Lancashire strike, and the political debate is interwoven with a portrait of everyday family life in which characterisation integrates psychological realism with roles which are representative of class background and political positions. In Lionel—the son of the mill owner—and Phyllis—the daughter of the working family—Monkhouse creates two characters who are willing to learn about the problems of each other's class; they are thus made to embody the possibility that a harmonious world in which capital and labour understand each other and work together can be achieved, and that civil war is not inevitable. They are contrasted with the other characters on both sides of the conflict, all of whom are entrenched in closed ideological positions. Inevitably, Lionel and Phyllis also provide the personal and romantic thread which was widely seen as an essential element in theatrical narrative—the necessity 'to punch the human note' which Frank Swinnerton had bemoaned as 'artistic betrayal' in discussing both Hutchinson's play and Galsworthy's *Strife*:

> Up to the present the only story that anybody has ever wanted to see or to read or to write has been a love story . . . These things have nothing to do with strikes, or, essentially, with plays about strikes . . . perhaps one day strikes and strike-breakers on the stage will be first of all human beings, instead of improvized sentimental figures who exist to sugar the dramatists's 'deep stuff'.[28]

Monkhouse may not succeed totally in combining political analysis with what Swinnerton called 'the exact reality of the personal drama', but the attraction between Lionel and Phyllis serves primarily as a device which enables the playwright to explore the strike within a naturalistic framework, by bringing together sympathetic representatives of the two sides in the dispute. The play could be criticised for suggesting that the problems of rulers and ruled are comparable and in need of equal understanding, and that romantic love can save us from class war, but at least Lionel and Phyllis actually talk politics to each other, and Monkhouse refuses to impose simplistic solutions.

First Blood articulates the need to change and reform political structures, but implies that such change must be slow and negotiated rather than confrontational. When the impetuous son insists that 'quick ways is best', his father reminds him that 'if yo' burn down a mill yo've got to build it up again'. However, the theatrical debate, which is carried on through action as well as words, allows space for contradiction and for spectators to draw their own conclusions. Points are countered by equally valid opposing arguments; when Lionel insists that for the workers to direct their violence against the wealthy is a gratuitous abuse of power, he is told that such behaviour is inevitable in a society where the workers have no real say, and are allowed 'only the power to smash'.

The fact that both Lionel and Phyllis are eventually shot while trying to prevent violence, during an attack by the workers on the mill-owner's house, offers a pessimistic prospect for future peace in Britain. Yet Monkhouse is too honest and complex a writer to condemn the Left's determination to challenge the system, or to have its representatives repent and capitulate. Indeed, he allows a forceful and passionate expression of the radical position:

> Year after year we go on with our little disputes and our little compromises. We get no further. The power's still where it was though we seem to be gaining. And now we're out for a real revolution, not a sham one. We've to be ruthless. You've got to go. You've got to learn that if you won't yield you'll be crushed.

Even after the violent conflict has led to tragedy and deaths, the subtly anti-climactic and understated ending provides no hint of an easy resolution:

> JABEZ: An' dost see where thy ways tak' thee?
> TOM: But we are in the right.
> LADY STOTT: Hush!
> [*Curtain*]

Since Monkhouse declines to feed his audience an outside agitator, the blame for the conflict cannot be so easily displaced. However, the Soviet revolution still stands as a warning model for Britain if the class conflict remains unresolved, as when Phyllis's father discusses with his sons whether or not the workers should restrict themselves to constitutional methods of challenging the status quo:

> JABEZ: What's your way? An' where does it lead? . . . To bloodshed.
> JACK: There's worse things than bloodshed . . .
> JABEZ: Is Tom Eden for bloodshed? Does he want us to be like them Bolsheyviks? What about Russia, Tom Eden?
> TOM: Russia's not done with yet.
> JACK: Russia's the land of great ideas.
> JABEZ: Are yo' for shooting and hacking? D'yo want to make this town a battlefield?

Monkhouse is not the first writer to suggest that the humanity of the British working class would prevent them from accepting in practice the blood and violence they are prepared to condone in theory:

> LIONEL: Theoretically you may be a Red or a Bolshevik or something nastier than that, but I'm sure you're not for murder and arson.[29]

Other dramatists treated the possible collapse of society in different ways. *Labour On Top* is a bitter fantasy from May 1926 which satirises the absurdity of a society which has reversed the social order.[30] It was set in a future 'which may be logically surmised in the movement of Labour to establish a supremacy of the Workers', where aristocratic parents put their sons' names down to be trained as bricklayers, and which is the direct result of giving the vote to women and children. Those who suffer from the reversal of a natural order include the head of a firm who must now expect to end up in a Home for Destitute Shareholders, and a Lord who is in love with a worker's daughter but knows she is hopelessly beyond his reach. A note from the author in the text instructs the cast that 'the distinctions of superior breeding in the characters who represent the old regime' must be 'starkly contrasted against the plebeian element of the others'.

Another political satire constructed along similar lines was H.F. Maltby's *What Might Happen*, which ran at the Savoy in the summer of the same year. Maltby again imagined a future in which former aristocrats live in abject poverty in leaking railway carriages or former army huts, and are oppressed by the wealthy but uncultured former working-class.[31] Pathetically delighted when they are employed for eighteen pence an hour to weed daisies from the tennis courts they once owned, the upper classes strive through fantasy to maintain the symbols of their wealth by ringing bells to call imaginary servants, and continuously converting their one small room from lounge to breakfast-room to bedroom at different times of day and as occasion demands. The Reader's Report for the Lord Chamberlain showed disappointment at the play's lack of ideological clarity:

> The topsy turvey business is fairly amusing, but it is rather spoiled by the aristocrats not really behaving 'as such'. They and the upstarts are satirised more or less impartially.[32]

Indeed, though the sympathies of the playwright are largely with the fallen aristocracy, he does allow the working-class oppressor to make a passionate and partially convincing justification of his right to oppress:

> Don't you see that that is what I'm out for to do—oppress them and oppress them . . . Because they've oppressed me . . . And now things 'as turned, they think it's a 'ell of a blinking shame they can't go on doing it any more . . . I've 'eard you sneer and laugh at blokes like me wot 'as made money at a time when you 'adn't the sense to keep yours. I've 'eard you saying 'Fancy that man 'aving salmon and asparagus to 'is dinner! What is things coming to?' You expected to 'ave all the salmon and asparagus all your lives . . . .[33]

Maltby blamed the relative failure of this play on the refusal of Mrs Patrick Campbell to learn her lines properly.[34]

Monkhouse's *First Blood* was written in 1924 and set in 'the uncertain future', but it was first performed in 1926. To some, the General Strike of that year must have seemed the harbinger of all the horrors that such plays had warned about, for while historians may dispute whether the stakes were really so high, the General Strike at least seemed to represent the moment at which the entire capitalist system was on the verge of being overthrown. Probably the first play to document that strike itself was *Shadows of Strife*, written in 1926 by John Davison, an engineer from Rotherham, which played in several northern venues before reaching London in 1929.[35] Davison's play purported to be a realistic and authentic examination of the effects of a strike on a working-class family, and was described by one critic as a 'study of war on the home front'.[36] The foreword to the published text links both the writing and the form to the work of Zola, and credits it with reflecting a growing interest in gritty realism at the expense of the heavily melodramatic. Once again, the play focuses on the connection between the wide political world and the narrower family one, and inevitably insists that the only hope for a prosperous Britain is compromise and reconciliation between the workers and the owners, in this case, largely on the terms of the management. While superficially offering a balanced view of conflict and acknowledging the existence of faults on both sides, the play becomes increasingly vituperative in its attack on the ignorance and motives of anyone who opposes the principles of capitalism.

The strike itself is provoked by unseen bolshevik agitators, who dupe ordinary workers into chanting empty slogans and singing songs which they do not understand. To these workers, the strike is a holiday and an opportunity to indulge their natural laziness. The voice of sense and reason in the play is clearly intended to rest with John, a working-class lad determined to 'better' himself, who is now the prospective agent for the local Conservative Party. John has the courage to stick to his principles in the face of much hostility, and is contrasted with his brother, Luke. At first, Luke's position seems to be afforded equal credence:

> It's us as goes down into t'bowels o' t'earth as provides all t'profits in this country. It's us as provides all t'royalties for dukes, and big estates.

But such views are made to appear extreme as the strike develops, and are discredited by Luke's selfishness and ignorance, and by the ease with which he falls into crime. John gives his savings to his mother to help with the housekeeping, while Luke demands money from her to buy beer and cigarettes; John stays at home to study and help his mother, while Luke returns drunk from the pub to shout his undigested political theories; John studies hard to become an engineer, while Luke sings The Red Flag, and sneers at education; John speaks of the need for harmony in society, while Luke declares with enthusiasm that 'the country'll be on its bended knees in a month', and naïvely dreams of a future in which every working man will be richer than Baron Rothschild. While John, according to the stage directions, habitually speaks 'earnestly', Luke and his comrades speak, 'hastily', 'blusteringly' or 'with a snarl'. When Luke knocks John out during a political argument, the physical action symbolises the Left's inability to respond to reason and rational argument other than with brute force.

Shadows of Strife comes close to endorsing John's reactionary convictions that all strikers are shirkers and that people should stop complaining and work harder. He is determined to 'make a lot of our chaps see a bit of reason, instead of 'em voting blindfold for t' Reds', and his prophesy of how capitalism will adapt in order to survive rings ominously true:

> A future British government will realise the enormous advantage in having a prosperous and well-contented working-class population.

However, it is the mother, finding her voice at the end of the play for almost the first time, who realises that there are faults on both sides, and presents the utopian and sentimental dream of a peaceful future:

> P'raps there'll come a time . . . when there'll be no such things as strikes, an' we can all live in peace . . . If both sides would use their brains a bit—both sides, mind . . . England would soon be same as Lloyd George promised us.[37]

The significance of the plays so far discussed should not be under-estimated, but no other political play of the 1920s occupied the mainstream of the theatrical Establishment to the same extent as *Yellow Sands*, designated by *Theatre World* in 1926 as its official 'Play of the Moment'. Barry Jackson's production of Eden and Adelaide Phillpotts's newest work ran for over six hundred consecutive performances at the Haymarket Theatre Royal and, after *The Farmer's Wife* which was also by Eden Phillpotts, became the most commercially successful and acclaimed play in London in the mid twenties.[38] Superficially, the play is a light comedy of nostalgia, romance and quaintly humorous rustic English eccentrics, but the plot centres on a self-declared English bolshevik who, in the final scene, renounces his political convictions in favour of love and capitalism. The confident conservatism of both form and content assert that politics is infinitely less important than romance, that radicalism presents no threat to the status quo, and that economic and cultural structures will remain unchanged. For London audiences, at a time of clashes on the streets and the threat of civil war, *Yellow Sands* must have provided comfortable reassurance; indeed, the fact that reviewers invariably described it as enjoyable and light entertainment rather than as a political drama is doubtless one of the main reasons for its success, even though the politics are central to both the narrative and the characterisation.

A world away from the harshness and menace of the northern strike play and the factories and mills of dark and dreary cities, *Yellow Sands* takes place in an old-fashioned, unchanging Devonshire fishing village, where the sun is always shining. The detail stipulated by the authors' stage directions reflects the careful construction for London audiences of an idealised, but supposedly authentic, image of a traditional English way of life:

The beach separates the hamlet from the sea. A strip of sand and shingle before a little road which runs in front of Thomas Major's cottage. On the foreshore is a wooden seat for visitors. To the left a boat is drawn up and round about are crab pots, oars and a litter of fishermen's things. To the right may lie the edge of a herring net, spread to dry on the shore. Against Major's house stands a shrimper's net. The road, after passing Major's cottage, turns up stage and, at back, are other cottages under low hills with trees rising behind their walls. To the right of stage another cottage stands.

The authors even require that

to suggest the life and movement of a fishing village, a few people should come and go behind the backs of those acting the play; children, a woman or two, an old fisherman, and the village clergyman.[39]

The characterisation itself was dependent on familiar rural caricatures, and the very familiarity was recognised as a crucial part of the appeal:

As usual with Mr Phillpotts, a tea-party of local characters provided the *pièce de résistance*.[40]

This is not the first time Mr Eden Phillpotts has presented us with this assemblage; but we can bear to see it oftener still.[41]

Anyone inclined to criticise the old-fashioned sentimentality of the style or narrative would doubtless have been dismissed as the sort of 'highbrow' who regretted that Strindberg's *Miss Julie* had just been refused a licence for public performance, and who failed to understand the true purpose of theatre.[42]

It is no good setting out to be superior about the sweet-meat comedies which Mr Phillpotts so industriously creates. The rustic fudge is toothsome stuff.[43]

The playwrights invite the audience not only to be amused by the portrait of rural Britain they gently evoke, but to be charmed by the nostalgic appeal of its quaint West-country dialect—doubtless rendered by actors more familiar with Oxford and public-school patterns of speech. The illusory threat to the idyllic atmosphere of village life is posed by Joe Varwell, but his left-wing convictions are constantly rendered laughable by his earnestness and lack of humour, his exaggeration, and not least his dialect. The communist fisherman is a well-meaning but not very bright young man of 'large heart and few brains';[44] a figure of fun at whom we can safely and patronisingly smile:

> If I was catching they crabs for the hungry, Emma, I'd be happy;
> but whenever I catch a whopper I says to myself, 'A damn capitalist
> will eat him', and I be half in a mind to put him back again.

Through Joe's insistence on dragging politics and injustice into every discussion and situation, the play mocks not only his socialist convictions but the very notion of living with a political commitment. He is

> oppressed by the woes of mankind, and somewhat like a bull in a
> china shop, rages at all the sweet simple people he lives among.

The effect is to deny that society's structures are in any sense manufactured or changeable, and since they are neutral and inevitable, it is pointless to worry about them; the impulse to change society, or for 'ordinary' people to worry their heads about politics, is condescendingly ridiculed.

Though the left-wing cant which Joe obsessively tries to inflict on the villagers of Yellow Sands occasionally provokes them, it is generally humoured by the other characters rather than interpreted as a serious danger. When Joe's criticisms become personally directed—as when he refuses for political reasons to give a birthday present to his aunt—he is put down much as a naughty child might be by its elders:

> JOE: If I had a present to give away, Aunt Jenifer, I wouldn't give
> it to you.
> JENIFER: And why not?
> JOE: Because—because you'm a blasted capitalist.
> THOMAS: Order, Joe!

Joe may huff and puff and say nasty things—he declares that 'you can only cure some things by killing 'em', and professes that he wants 'to see the guillotine set up on this beach'—but these are only words and therefore harmless. The community has no doubt that he is powerless:

> The Socialists be like the steam whistle—smallest part of the
> engine—and the noisiest.

From early in the play, the audience is made aware that Joe is suppressing his romantic feelings for Lydia, a servant girl, and it is clear that his efforts and energies should really be going into that relationship rather than into politics, and that he is lucky Lydia is prepared to wait until he himself realises this. In fact, the way in which Joe determinedly refuses to give in to his affection for Lydia, so that he can devote himself fully to politics, is one of the main sources of humour, signifying the socialist's denial of instinct and human nature:

> Don't you Socialists never kiss each other, or be you only built to bite the rich?

His cousin shrewdly reminds him that 'love will creep in, Joe, even though there's a million men out of work', but Joe ridiculously insists, even when he is alone with Lydia, that reforming society must take priority over personal sentiments:

> I'm out for something a good few sizes larger than love; and that's justice for the under-dogs.

He declares that there's no time for marriage as long as 'the capitalists have still got us on their chains', and rails against those union leaders who have families:

> Us don't pay 'em to have children, nor yet to fondle t'em; we pay 'em to smash the capitalists.

Most ludicrous of all, he actually tells Lydia of his feelings for her—'You know love, same as you know whooping cough'—but announces that in no circumstances must this 'darned queer thing' get in the way of his plans:

> I won't marry you. There's only the Cause for me.

Meanwhile, in political disputes with his uncle, Joe is seen to rely on empty slogans which are unable to withstand debate or common-sense logic:

> JOE: England's a cannibal country.

> DICK: Capital don't eat Labour, my poor Joe. It's Labour eats Capital . . .
> JOE: All masters are bullies and dock their men's liberty.
> DICK: It's your bosses dock your liberty, not your masters.
> JOE: Our bosses protect us.
> DICK: Against what? They protect you against your own freedom and independence, against your will to work and your power to earn . . .
> JOE: They protect the weakest members.
> DICK: Does it help the weak to cripple the strong? Never!

Beneath the misguided and parroted slogans, Joe is an essentially decent and caring young man. Though he is reluctant to attend the celebrations for his Aunt Jenifer's eightieth birthday—'there's only one party I know about, and that's the Socialist party'—he ultimately puts family relationships before politics and gives her a present of a book entitled 'The Heart of the Under-Dog'. It is because she recognises the good intentions cloaked by his gruff and aggressive exterior that she leaves her money to him, knowing this will require him to face up to the reality of how the wealthy can best help the unfortunate poor. As she says in her will, she is confident that Joe will 'do what little he may in reason to right the under-dogs without wronging the upper ones'.

When his aunt dies, the effect of the inheritance on Joe is devastating, and the propaganda of *Yellow Sands* becomes even more explicit as he undergoes an almost instant political conversion. The lawyer remarks that it is 'easy to share if you've got nothing yourself', and Joe's uncle is quick to tease him:

> JOE: What do it mean?
> DICK: It means you're a bloated capitalist, Joe—a profiteer, rich with money you never earned—a chap battening on the sweat of the poor—a rascal with four thousand quid in the bank, who ought to be taken out to the first lamp-post and strung up.
> JOE: Hell!

Having first tried to refuse the money, Joe then decides to give it all away to the poor, but with Lydia's help his uncle is able to demonstrate to him the illusion under which all socialists patently labour. As they work out together how to 'get Utopia started on a solid monetary basis', Dick explains to an astonished Joe that if they divide the inheritance between all the unemployed in the country it will be barely enough to buy them a box of matches each. Through this somewhat specious argument the playwrights ridicule the principle of sharing wealth and reassure the audience that the existing system is already designed to help the less fortunate:

> If you was to dole 'em out pennies, Joe, there'd still be forty thousand penniless . . . to help a million all at once, you must look to they rascals who pay income tax and super-tax, and all they villains and scamps who have had the wit enough to earn big money, or the luck to inherit it. The levy on capital is going on fine, Joe, while everybody pretends it can't be done.

Joe is soon persuaded that the best way to help his fellow-workers is to build them a cafeteria; by setting up a capitalist enterprise, he will be providing both a service and employment for local people. For Joe, the political penny finally drops:

> LYDIA: There's nought like money to find work for others, Joe.
> JOE: By Gor! I believe you're right. When it comes to finding work, the first thing is to find wages, ain't it, Uncle Dick?
> DICK: Well, to my simple, backwoodsman's mind it looks like it, Joe . . . The business of capital, Joe, is to find work, and the more capital, the more work. That's what you don't understand. Try and get that.

Within moments, Joe has become a potential employer, promising to deal firmly with what he now perceives as an idle work-force:

> JOE: I'll darn soon larn the masons how many bricks a man did ought to lay in a day!
> DICK: Spoke like a damned capitalist, Joe![45]

As *The Times* delightedly put it:

> Joe the dull-witted but generous-hearted fisherman, who babbles of the social revolution . . . finds himself a capitalist and is compelled to abandon most of his cherished convictions.[46]

He can now be re-absorbed into an English village life which will continue unchanged for ever.

In the final scene, Joe not only turns from communist to capitalist but also from angry young adolescent to contented fiancé. A stage direction describing the final image of the play demonstrates how political commitment makes you morose and sullen while love brings happiness:

> *For the first time in the play Joe's face breaks into a smile, and he embraces and kisses her.*[47]

The conversion of the 'charming Bolshevist' is complete, and the audience has had its assumptions validated. As the *Sunday Times* significantly admitted:

> The time is not yet, in the theatre, when we shall cease to believe that a legacy of four thousand pounds can turn the most frenzied Communist into a rapturous Individualist.[48]

The reception of *Yellow Sands* is a classic demonstration of the fact that while left-wing plays are always identified as political, right-wing plays are not. Yet perhaps the most striking accomplishment of the play is the way in which it contrives to absorb a revolutionary communist into a familiar framework of stock characters and comic dialogue. In constructing Joe as an object of affectionate mockery both for the other characters and for the audience, the oppositional and most threatening element of society is disarmed and made safe. The refusal to take Joe seriously not only renders his ideas unimportant but also denies the need to be concerned about the power and threat of British radicals. In practice, all the socialist can do, like Bolshevism and King Discontent in *It's All Wrong*, is to upset people needlessly just for the sake of it, and to make them feel miserable:

> EMMA: You do cast one down, Joe.
> JOE: That's what I be here for—to cast people down.[49]

Yet it was crucial to the consciences of audiences at *Yellow Sands* that Joe's abandonment of impractical and idealistic left-wing theory should not be seen as betraying his commitment to help the poor. Since the message must be that a system of benevolent capitalism benefits everybody, Joe cannot be allowed to turn into a selfish individualist, but must be seen rededicating himself to help those less fortunate than himself in a more effective way. Communism is seen to consist of enviously complaining and trying to reduce everyone to equal poverty, while capitalism can take care of the whole of society, with the rich using their wealth to help the poor—just as Sir Reginald's daughter had advocated in *Reparation*.

While audiences can hardly have believed that British political agitators were all like Joe, it was doubtless a relief to be reminded in the winter of 1926 that some of the most threatening extremists who shared his 'horrible Bolshevik notions' might in reality be 'the mildest of lambs in the most ferocious of wolf's clothing'.[50] Revolution and socialism are no longer a threat, and can be safely and reasonably dismissed, because we can all see that, as Uncle Dick patiently explains, benevolent and common-sense capitalism is the only realistic way of alleviating hardship:

> Let charity begin at Yellow Sands, my boy. And since Communism's no more than a bad smell from the north-east, just put what you can do before what you'd like to do.[51]

For this soothing message to have been such a commercial success in the mid twenties is a reflection of either the confidence or the desperate wish-fulfilment which existed in certain circles.

4

Wakening the Devil

It is so easy to make a revolution, but to bring one to a full fruition,
that has still to be done.[1]

As we have already seen, plays dealing directly with the events of 1917
were not welcomed by the censors, and it was twelve years after the
revolution before the characters of Lenin or Trotsky or the Czar
appeared on the British stage. Even then, they did so in clubs rather
than public theatres and without being licensed. However, it was
sometimes possible to write about the revolution less directly, by using
a fictitious setting and characters. It is on such plays, written or staged
during the twenties, that this chapter will focus, remembering that it is
not only unlikely that a play supporting any kind of left-wing revolution
would have been licensed, but that this fact would have been well known
by playwrights and theatre managers.

Despite this, the first play to represent the Soviet revolution was
performed as early as January 1918, and even if it was not quite a
celebration of the new regime it was certainly not sympathetic to the
old order. *Annajanska, The Bolshevik Empress* was a one-act piece written
by George Bernard Shaw, and was less concerned with factual accuracy
than with imaginative speculations. The issue of whether it could be
granted a licence for public performance never arose since it was
presented as part of a revue in a variety theatre, over which the Lord
Chamberlain had no control.[2] One of the more provocative and
interesting political dramas of its time therefore appeared as the ninth
of twelve items on a bill which also included Herculean Gymnasts,
Dainty Doris, and an assortment of performing animals. Yet the
surprising twists and relative complexity of *Annajanska* show little
attempt on Shaw's part to compromise his intellectual approach or to

patronise his audience. The context was violent revolution and war, but Shaw's play centres not on action but on debate.

Shaw chose to identify himself with the Soviet revolution, declaring elsewhere of the new leaders 'they are Socialists: we are Socialists: we must be on their side'; indeed, his continuing apparent support of Stalin is hard to explain. In *Annajanska*, however, he is not concerned with offering a naïvely utopian vision, and the play can hardly have pleased those on either the left or the right of the political spectrum. Certainly the disintegration of the aristocracy is seen as inevitable, and Shaw shows even its own members welcoming their collapse:

> We are so decayed, so out of date, so feeble, so wicked in our own despite, that we have come at last to will our own destruction.

Annajanska herself, the deposed Grand Duchess, shocks her followers by declaring support for the revolution and even encouraging it against her own regime:

> When will you learn that our strength has never been in ourselves but in your illusions about us.

She is not blind to the horrors of the new system, pointedly observing that it is 'as cruel as we were', and accepting that the new rulers, in their turn, will employ systematic terror and oppression to establish and maintain their power:

> GENERAL: How much liberty is there where they have gained the upper hand? Are they not hanging, shooting, imprisoning as much as we ever did? Do they ever tell the people the truth? No: if the truth does not suit them they spread lies instead, and make it a crime to tell the truth
> DUCHESS: Of course they do. Why should they not? . . . We did it.

In allying herself with the aims of the revolution, Annajanska proclaims her support for 'anything that will make the world less like a prison and more like a circus', but perhaps a more accurate recognition of what the real revolution would turn into is voiced in Annajanska's threatening and disturbing prophesy:

I say that if the people cannot govern themselves, they must be governed by somebody. If they will not do their duty without being half forced and half humbugged, somebody must force them and humbug them. Some energetic and capable minority must always be in power.[3]

The first play to use an imaginary country as a way of writing about the revolution was a fairly obscure piece called *Joan of the Sword*, performed in 1919 at a time when British troops were still fighting the bolsheviks.[4] This is an implausible story of romantic love and adventure, but the political references and messages are explicit, as the revolutionary government proclaims that 'all men shall be equal', that 'private capital and masters are abolished', and that 'all wealth, men, women and things are the common property of the State'. The play opens on the barricades, with a group of drunken louts waving the red flag and singing revolutionary songs, and while the defeated aristocrats are shown as polite, brave and gentlemanly, the revolutionaries are invariably rough, cowardly and lecherous, and given to calling each other 'comrade' and boasting about the 'accursed royalists' whom they have been shooting 'like rabbits'. The principle of equality is depicted as an attractive but absurd illusion—'Ah, it's all very beautiful and ideal—the pity is that it can't be true'—and we quickly see that a society without rulers and ruled could not even defend itself effectively since without superiors there would be no reason for an ordinary soldier to obey orders:

> This paper says that all men are equal. That means that there are to be no more Officers, so you can go to hell.

The main political thrust of the play is its demonstration of how the naïvety of the peasants is manipulated by a cynically hypocritical dictator, who seeks power only for himself:

> First the rabble must have their heads. I shall supply them with plenty of wine—give opportunities for excesses in all directions —advocate the gospel of equality and all that sort of rot, until a reign of terror has been established. The people who matter will begin to sicken of the orgies of wine and blood, and wish for a more stable form of government. That is the moment I'm waiting for.[5]

The attempt to redistribute wealth is shown to be doomed to failure because of humanity's unchanging and unchangeable nature, and most of the poor do not even support the revolution, because they recognise the differences between the classes as natural and unbridgeable. Ultimately, even the revolutionaries admit that they are incapable of pretending to be royalty, because they don't have the right faces or physiques for it.

Equally didactic and melodramatic was *The Terror*, a one-act play by Clemence Dane produced at the Liverpool Playhouse in September 1921, and written for Mrs Patrick Campbell to play the part of a suffering Russian aristocrat.[6] Censorship required that the setting should be described as an anonymous country 'in time of Revolution', but even the Reader's Report for the Lord Chamberlain, which found 'nothing whatever to censor', described it simply as 'A play of Bolshevik Russia'.[7] Again, Dane depicts the revolution as a reversal of the natural order of things, which has allowed 'the mob', with its animal instincts, to take power. The terror on which the play focuses is primarily to do with individual sexual lust rather than with politics, though the two are linked in that the lust is directed against a former aristocrat by her ex-servant. Sexual licence is directly equated with class anarchy, and is seen as either the aim or at least the main result of the revolution. In the words of the heroine, the revolution has 'wakened the devil in us all', and the new society sneers at values such as honesty and loyalty, while celebrating lying, robbing and cheating. The former aristocrat, Sonia, earns her living as a singer who is 'graciously permitted to amuse a Bolshevik mob for a half a loaf of bread a week', and believing her husband murdered, her only comfort is a faithful servant who refuses any attempt at liberation, and remains loyal to her mistress; together, they are 'helpless women in a city full of wild beasts'. The villain, Bergman, was previously her husband's bootboy, but as a high-ranking and sadistic official, he spares their lives only in expectation of sexual favours. As in *Joan of the Sword*, he has no respect for his own followers:

BERGMAN: These are tiger-cats, these men! I must give them mice to play with now and then or they'll turn on their trainer . . .
SONIA: But what will they do to him, the man you're hunting?
BERGMAN: There are many ways of getting rid of the troublesome now-a-days.
SONIA: [*shivering*] You'll let them—
BERGMAN: Play with him? Why not? The man's a reactionary, rich, a landowner, an enemy of the people.

Fortunately, Sonia's husband eventually escapes from prison, and together they manage to trick and kill Bergman, and set off towards the one haven of safety and freedom: 'To England—there's real freedom there!'[8]

In portraying the dire effects of revolutions in real or imaginary countries, it was not unusual to hold up Britain as a land of liberty and freedom, and many White Russians did indeed look to Britain as a bastion against communism. In 1921, three short plays were presented at the Ambassadors' Theatre specifically to raise money and provide comforts for refugees from bolshevik Russia, which again show England as the source of hope for true Russians and the ultimate enemy for the bolsheviks, who 'hate the English worse than anybody'. The cover of the programme depicted a weeping and frightened woman escaping into a sanctuary from an octopus-like creature with the face of Lenin, and the slogan: 'British Refugees From Russia: The Queen Has Helped Them—Will You?' One of these plays, *The Silver Lining*, was pure propaganda on the need for British soldiers to destroy the Soviet Union, whatever the individual cost.[9] The hero, an English soldier, is in despair after being permanently blinded in fighting the bolsheviks, but his Nurse tells him he must not be a coward and should remember the much greater distress of all who live under Soviet rule:

> What are your sufferings in comparison? You are not cold, starving
> or penniless . . . Petrograd is like a city of the dead.[10]

The soldier duly announces he will do all he can to help 'exterminate the whole breed', whereupon his fiancée, by whom he thought he had been deserted, assures him that she 'can't imagine anything more exquisite' than to nurse him for the rest of his life.

All of these plays clearly delighted in employing the crudest conventions and stereotypes, taking advantage of topical events to provide superficial variations on well-worn stories, and failing to engage in any kind of political argument. In 1922, Austin Page's *The Beating on the Door* ultimately descended into familiar clichés—more than one review suggested it 'could be turned with very little trouble into one of the old stock melodramas of the French Revolution'—but in its study of the effects of the Russian Revolution on an invented family of aristocrats it does at least engage in a real debate and dramatisation of ideas.[11]

The action of Page's play begins in November 1917, immediately before the fall of the Kerensky government, and the first Act exposes the uncaring and arrogant life-style of the wealthy Rosanof family in their sumptuous palace. Sacha, a family friend, is a disciple of Tolstoy who has written a book expounding socialist principles, and he tries to warn them that a violent revolution is about to destroy their way of life. Though he is promptly banished from the house as a traitor to his class, Sacha's prediction is fulfilled at the end of the first Act, as we watch the family being stripped of their wealth and dressed in sackcloth by the bolshevik leaders of a violent crowd threatening revenge.

> KRASNO: And now, line up all of you. (*A stone hurtles through one of the panes—the wind howls through*). Ah, you shiver! They have been shivering out there for centuries! It is your turn now.

In the second Act, the Rosanof family are labouring on the land they used to own, again obeying the orders of a former servant sadistically exacting his revenge. Sacha has joined the bolsheviks, but torn between politics and loyalty to the family, he manages to secure less physically demanding work for them. The third Act shows the utopianism of the revolution descending into horrific and violent atrocities, and the Rosanofs are arrested and sentenced to death for plotting a rebellion. The brutal campaign of terror drives Sacha to renounce his allegiance to the bolsheviks, and the final Act takes place in the prison where the family await execution. In an implausible climax, Sacha enables their escape by bribing the revolutionary guards, while he and the daughter, Tanya, discover they are in love with each other and stay behind to fight against the bolsheviks and for freedom. The title of the play is explained in the final image, as Sacha and Tanya listen to the sound of a guard whom they have locked inside a cell:

> SACHA: The beating on the door, It typifies the Russia of to-day. A poor, ignorant official doing what he's told, not knowing why— caged, caged!
> [*Slow ponderous knocks*]
> There he beats, beats, beats—begging for liberty and for light—we must fight for him out there![12]

Most theatre critics complained about the play's 'wearisome talk and argument', and accused it of being 'not vigorous nor lurid enough to make downright melodrama'. But though the combination of political discussion, sentimental romance and heightened action is not always sustainable, Page does allow for debate both on stage and in the auditorium. The unflattering portrait of the aristocrats' excesses and arrogance in the first Act—with their ninety-room palace, their two dozen servants, their golden finger bowls and their caviar breakfast served at noon—makes the revolution not only comprehensible and inevitable but probably deserved. Criticisms of the old order are forcefully expressed through Sacha:

> Your names are on the list of what they call—'wasters'—and when one sees the senseless, aimless lives you lead, can one blame them?

There is no doubt that we are intended to find both his rejection of their decadence and his idealism about the need for education and reform theoretically attractive, if not necessarily practical:

> TANYA: But you know, you're an awful Utopian, I wish I had the faith in human nature you have . . . Your ideas are wonderful, but not for the world we live in.

Sacha's eventual disillusionment with the bolsheviks does not mean an abandonment of principles, and even at the end of the play, he and Tanya are planning not to restore the old order but 'to educate and enlighten' in order to 'bring true brotherhood and equal opportunity' to all.

Page even allows strong arguments to Volsky, the intellectual leader of the revolution who is presumably modelled on Lenin. For example, Volsky produces a convincing if simplified justification for centralised state control of the economy, and gives even the confiscation of property an obvious logical base:

> We seize only what is superfluous. If the peasant has too much, we seize his surplus, and with it feed the famishing.

Certainly Volsky's ideals are initially allowed more credence than the Rosanof family's facile and bitter definition of the new system as 'anarchy', or 'take what the other fellow's got and say it's for the people'.

But crucially, Volsky is dependent for his power on a brutal and corrupt system imposed through force, and he too becomes a dictator, prepared to use threats and violence against anyone who questions his policies—including the workers on whose behalf the revolution has supposedly been fought and won:

> You'll go back to your work, and do as you are told. I shall take no
> dictation from you lot—remember it is I who decide, you who follow,
> and any disturbance or insurrection will be put down with an iron
> hand. We showed no mercy to your oppressors, when they refused
> to obey orders—we will show none to you if you disobey them.

Sacha's rejection of the bolsheviks when he realises how their intentions have been corrupted provides the example for us to follow:

> If communism, which should mean brotherhood, must wade through
> a sea of blood to accomplish its end, then the end is lost sight of at
> the very outset, and I refuse to go on.

Meanwhile, Tanya's rebellion against the brutality of the new regime forces Volsky into exposing the implications for society and the individual of communist rule:

> VOLSKY: If I could only bring you to think in the modern way,
> you would be a great acquisition to the cause.
> TANYA: The modern way! You're going back to the medieval, and
> the horrors of the Inquisition are as nothing to yours! . . .
> VOLSKY: We have no use for those who disagree with us.
> TANYA: And yet you cried out against the autocracy of the Tsar!
> You're a million times worse than those you overthrow!
> VOLSKY: Their autocracy was a synonym for reaction and
> corruption—ours is for progress and light, and the end justifies the
> means.
> TANYA: No end can justify such means!
> VOLSKY: If a million lives have to be sacrificed to attain our ends,
> they shall be sacrificed. The principles of Bolshevism must prevail,
> and for whatever we suffer, posterity will benefit—those are our
> ideals.

The message of *The Beating on the Door* is that a corrupt and unfair society has been replaced by one which has proved to be even worse. The revolution may have been motivated by genuine idealism, but it has been perverted by leaders who are at best arrogant, cynical and ruthless, at worst, corrupt, stupid and vicious. Yet in terms of audience reception, some of the play's assumptions were publicly questioned. One review mentions that 'the upper parts of the house seemed rather inclined to scoff' at Tanya's brave but somewhat unlikely defiance of Volsky, while the familiar and patriotic identification of England with freedom provoked a perhaps healthily cynical reaction:

> The first night audience was unusually hilarious during the closing scene, where the aristocrats escape from prison on their way to the frontier, and when one of them mentions that they are bound for England 'where there is real freedom', a shout of delighted laughter went up from the house.[13]

Certainly, Page's play was seen to have a contemporary relevance. Historians may suggest that any realistic likelihood of a major upheaval in British capitalist society had effectively vanished by the beginning of the 1920s, but it did not seem to everyone that revolution was something which could occur only in distant or fictitious countries. As the *Sunday Times* reported in its review of *The Beating on the Door*:

> many of the well-clad and bejewelled ladies in the stalls shivered as they watched the Communists seizing the pearl necklaces, confiscating the gold plate, and stripping the women of their furs.[14]

It was not just sympathy for the Russian aristocrats on stage that made them shiver.

A similar theme of high ideals becoming corrupted by power is at the centre of Israel Zangwill's *The Forcing House*, another play about communist revolution set in an invented country, which was written in the same year as Page's play, though not performed until 1926.[15] A political philosopher and campaigner, and a writer of considerable renown, Zangwill had argued for a serious theatre of ideas and debate. He had also previously shown public and political sympathy for at least some parts of the bolsheviks' programme in the Soviet Union, and in February 1919 he had been a principal speaker at a meeting in the Albert Hall organised by the 'Hands Off Russia' campaign, which was attempting to prevent the British government from sending financial and military support to the White Russians to help them defeat the Red Army.[16] While insisting that he was not a bolshevik, Zangwill had strongly attacked the hypocrisy of those who criticised bolshevism for a violence which they condoned elsewhere, maintaining that 'the bloodiness of their regime has been as exaggerated as its bankruptcy', and suggesting that if the British government had officially recognised Lenin's regime instead of setting out to destroy it then the revolution might have been 'comparatively bloodless'. Communism, claimed Zangwill, had already produced beneficial effects by shifting capitalism into a more liberal mode, and while not oblivious to the negative aspects of the revolution, Zangwill's excitement about the possibilities and the future shine through his Albert Hall speech:

> I regret their methods. I would not have raised a finger to help them. But now that they have helped themselves I would not undo their work . . . it is still in travail, a revolution still in evolution, a birth that is half an abortion, a chaos of capitalism and socialism, of idealism and materialism, of wisdom and folly.[17]

By 1922, when he published what he himself called his 'tragi-comedy of Communism', Zangwill's optimism had collapsed.[18]

The Forcing House shows the country of Valdania shortly before and after a left-wing revolution has overthrown an aristocratic government and replaced it with a republic. The two leaders of the revolution, Riffoni and Salaret, are highly intelligent and inspired by a genuine concern to create a better society. Riffoni cites Marx, insisting that even a benevolent capitalism, dependent on the generosity of individuals, is an inadequate basis on which to found a just society, and represents no more than 'blackmail to ward off revolution'. Yet once they have achieved power, their commitment to peace is transformed into an enthusiasm for punishing and repressing all dissenters, and Riffoni's determination to 'make a new heaven and a new earth—by making heaven upon earth' is dependent on the ruthless imposition of a dictatorship:

> Terror is the only shaping-tool. The Earthly Paradise we plan must be cleared of weeds: pitilessly—for pity's own sake.

The revolution literally replaces one set of icons to worship with another: the throne-room becomes 'The People's Hall', flying the flags and banners of socialism instead of those of conquered nations, the throne itself becomes a business seat, and the busts of royalty are supplanted by figures of Marx, Luxemburg and others. Similarly, the beautiful and sacred images of what Riffoni terms 'grotesque beliefs' are replaced with those of reason as plain glass replaces a stained-glass image of the Madonna and child, and the churches are transformed into cinemas showing socialist propaganda. Significantly, the stage description which opens the post-revolutionary second Act tells us that there is 'no visible alteration in the line of guards that stand with fixed bayonets', while the promised equality is achieved only through a general fall in living standards, as peasants and workers are cynically duped into accepting policies and conditions which they would refuse if they understood them. Before long, the surviving leaders of the previous regime have been welcomed back into office.

In a dimension rarely touched on by other playwrights, Zangwill is concerned not only about material freedom under a communist government, but also the freedom of the artist and the philosopher, recognising the danger that a revolution which unreservedly celebrates the values of those who have been oppressed and uneducated may fascistically deny the worth of all that has gone before:

> RIFFONI: We won't be nipped in the bud by your aristocratic artists and thinkers!
> D'AZOLLO: [*blandly*] Are there any others?
> RIFFONI: [*passionately*] Their art is worthless. Art and Thought must be of the People.
> D'AZOLLO: Good God! My peasants turned my library into cigarette-papers and my grand piano into a manure-sleigh. Aren't you satisfied with handing politics over to the People—the lowest thought of the greatest number!
> CAZOTTI: [*seeing the others a bit disconcerted*] The voice of the People is the voice of God.
> D'AZOLLO: Then the voice of God needs training.
> RIFFONI: [*unsmiling*] Exactly.

Ultimately, however, the revolution is confounded by the gap between theory and actuality, as its leaders betray their rationality to sexual desire; thus Salaret creates a harem of former aristocrats on the luxurious royal yacht, while Riffoni struggles to avoid being deflected from his ideological beliefs by his attraction to the imprisoned Queen.

> Who knows if it was not really your face that drew me back from exile? Perhaps my whole Revolution was only a bridge to span the gulf between us.

Before the revolution, the aristocratic Duke D'Azollo is an unexpected sympathiser with Riffoni's principles, but he recognises them as utopian and impractical. Arguing that socialists base their beliefs on theories rather than on an understanding of the real world and human nature, he compares their attempts to fashion a better society to climbing a mountain by telescope rather than in reality:

> D'AZOLLO: Wait till you are actually among the crevasses and glaciers—
> RIFFONI: We shall be roped together.
> D'AZOLLO: And together you will tumble.

Most tellingly, D'Azollo insists that the new system cannot last, and that capitalism will survive and return:

> Scarred perhaps, but titanically strong and crafty, like one of those great old whales that go careering about the oceans, stuck full of harpoons. Believe me, Capital has a long swim before it, and will yet upset your boat with a flick of its mighty tail.

By the final Act, the leaders of the revolution have all admitted that socialism is unworkable because it 'presupposes a quality which is not in human nature'. Trying to suppress its critics, admits Riffoni, is like trying to extinguish a volcano with a hose:

> As I mowed down the poor stupid peasants, who could not understand that the crops must be communised as well as the land . . . I wondered . . . whether the Workers' Republic was indeed only a forcing house.

Riffoni eventually shoots himself in despair, and in the final images Salaret symbolically tears down the red flag and, to the cheers of the populace, a new King is crowned. The message is the familiar one that humanity is too corrupt to live up to the ideals of communism; a fairer society may one day evolve, implies Zangwill, but the attempt to impose such a society is bound to fail. This point is encapsulated in the metaphor which describes the short-lived republic and gives the play its defining image:

> It is Socialism while you won't wait. Not a Paradise of blossoming brotherhood, not a natural growth under God's heaven, but a

Socialism ripened prematurely under the heat of compulsion and watered with blood: a Socialism under a sky of glass, unstable, sterile, without spontaneous sap, that can be perpetuated only by ever-renewed compulsion. And forced—good God!—from what seed? Constricting figs in greenhouse pots will precipitate them artificially, but there is high authority for doubting if they can be gathered from thistles. And human nature is unfortunately thistly.[19]

In his introduction to the published text, Zangwill reminds us in unequivocal language that Russia is 'not the only country where the dread "new" disease has raged' and mocks the dismay of socialists who now seek to 'disavow their progeny'.[20] The *Saturday Review* described the play as 'the profoundest and curtest criticism Russia has been subjected to' and compared the incisiveness of the writing to scorpion stings.[21] Indeed, when the play was eventually staged four years later, a Tory MP judged its importance and persuasiveness sufficient to make it worth his while to book the entire theatre for one performance, and to invite fellow Members of Parliament from all parties to attend at his expense.[22] Yet Zangwill's treatment of his subject is, at least in some respects, much more probing and complex than that of other writers from the early twenties, and he refuses to allow us to read the play in simple didactic terms. Even when they rule by terror, we are attracted by the rhetorical power of Riffoni's assertion that one day 'slave Socialism will beget free Socialism', and Salaret's conviction that 'the end does not resemble the means any more than a fruit resembles its seed'. Zangwill even gives Riffoni an argument which is reminiscent in the power of its image as well as its philosophy of Brecht's advice to revolutionaries to 'embrace the butcher' and 'sink into the mire':

The pioneer's hand can never be clean, and we who create civilisation are like the swine-grease through which perfumes are distilled for the delicate nostril.

Ultimately, however, *The Forcing House* suggests not only that communist ideals are impractical, but that socialists are, if not yet corrupt, at least inherently corruptible.

The middle of the decade saw two historical dramas about nineteenth-century Russia which depended partly for their interest on audiences making parallels or connections with more recent events. *Such Men are*

Dangerous by Ashley Dukes and *Paul I*, translated from the Russian of Merezhkovsky, both dealt ostensibly with the overthrow of Czar Paul Alexander, but the assassination of a Czar who is autocratic and weak, to the point of madness, invited the audience to approach the text in search of signposts pointing towards 1917.[23] Thus in *Such Men are Dangerous* the doomed Czar prophesies:

> My father was murdered, and maybe my son will be murdered, and my grandson . . . and all the Romanoffs will be murdered . . . and last of all, Russia herself will die.[24]

In *Paul I*, the Czar maintains that those who oppose him are 'preparing the way for the Beast, the Antichrist!', while a group of aristocratic conspirators debate the need to overthrow a despotic Czar who is like 'a madman amok in the world with a razor in his hand'. One of their more extreme members insists they must behave with cruelty in order to gain eventual freedom from it—'While we are dethroning the tyrant, let us be tyrants ourselves'—and warns what the future will bring unless they act effectively now:

> MARIN: The day of reckoning will come—the slaves will rise—they will break their flails over our heads; our blood will water their fields. The gibbet and the block, fire and the sword, these are what await us. And it will come, it will come. I see into the future—I see a hundred years ahead.[25]

In *The Grand Duchess*, a light romantic farce about the Russian royal family in exile in Switzerland, all specific references to the Soviet Union, the bolsheviks and Trotsky were removed by the Lord Chamberlain, though the play offers a sentimental and sympathetic view of how the aristocrats adapt to a world in which they have lost their inherited and absolute authority.[26] While one prince remembers nostalgically how footmen used to faint if he looked at them, a younger one rather enjoys the novelty of being treated as an equal and 'the more modern free-and-easy attitude adopted by the lower classes'. Communists, meanwhile, can now be recognised as the people wearing the largest diamond rings, having abandoned their principles and adopted policies indistinguishable from those of their predecessors:

It's the end of everything! . . . The Communists have decided to recognise the right to private property . . . They can't do a thing like that. Either they're Communists, or they're not . . . If these wretched creatures, after taking everything from us, adopt our methods as well, there's no knowing how long they may last.[27]

Some old-fashioned melodramas, such as *The Volga Boatman*, continued to attack the bolsheviks from a more traditional perspective.[28] Set on the banks of the Volga shortly before the revolution, this play depicts a largely exploitative aristocracy which regards the peasants and workers as mere beasts. The rebellion has two leaders, one a moderate, who seeks to improve conditions through negotiation, and the other an extremist, who desires a complete over-turning of society, and who lusts after wealth and revenge:

> Shoot these torturers, let's live in ease. Think of the riches in the palace . . . We are the bosses now. Let these fools wait on us. Have we not slaved for them till the flesh has worn off our hands? Let them slave for us.

A noble princess is shocked when she discovers the terrible conditions in which the majority of people live and work, and of which she has been kept ignorant, and conveniently falls in love with the moderate leader of the rebels. She warns her family that 'the day will come when we shall pull the boats and toil like beasts', and ends the play committed to improving the lives of the boatmen, and pulling boats alongside them:

> Now I see a purpose shown me: to bring light, hope, beauty into the lives of those whom the world seems to have forgotten—whom God seems to have forgotten—the Boatmen of The Volga.[29]

Even the Reader's Report for the Lord Chamberlain described this piece of naïve fantasy as 'an absurd, machine-made melodrama about Russia', though it found 'no harm in the rubbish'.[30] On the other hand, the single speech cut from *Red Nights of the Tcheka*, a piece of French Grand Guignol produced by Terence Gray at the Cambridge Festival Theatre in 1927, was the one which offered an element of justification for the viciousness of the bolsheviks, by pointing out that the Czars had been equally oppressive.[31] The Lord Chamberlain also insisted on changing the names and identities of characters and places, in order to avoid reference to actual Russian aristocrats:

To suggest, even in a melodrama, that a child of the Czar became a spy for the Soviet Government seems to me to be an outrage and unless this ending is altered I do not recommend the play for licence.[32]

The narrative deals with spying and counter-spying in the Soviet Union by bolsheviks and monarchists shortly after the revolution, and revolves around the recurring hope that the old Russia might be saved by relatives of the Czar who have escaped and will eventually return in triumph.

MICHEL: The whole of fallen Russia, crushed and enslaved, places her hope in you! . . .
WASSIL: Your name will raise the whole country!
SONIA: When it is known that you are alive, there is not a peasant in Russia who will not rise and follow us into the battle.[33]

Loyal Czarists have infiltrated both the government and the Red Army to plan a coup which will restore the monarchy and assure 'the deliverance of Russia from the yoke of the Barbarian', but the woman whom they believe to be the Grand Duchess is subsequently identified as a notorious bolshevik agent. In despair, they leave her buried alive in a cellar, before a final twist reveals to the audience that this really is the former Grand Duchess after all, who had become a Soviet spy in order to survive.

Towards the end of the twenties, a growing number of prominent and public figures began openly to express their admiration for the Soviet Union. John Strachey visited Russia in 1928 and believed he was witnessing the dawn of a new and better age, while one Labour MP found 'a sort of Book of Revelations ' when he visited to celebrate the tenth anniversary of the Revolution:

The impossible has happened. The things of which prophets have spoken have come to pass. The mighty have been pulled down from their seats, and those of low degree have been exalted.[34]

Culturally, formal and informal links with the Soviet Union had increased following the founding of the Society for Cultural Relations with the USSR in 1924, with H.G. Wells as one of its vice-presidents, and regular London seasons of the Russian Ballet drew crowded houses. At the same time, Soviet films began to emerge as a strong minority interest at independent London societies, and both Pudovkin and Eisenstein visited Britain in the late twenties to lecture about their work. In 1928, the Moscow Arts Theatre came to London with a repertoire of eight plays by Chekhov, Ostrovsky, Tolstoy and Gorky presented in Russian, and it is interesting to see *The Times* joining the praise for the company's apparent rejection of individualism, and identifying in particular the

> quality of collective understanding conveyed to the audience in a group of performances so fused in imagination that they give an impression of one performance, not of an aggregate of personal achievements.[35]

The staging of Russian plays by British companies also increased as the growing number of experimental theatres and Sunday Societies began to challenge British insularity by introducing foreign plays absent from mainstream repertoires. *The Cherry Orchard* had barely been seen in Britain before its run of 136 London performances in 1925, but in the second half of the decade all of Chekhov's major plays received significant productions in London and beyond. While Chekhov, the Moscow Arts Theatre and the Russian Ballet did not necessarily reflect revolutionary aesthetics or ideology, they perhaps offered a reassuring signal that the culture of a previous era had not necessarily been swept aside by a regime of uncivilised philistines. It was in this context that the last year of the decade brought four plays about Soviet Russia to the London stage, focusing on contrasting aspects of the revolution. Two of these were translated from Russian and one from Polish, though only one of the four could be licensed for public performance.

Rasputin, based on the Russian text by Alexei Tolstoy and Pavel Shchegoleff, was perhaps the least interesting of the four 1929 London productions, concentrating primarily on events and trivial action and described by the *Stage* as 'alternately dull and crudely realistic'.[36] However, this probably reveals as much about the conservative strait-jacket dominating performance styles on the British stage as it does about the play itself, since Piscator had used the script two years earlier in Berlin as the basis for an innovative theatrical and cinematic montage about the revolution. By contrast, the London production was a somewhat tedious translation of the text, staged according to established conventions. Nevertheless, the play did provoke debate concerning the appropriateness of dramatising real and recent events, with *The Times* asserting that history plays were 'apt to be dull' unless they were 'enlivened by pageantry', and the *Saturday Review* conversely suggesting that 'being history, recent, remarkable, and tragic, it can only fail to be interesting if the authors insist'.[37]

The extent of the debate was limited by the Lord Chamberlain's refusal to license *Rasputin* for public performance because the narrative and characterisation were not only critical of the pre-revolutionary regime in Russia but were also seen as anti-German.[38] The Czarina speaks with a German accent, connives with Rasputin for German ends, becomes the butt of vulgar army songs about her sexual liaisons with him, and is thoroughly machiavellian in her manipulation of events. Indeed, a more accurate translation of the original title would have been *The Empress's Plot*. In one speech, specifically marked as unacceptable by the Lord Chamberlain's Office, she expresses both her certainty that the revolution will fail, and a vindictive lust for the revenge she will take:

> Just a day or two more, and these clever Deputies, these wonderful Socialists, these magnificent Revolutionaries, will come crawling on their knees and begging me to take over full power. And I'll teach them a lesson that they will never forget,—these miserable workmen, these disgusting Soviets.[39]

The Lord Chamberlain's Office found the play 'sordid, nasty and offensive'.[40]

The only one of the four plays able to enjoy a sustained run was *Red Rust*, by Vladimir Kirchon and Andrei Ouspensky, which was promoted as 'the first play of Soviet Russia to be produced in England'.[41] The play had none of the theatrical energy and excitement of the Soviet experiments with form which had been passionately explored in the early years after the revolution, but its rather pedestrian style— somewhere between realism and melodrama—did not discourage British reviewers. Furthermore, having assumed that any Soviet play would be crudely propagandist, most of them were surprised by the play's willingness to critique its own society, even querying the accuracy of the translation and mistakenly suspecting that the original pro-Soviet propaganda must have been 'removed by our lynx-eyed authorities'.[42] *The Times* was confident the play could not 'pervert anyone of normal intelligence' and the critic W.A. Darlington contrived a particularly unlikely explanation:

The play is supposed by its Russian authors to be a pro-Bolshevik play, while its English adapters regard it as likely to be excellent anti-Bolshevik propaganda . . . The play is . . . a picture of a corner of modern Russian civilisation. That civilisation seems a fine thing to Comrades Kirchon and Ouspensky, who doubtless hope that we shall be persuaded to see it with their eyes. But we insist on looking at it with our own eyes, and so see it as a crude, lopsided Utopia which doesn't work.[43]

However, other reviewers focused on the surprising similarities between Moscow society of the 1920s and their own. 'Soviet Russia seems just like one's Public School', mused one, and the *Observer* similarly commented 'As at Eton, so at Moscow'.[44]

Red Rust is set in 1926 amongst students at Moscow University, and stages a complex and detailed debate about the merits and faults of post-revolutionary Soviet society, and the need for that society to continue evolving and not rely on the past to sustain it. The students complain that Party meetings are now dominated by business men rather than idealists: 'Thanks to them the whole revolution is becoming a matter of Kopecks.' The metaphor of the title refers to the stagnation which has crippled the glorious triumph of 1917, and especially to those who hold power:

The rust has eaten into them, and it will eat into all of us. This is not my Russia, not the Proletariat for which thousands of our dead lie all over Russia.

Some of them believe the future lies with science and the 'complete mechanization of man', and are ready to discard such concepts as humanity and justice in order to achieve a state in which 'not one vestige of this individualism remains'. The play raises questions about the appropriate models for morality and human relationships in a society which is determined to sweep away hypocrisy and to avoid the domestic structures of the past, but which has given birth to an alternative which seems to be excluding both the personal— 'I suppose it is bourgeois to want to be happy—everything must be for the mass'—and especially the emotional:

In the old days there was something called Love. [*There are groans in the darkness*] I know, Comrades . . . We can leave that to novels and poems.

One student argues forcefully against the traditional 'trapping and holding of one individual by another', and insists that 'we've got to live freely'; for her, any wish to preserve exclusivity in sexual relationships threatens to

> drag us back to the days of the slave owners when the Capitalist encouraged breeding so that he would have more human beings to put into his grinding machines.

Yet *Red Rust* also exposes the hypocrisy of a society in which men use the breakdown of traditional moral codes as an excuse to exercise their power over women.

In placing at the heart of the play an unpleasant and immoral individual who is a senior member of the Party, the playwrights deliberately draw our attention to the corruption and decadence of Soviet society. Terekhine is in some ways a conventional stage villain, and one critic described him as 'the bad Sir Jasper of a hundred English melodramas dressed in Red's clothing'.[45] He has abandoned his wife and child before the play starts, and continues by secretly committing bigamy, even while dismissing marriage as a bourgeois institution. Terekhine sneers at his detractors for their old-fashioned and middle-class morality, yet intimidates his new wife for having a platonic male friendship. Having forced her to undergo an abortion, he deliberately drives her to suicide through his philandering excesses and persistent abuse. However, *Red Rust* exposes the immorality of more than a single individual, for not only Terekhine's corruption but also that of the whole Soviet system is revealed when he silences and terrorises his first wife by threatening to inform the authorities that her brother fought for the Whites and that her father believed in God. Crucially, because he is a veteran who fought in the Red Army, Terekhine enjoys the automatic and unquestioning respect, and the misplaced trust and favour, of Party leaders.

Terekhine is finally trapped by his fellow-students and dragged off to pay for his crimes. In melodramatic terms, the villain gets his just desserts. Perhaps more significantly, the Soviet audience is encouraged to re-examine and criticise its heroes, warned against assuming that the revolution has solved all problems, and reminded that the process of change must not be allowed to stagnate:

Bad things have been carried out of the past ages. We can't outgrow our past overnight. But we must outgrow it. We will outgrow it.

Yet it is harder, perhaps, to see the relevance of this play to a non-Soviet audience. From another perspective, and with the benefit of historical hindsight, the play's construction of the committed and veteran Party member as a monster who must be destroyed could be read as an ominous justification for the purging of all dissident elements from society:

> Among us are certain individuals who are more dangerous than our millions of enemies outside the frontiers of Russia . . . we allow them to express theories which are like abscesses in a healthy body . . . This party is a body into which some foul microbe has penetrated, and most of us are like the healthy corpuscles of the blood. We are throwing ourselves upon the infected spot—we want to get rid of the malady.[46]

In 1941, according to his own account, the Polish writer Waclaw Grubinski was imprisoned in the Soviet Union for attempting an illegal crossing of a frontier, and condemned to death for having written a play some twenty years earlier which had 'blackened "the genius of humanity, Lenin"'.[47] *Lenin* had originally been written for performance in Warsaw, and was presented in London in 1929 as part of a trilogy with the collective title *Peace, War and Revolution*.[48] Under Soviet interrogation, Grubinski was to deny that his play was political, claiming that the choice of Lenin and the Soviet Union had been arbitrary, since his real subject was 'the psychology of revolution' rather than a specific ideology. However, it would be naïve to expect a writer to comment honestly on his work when his critics are armed with machine-guns, and it is hardly surprising that the court was unconvinced, for no-one seeing or reading the play could fail to interpret it as a concerted attack on the bolshevik government. Indeed, Grubinski concludes the account of his trial with the following observation, which he had understandably not admitted to his prosecutors:

> In the persons of Nicholas II and Lenin, I dramatically confronted the rule of the Czars with Bolshevism, and then, in the course of the play, in the dialogues between Lenin and Nicholas, the horrible truth inevitably shines out—that Bolshevism is Czarism, that Lenin is a more quintessential Czar than Nicholas.[49]

In part, *Lenin* rehearsed the familiar argument that human nature is too selfish for communism, and that everyone is a would-be capitalist —'in the meanest beggar crouches a bourgeois'. Lenin himself is compared in a stage direction to 'a machine running with inexorable regularity', producing manifestos as a substitute for bread, and seducing people through oratory and rhetoric. Ironically, and fantastically embodying the point Grubinski himself was to make, Lenin's most loyal ally is the former Czar Nicholas, now a committed socialist working as his secretary. But where Nicholas believes in freedom and equality, Lenin is devastatingly cynical:

> To become a Bolshevik you must gain an understanding of the unlimited contempt merited by man. Without this deep understanding you cannot be initiated into Bolshevism.

He freely admits that he has 'brought back to Russia the tortures of Ivan the Terrible', and that his policies have caused the deaths of tens of thousands of people through starvation, persecution and mass executions. In his own words:

> Before you were whipped like slaves and cattle in order to keep you as slaves and cattle. Now you are tortured to make you into free and equal people.[50]

Hubert Griffith also centred his play about the events of the revolution on Lenin, but where Grubinski shows him as a self-serving megalomaniac, *Red Sunday* emphasises how his every thought and action are dedicated to the revolution.[51] The play ends with the attempted murder which paralyses Lenin and, metaphorically, the revolution, and Trotsky helplessly asking 'Who is going to save our revolution now?'. In Komisarjevsky's production, Lenin's first entrance was in a symbolic red spot, and stage directions insist that he looks 'rather like Satan', and that 'his manner is autocratic as a Czar's'. Yet he is also depicted as hard-working and altruistic, combining high moral principles with a flexible pragmatism.

The ten scenes of *Red Sunday* unfold chronologically in nine separate locations, starting in 1906 with the first meeting between Lenin and Trotsky, and the settings include an underground cellar in Odessa, the Winter Palace, Trotsky's lodgings in Siberia, and a street in Geneva.

Griffith traces the events of 1917 to the brutality of Bloody Sunday in 1905, and shows that while Lenin is an important catalyst, the revolution is the outcome of a struggle which has been waged by many people over a prolonged period of time:

> Were we all mad? A hundred people can be mad. A thousand people can be mad. The mob itself can be mad. But when thousands of people, separated, spread over many years, all drive independently towards the same idea—then it's a madness that looks too much like common-sense.

The eventual coming of revolution is simply a question of time, as the Czar's incompetent handling of the European war, the murder of Rasputin by Russian aristocrats, the decision of the Germans to allow Lenin back into Russia, and even the arrest of Trotsky in 1906, all somehow lead directly towards it. But Griffith goes to considerable lengths to absolve the Czar from blame, making Nicholas a sympathetic if somewhat spineless figure, a devoted husband and father, who is aware of his faults and those of his ancestors. He is simply the wrong person in the wrong place at the wrong time, who would really have preferred to be a gardener. Even the Czarina is described in Griffith's stage directions as a 'tragic woman', out of touch with the real world and suffering from sickness. She may be misguided in her blind insistence that Russians long for an absolutist ruler to 'make them bow before the whip if they disobey', but she still attracts our compassion.

Simplistic though it sometimes is, *Red Sunday* embraces an unusual level of detail and analysis, distinguishing strongly, for instance, between the relative significance of Lenin and Trotsky. Even before he speaks, Trotsky/Bronstein is presented as an impractical romantic, attracted by the idea of a revolution and of himself as a revolutionary, and ostentatiously identifying himself with the oppressed by wearing a peasant-blouse which is actually made of silk. His passionate speeches are rhetorical and over-rehearsed, and when introduced to an uneducated peasant whose brother has been killed by Czarist soldiers, he launches into an abstract analysis of the political situation which all but alienates a prospective disciple. By contrast, Lenin is down-to-earth, learning from the peasants and workers rather than lecturing to them, and pointedly telling Trotsky that for a revolution 'one technical expert is always worth ten socialists'. Yet Lenin also uses theatrical devices to inspire others—as when he predicts the coming revolution:

About its coming there is no more doubt than about tomorrow's light! It will come! Look. Like a match flames when one rubs it on the box. [*He strikes a match on a box at the table, and the company, entranced, watch it burst into flame*]

Since the audience knows what will happen, Lenin's prophecies appear as uncannily accurate; in 1906 he confidently predicts:

I give the Czar eight years, ten years more—and then he and his whole imperial system will, of their own accord, go crashing to ruin.

The second Act focuses on the murder of Rasputin, as the political debate retreats into the background. Several reviews relished these scenes of action as the highlight of the production, but although the attention seems at first to shift from Lenin to Rasputin, events are constructed so that we continue to view them through Lenin's eyes; he predicts Rasputin's murder:

Who'll kill him?—what does that matter! The country's half in revolt already. We've only got to wait. To wait, to wait, to wait . . .

Then a stage direction indicates that 'the stage gradually darkens, as Lenin gazes into the night', and we see the plotting of the conspirators against Rasputin as if through Lenin's gaze. This effect is further enhanced when we subsequently cut back to Lenin and Trotsky exactly where we left them.

The climax of *Red Sunday* occurs three years after the revolution, as Trotsky challenges Lenin's momentous decision to compromise his economic policies. Griffith interprets this not as the policy of a hypocrite or of a dictator desperately hanging on to power, but as a necessary adaptation to the reality of changing circumstances. Just as in the opening scene, Lenin is contrasted with his idealistic but impractical colleague:

TROTSKY: The New Economic rot of yours is a return to Capitalism.
LENIN: Yes . . . How clever of you!
TROTSKY: We can't do it!
LENIN: We must.
TROTSKY: It'll lose the revolution. It's turning round against everything we've ever fought for . . .

LENIN: We're not giving way. We're turning round . . . Pure
Communism has failed.
TROTSKY: No!
LENIN: It doesn't work, which is the same thing! . . .
TROTSKY: It's the loss of an ideal.
LENIN: It's the loss of an illusion!

Lenin explains, more, presumably, for the audience than for Trotsky,
how he has had to overcome both the legacy of the Czar and the active
opposition of other nations:

> The Czar's government left us with a hundred years of debt when
> it fell. A disastrous war—that hardly helped us much. Then a
> disastrous peace! Then the nations of the world blockading us. Then
> the entire vast populace of the most backward country in the world
> to be governed for the first time by a new system. One has need to
> be an 'opportunist' to make much good out of this!

Yet Griffith suggests that in spite of these problems, Lenin has already
created a more open and honest democracy than exists in capitalist
societies:

> I do what a ruler has never dared to do before! I take the people
> into my confidence . . . I tell them what's being done! I go before
> the workers and I say: 'We're going to do this and this'; and then
> we do it. We make mistakes—ghastly or ludicrous mistakes
> sometimes—and then I go before the workmen again, and I say:
> 'We have tried to do this and this, and we have failed; now we are
> going to try something else'. And they begin to think; and they trust
> us . . . And they see that at least we are not out for ourselves.

In a final soliloquy just before he is shot, Lenin imagines himself
undergoing an interview with a hostile Western journalist. This device
allows Griffith to criticise countries such as Britain, which have been
covertly carrying on the war against the Soviet Union, and he even hints
that it may be this external threat which has caused Lenin to institute
the reign of terror, and prevented the Soviet Union from achieving its
utopian ideals:

> 'Not war, not war, Mr Journalist?' But as your peoples are still cutting
> us off from books and medicines, from steam ploughs and railway

engines—from anything that might make our State a little better
. . . perhaps you'll tell me, then, what war is? . . . 'I'm a demon, a
destroyer?'—but I had to make the land safe for the revolution, and
now at last, after this, perhaps the killing can stop.[52]

Red Sunday has many weaknesses as a piece of theatre. The writing
suffers from the strait-jacket of naturalism which sometimes forces the
author into clumsy expositions designed to give historical information
to the audience, and Griffith was not always able to incorporate effective
political debate into the dialogue. There is little discussion of what the
bolsheviks or Lenin actually stand for, apart from a vague commitment
to a fairer society, and the perceived need to emphasise dramatic action
means that the issues sometimes disappear into the background.
Nevertheless, Griffith opened up perspectives which challenged those
normally expressed in the British media, and it is no wonder that the
Establishment found the play too dangerous to allow.

If daring to put the Russian royal family on stage was the ostensible
cause of the official outrage at *Red Sunday*, it was the characterisation
of the two leaders of the revolution which most obviously challenged
the accepted truth. *The Times*, for instance, found them 'contrary to the
usual notions, intellectual men of high ideals and sincerity of purpose'.
As the first British dramatist to present a predominantly positive vision
of the revolution, Griffith was bound to provoke controversy. He
claimed an impartiality, and that the facts and personal details were
authentic, but *The Times* accused him of having 'gone to the Soviets for
the morals', and complained that the final curtain 'falls on a note of
ecstasy'.[53] Other critics suggested that it was still too soon after the
events for a writer to achieve the balance and distance which was
essential to good writing:

> Mr Griffith might have profited by his admiration for Ibsen, who
> began the best of his plays twenty years or so after the crisis. The
> author of Red Sunday may be said to have started ten years too
> soon.[54]

Alternatively, one might suggest that the British theatre was ten years
too late in trying to find an effective form for exploring politics on the
stage. The urge to build up a drama through montage and by
intercutting short scenes is implicit in *Red Sunday*, but such a style
would simply have seemed perverse to most reviewers, who felt that the

task Griffith had taken on was unachievable in theatrical terms. The *Observer* described the play as 'scrappy', and accused Griffith of having 'taken "bits" and put them together rather clumsily'.[55] He surely needed a more fluid, or epic, style of theatre than had yet been conceived of in British theatre, for the production was hampered by the obligation for each scene to be presented in a frame which necessitated regular and unacceptable delays as sets were changed:

> It was almost immediately obvious that what Mr Griffith had assembled was the scenario of a film. And how much better, we reflected, it would all have been as a film! . . . here are the notes for a scenario to rejoice the heart of a film producer . . . are these notes quite sufficient to make a play in the theatre? Quite frankly, they are not.[56]

In his introduction to *The Forcing House*, Israel Zangwill had admitted that although his play engaged philosophically and ideologically with contemporary issues, the form and theatrical language were traditional to the point of being old-fashioned: 'a modern picture', he had claimed, 'is infinitely more important than a modern frame.'[57] Yet the frame and what it encloses are not as independent of each other as Zangwill implies, and the imposition of, say, naturalistic or melodramatic conventions necessarily defines how an argument can be presented and even what the argument is. As *The Times* was to put it in discussing another anti-communist play in the early thirties: 'a problem that is at root economic cannot be debated in the terms of Adelphi melodrama.'[58] But that, perhaps inevitably, was what most of the plays about revolution in the 1920s had attempted to do.

5

When England goes Communist

> CHARLES: Do you believe all that tripe you hear about Russia
> being Heaven on earth?
> ANNE: Do you believe all that tripe about it being hell on earth? . . .
> CHARLES: I've got an idea that Asia is feeling its way to a better
> state—it may be hell now, but heaven's coming along.[1]

If the dominant tone of plays about communism during the 1920s had
been fear and horror, that of the 1930s is more varied and often more
ambivalent. This was, after all, the 'Pink Decade' during which, as *The
Times* obituary of Stephen Spender was to put it, 'politics invaded the
innermost recesses of literature'.[2] *Left Review*, which began publication
in 1934, is only the best known of a number of journals in the thirties
which discussed art from a left-of-centre perspective, announcing that
'we no longer believe in "detachment" ', and insisting on the indivisibility
of art and politics:

> I imagine that it is generally accepted by readers of *Left Review* that
> 'literature is propaganda.' But I am not sure that we emphasise often
> enough the converse that the most lasting and persuasive propaganda
> is literature . . . it is the job of literature to influence readers, to
> work a change, and to record change in both reader and writer.[3]

The journal appealed for contributors who recognised that fascism was
simply the last bastion of capitalism, and even established what it called
a 'Writers International', designed to 'bring writers into touch with life'.[4]
It was not merely convinced fellow-travellers who began to predict
the coming of communism and the death of capitalism in Britain. In a
radio talk in 1937, Frank Birch summed up the uncertain and con-
tradictory feelings shared by many:

The more one reads about Bolshevism, the more one is astonished
—partly horrified, partly filled with admiration, but wholly
bewildered. It is barbarous, and it is ultra-modern. It is completely
materialistic, yet it is saturated with idealism. It is atheistic, but it
has all the fanaticism of a religion. It is tyrannical, but in the name
of freedom . . . In many ways it revolts me. But I do feel that it
makes a lot of the current coinage of our social creed sound like dud
half-crowns on a counter.[5]

Instead of endlessly repeating horror scenarios, some commentators and
playwrights began to question more seriously what Britain might really
be like if the communists took power, and whether things would really
be so very different. As Douglas Goldring observed:

When England goes Communist . . . no doubt the party in power
will call itself the 'Conservative Co-Operative Party', and, as usual,
half the Government will be Old Etonian.[6]

Not the least interesting thing about Goldring's remark is his use of the
word 'when'. Similarly, Beverley Nichols prefaced the published text of
his 1934 play, *When the Crash Comes*, by affirming his conviction that

sooner or later the whole world will be forced to adopt the general
principles of Communism, and that therefore, in our own interests,
it is high time that we stopped talking about the Bolsheviks as if
they were merely a collection of bogies and blasphemous savages,
and began seriously to study their ideals, their methods, and their
achievements.

Like Goldring, Nichols argues that when the communists do take power,
little will actually change, and that neither the process nor the result
will resemble what has occurred elsewhere:

The English character is so strong, so solid, so ingrained with a
curious fatalistic humour that any scenes of hysteria and violent
excess are literally unthinkable.

He also claimed that his play would redress an imbalance, since the
British press had hidden the 'tremendous miracle' which had occurred
in the Soviet Union:

Day after day they print, in flaring headlines, accounts of the appalling conditions under the Bolshevik regime . . . when precisely the same conditions exist within a hundred yards of their own front doors.[7]

When the Crash Comes is a drawing-room comedy, which opens as the Communist Party comes to power through a general election; this itself is a typically British compromise since, as one of the characters says, 'you can't make a revolution by act of parliament'. The upper-class and working-class families billeted together after the 'Redistribution of the People Act' divide the drawing-room by a line on the floor, and the drive for equality leads to petty and farcical squabbles as they debate who should have the second half of the *Encyclopaedia Britannica*, which contains the lives of both Lenin and Queen Victoria. However, Nichols shows that although they think of themselves as bitter enemies, the families soon develop relationships of trust and sympathy once they have the chance to get to know each other.

When the Crash Comes implies that the British are too impatient and apolitical to give an alternative to their present political system a fair try. At the centre of the play, and its tragic hero, is Jim, a Communist MP who discovers that support for his government quickly evaporates with the onset of shortages and rationing of supplies:

> They didn't realize . . . that in a country like this, you can't bring about a revolution in three weeks . . . Nor can you avoid extreme suffering . . . They want to go back to their old masters . . . What do they expect? Paradise in a couple of weeks? . . . I never promised them that . . . I always said there'll be suffering, and chaos, and agony, and disillusionment . . . What do they expect me to be? What did they elect me for?

Public attitudes are typified by three supposedly communist supporters, who curse the British aristocracy while being simultaneously fascinated by every detail of their private lives. Confronting the doubters, and supported and inspired by his love for the aristocratic Celia, Jim tells them that to renounce the revolution will

> not only destroy the ideals for which the people of this country declared themselves a few weeks ago . . . not only strangle the revolution at its birth, but . . . set back the clock of progress for a hundred years—perhaps for ever.

However, as he stretches out his arms 'like a figure on the cross' and tells the crowd 'I want your faith', he is assassinated; his death signals the end of the communist experiment, which is yet again shown to be utopian and impractical. Celia tries to maintain his ideals, but after six months of failing to convert the wives of workers, she realises that people are simply not interested in reorganising society:

> All they're interested in is the way I dress . . . Just because things are a bit better . . . because the unemployment figures are going down, because a lot of them are getting three and four pounds a week, they've forgotten all they ever learnt.[8]

Nichols blamed the weather and the English character for preventing a revolution. One of the characters in F.L. Lucas's 1932 play, *The Bear Dances*, is similarly scathing and cynical, suggesting revolution would interfere too much with the football and the urge to frivolity:

> No use preaching the class-war to the English workers. You can make them angry—but then someone else makes a joke—and they laugh—and it all flies out of their heads. Besides, the English think all people with theories mad anyway.

Lucas himself was unable to decide 'whether Soviet Russia inspires more vivid admiration or contemptuous disgust, so strongly does it inspire both'. He was particularly appalled by what he saw as the subordination of art and culture to ideology, and the absolute faith in materialism as the key to happiness:

> Few spectacles are more extraordinary than this passionate faith that Heaven can be reached by the world-proletariate in a sufficient number of sufficiently large omnibuses and the divine fire descend from an electricity-grid.

Yet he also expressed great admiration

> for the moral courage that sets out to redeem a world over which cleverer men only shake their clever heads . . . for actual achievement in lessening infant mortality and illiteracy, in liberating women from inferiority, in handling boldly, if crudely, marriage and divorce.[9]

Lucas argued that the Soviet Union had so exposed the injustices of capitalism, that communism was bound to become the dominant system of government in the future, and it was in the spirit of contributing to its reform and improvement that he set out to criticise the Soviet system.

The Bear Dances is a determinedly balanced play, self-consciously Chekhovian in its theatrical language, which sets out to reveal the nature of everyday life in the Soviet Union, and to contrast it by implication with the world familiar to its audience. Set entirely in the Soviet Union, Lucas's play shows a society in the grip of a restrictive and extreme ideology in which a professor loses his job for making jokes about Lenin and not mentioning Marx in his Shakespeare lecture, and children are given such names as Antichrist and Dialectic Materialism. Artistic suppression and control is such that poetry is allowed only if produced by groups rather than by individuals, music by orchestras without conductors, and plays by actors who model themselves on machines. It is also, as one of the visitors from England sees, a society riddled with jealousy, murder, prejudice, corruption, revenge and poverty.

> ANDREY: Remember this—that you cannot build on hatred . . .
> Level everybody, if you want; leave everybody with sixpence in the
> world; but have done with this devil's nonsense about the class-war
> and the nobility of hate.

Andrey identifies the potential for a healthy society which is in danger of being wasted:

> ANDREY: Why are human beings such fools? Here was the real
> chance for Socialism—and to spoil it all like this, with spies and
> hate and hangmen! All the cruelties of the old Russia poisoning the
> new! It's foul.

Meanwhile, Vera, an unquestioning Soviet apparatchik with whom Andrey falls emotionally if not ideologically in love, may be shown as foolish and deluded, but she is also allowed a long and sincere speech in which she cogently attacks the Orthodox Church for spending its money on churches rather than the poor, science under capitalism for building machines to 'squeeze the workers in peace, and to massacre them in war', and the Russian intelligentsia for having tried to sabotage the revolution:

Russia's not a tea-party; it's a battlefield. We're fighting to do
something the world has never done . . . It's being born again, and
that means agony . . . Communist Russia is the only country in the
world today where there's work for all. And if there's suffering for
all—at least it's shared. And we know what it's shared for, and that
we are bearing it now to abolish it for ever.

When asked why the new society must be built 'on a foundation of
screaming bodies', Vera asks in turn

if a few thousand perish—what's that compared with the millions
in Capitalist wars?

Andrey, returning to the country he had fled in 1914, discovers how
easy and foolish his communist sympathies have been as 'a Bolshevik
in Berkeley Square'. When Vera expresses surprise that there has been
no English revolution, he replies by advocating a process of gradual
evolution:

There's always a revolution in England. Only like the hands of the
clock, it's too slow to see.

Despite herself, Vera is moved by his recitation of classical poetry, which
he sarcastically tells her is excluded from the Soviet Five Year Plan, and
echoing Lucas's own insistence, Andrey ridicules her materialist belief
that happiness can be the result of external progress:

You who dream the world will live happily ever after, when
everybody has a tractor and nobody has lice! Machines!—how they'll
mock you, one day, with their winking wheels and humming throats,
for having sold your souls to them.

By the end of the play, Vera, the dedicated Party member who was
previously upset and insulted by any criticism of Lenin and who spouted
his phrases by rote, has begun to question things she took for granted,
and 'in a voice broken at first, strengthening as she goes on' she makes
an inspiring and idealistic speech about justice, to her fellow farm-
workers:

For we shall win the world by that, Comrades; not by tanks or
poison-gas; but by justice—because our motto is the only just

one—'From each according to his abilities; to each according to his needs.' Poverty is a crime; riches are a theft. And yet injustice is strong . . . The world isn't so simple as we think it, Comrades . . . But we must understand. For if we don't, we shall hate. Life's too short and too harsh to make it bitterer with that. Let's hate only one thing, Comrades—injustice; and no people, not even the bourgeois . . . Let's work, indeed, for the day when the word 'wealth' is abolished, and the word 'war' forgotten too.[10]

The hope of reformation eventually resides with two women, one British and one Russian, who dedicate themselves to living and working for a fairer society within the Soviet Union. For while *The Bear Dances* may be critical of many aspects of life there, Lucas shows little sympathy for the mundane oppression of British society, recognising the deliberate distractions encouraged by the Establishment to secure their own survival. Listening in Moscow to the BBC, the empty rhetoric of a bishop and a 'peculiarly senseless piece of jazz' reflect the emptiness of Western society and culture:

VERA: We don't need your sex-films and your fox-trots here in Russia to keep the idle busy, while the workless tramp the streets.

Indeed, the commercial failure of his own play typified for Lucas the mindlessness which he despised and derided in British society:

The first night coincided with a musical comedy at Drury Lane about a girls' school . . . With such preoccupations of an imperial people it was, I see now, tempting Providence to compete.

Unable to comprehend why so few plays were being written about such an important issue, Lucas identified a will to ignorance among the British people:

It is not so much that the ordinary public fails to see the importance of what is happening in Russia, as that it does not want to see. It might sleep worse.[11]

Another play from the early thirties which contrasted British and Soviet societies was Hubert Griffith's *The People's Court*, but Griffith's argument is much more heavily loaded.[12] In 1929, his epic *Red Sunday* had already implied that the Soviet Union under Lenin enjoyed a fairer and more democratic society than that of the Western powers. On the face of it, *The People's Court* was much more limited, with its single Act focusing entirely on one apparently domestic trial in a Moscow courtroom. Yet the play's implications were equally broad, questioning British assumptions about the inferiority and immorality of Soviet society.

The trial with which Griffith's play deals concerns an unmarried girl of nineteen who is bringing a claim for maintenance against a man who denies being the father of her child. The identity of the Judge alone is intended to shock London audiences; not only is she a woman, but also a shabbily dressed and middle-aged peasant, and Griffith notes in an ironic aside that 'society instead of asking her to scrub floors or dig potatoes, happens to have placed her in a situation for which she is admirably suited'. Moreover, by contrast with British judges, she has not lived at a distant remove from ordinary people, and is therefore better equipped for her role to judge the truth of a situation:

> I didn't spend half my life dealing in cattle in a village market without knowing when a man was telling lies to me—before the lies had even got as far as his mouth.

Because ordinary people administer justice in this society, they take it seriously; drawing an obvious comparison with the vested interests which dominate capitalist society, the Judge defends the fairness of the Soviet system:

> As in a state of Communism nobody has anything to gain by bad decisions being made, and everyone stands definitely to gain by good decisions being made, it follows that we are likely to be as fair about the whole thing as human beings are ever able to be.

At one point, the court mocks the naïve ignorance of a recent English delegation which had questioned whether women in Soviet Russia received the same pay as men for the same work:

> There was such a shout of laughter at the idea that a woman should not get the same pay as a man. But that, too, was to the English apparently one of our innovations.

Meanwhile, the Judge produces statistics to demonstrate that government policies have halved infant mortality, that mothers are paid and cared for better than in any other society, and that the system of marriage and separation is being improved:

> Divorce, frequent as it is, is at least free and not hypocritical. We have abolished the swamp of lies and perjuries and degradations necessary to get it in almost every country in the world but ours!

At the end of the trial, the Judge challenges the accused man to tell the truth on his honour as a member of the Communist Party, reminding him

THAT THE WORD OF HONOUR OF A MEMBER OF THE PARTY IS THE MOST VALUABLE THING THAT HE POSSESSES, AND THAT TO USE IT IN VAIN IS A SIN AGAINST THE WHOLE OF HIS LIFE.[13] [*Griffith's capitals*]

Faced with this, he immediately confesses his guilt and begs for forgiveness. Such an easy ending may seem implausible, but in a preface to the published text, Griffith insists on its authenticity and that the play 'is at least as much a literal transcript as a work of imagination'.[14] Despite these claims, there is surely a tragic naïvety or disingenuousness in the playwright choosing a court-room as a setting in which to demonstrate the supposed justice and superiority of Soviet society.

One play which reads as a relic from the previous decade was *The Red Light*, co-written by H.F. Maltby and John Trevor. Indeed, it is striking how old-fashioned and inappropriate the simplistic message of this desperately anti-communist drama from the early thirties seemed, even to those who might have been expected to share its political assumptions. Maltby had already written *What Might Happen* in 1926, a fantasy about the demise of the aristocracy and their replacement as rulers and decision-makers by a greedy, crude and uneducated working-class. *The Red Light* was several stages darker in showing the dire consequences for Britain if the bolshevists should ever come to power.[15] The play's production was financed by John Trevor, a wealthy lawyer, whose intentions were explicit:

> Mr Trevor states that his main object is to be of service to his country, and he certainly proves his sincerity by standing the cost of the play. It is a warning against us to be on our guard against a Communist or Bolshevik Revolution.[16]

The programme showed a globe whirling to destruction in red flame, and audiences were advised that police were 'scattered about the theatre to deal with a possible uproar'.[17]

Maltby was primarily concerned to warn audiences that they needed to take the communist threat much more seriously. Of the aristocrats on whom the play focuses, only the elderly Sir Herbert realises that Britain is in danger; to the rest of his family and friends, revolution is 'what happens in Russia and places like that', and his dire predictions are ignored:

> SIR HERBERT: You don't believe it could ever happen in England?
> GROOMBRIDGE: Of course not.
> VERA: Of course not! Bertie, have some more strawberry flan.

Sir Herbert tells them to change their behaviour before it is too late, and especially to be more discreet about their wealth:

> If you know a man is hungry, don't grill a rump-steak under his nose and then eat it yourself. If you want an expensive dinner don't have it at the next table to people who can only afford bread and cheese. If you want to wear furs and diamonds don't flaunt them about and make others envious! Whenever I see an overdressed woman driving in her limousine through the poorer quarters, I wonder what seeds of Bolshevism she is sowing.

But his relatives are too busy betting on the chances of a General Strike taking place to worry about its social and political implications. The massed marches, the demonstrations and even the military organisation of the workers—'much better for them than hanging about at the street corners'—are blindly and patronisingly treated as mere entertainment:

> Oh, by the way, what is that latest song that everyone is singing . . . something about a 'Red Flag'? . . . What funny songs the common people get hold of.

When it comes, the revolution brings queues, shortages, revenge, poverty, prostitution, sexual blackmail, illiterate local despots, the loss of individuality, and the collapse of all standards of hygiene and of social and moral values. The absurdity of 'the war for an equality the creator never made' is revealed too late, as the impracticality of communism dawns even on those who had supported the revolution:

As soon as you're given an extra good job or put in a bit of authority—you have all the rest of them, like a pack of hounds —howling you down until they've got you level with them again. It's those who had nothing to lose who are profiting by all this—I ought to have rumbled that before. We can't all be on top, but we can all be at the bottom and that's where we all are.

The last Act of *The Red Light* resolves the situation through the oldest of devices, when we discover we have been watching Sir Herbert's dream, and that the impending strike has been averted:

I knew all along that people were making too much fuss about it. I knew that everything was bound to come out all right—it always has done and it always will. As my husband always used to say—'Have faith in England—and England will always pull us through!'

However, we are invited to view such certainty as misplaced and arrogant, when a final twist—in a pre-echo of the famous climax of Priestley's *An Inspector Calls*—implies that the 'fictional' events which we have witnessed are about to become 'reality'. Only Sir Herbert and the audience can hear the singing of 'The Red Flag' from under the stage which accompanies the final scene; as the music swells, he turns to address us directly, and the breaking of the naturalistic convention which has operated throughout the play heightens the sense of shock and warning:

Are they all mad? Or am I? (*Straight to audience*) Why am I the only one who seems to hear it?

On the face of it, then, *The Red Light* is classic right-wing propaganda hitting predictable targets. The language used to describe working-class characters reveals the prejudices and assumptions of the playwrights; one is 'a dreadful looking female', another 'a working bootmaker and looks it', while the regional communist committee 'might have been picked out of a common doss house', with its female member 'of the virago order'. One of the intended shocks for the audience is the visual image of Burlington Arcade transformed into Poverty Corner, the tone of the stage direction confidently assuming shared values between playwrights and audience, and dismay at the erosion of those values:

The shops we know are there, but their well-dressed windows are gone and fish and chips, tripe, potatoes and onions are displayed in their places.[18]

Yet the play's lack of political subtlety actually proved an embarrassment to many who had no wish to defend the ideology Maltby had set out to discredit. *The Times* described it as 'a crude and tawdry entertainment' and talked of 'dingy sketches' and 'satirical bludgeonings'. Even the lighting was criticised on ideological grounds:

A glow so infernal and artificial at the end of the first scene causes the experienced playgoer to abandon hope. Propaganda . . . where plastered with this kind of emphasis, is going to be exceedingly uncomfortable.

Perhaps even more significantly, the newspaper argued that the very form in which the play had been written inevitably led to a simplification of the issues, pointing out that 'a problem that is at root economic cannot be debated in the terms of Adelphi melodrama'.[19]

Just as crucially, the propaganda itself was seen to be fundamentally flawed. Before licensing it, the Lord Chamberlain had sent the script to the Home Office, concerned that showing a British revolution might be too dangerous. However, the main complaint of the Home Office was that the play did not achieve the effect intended by the authors; the problem was that the aristocrats were

not attractive people and they break up so badly under stress that if they were really representative of the upper classes the public might well think that there is something to be said for revolution![20]

The same point was made by several reviewers, with James Agate being particularly scathing and thorough in reaching his paradoxical conclusion:

Since this play was to be propaganda on behalf of the existing social order, our authors must surely have shown . . . a social order preponderantly and overwhelmingly worth preserving. The failure to do this was Mistake Number One. Mistake Number Two was to depict Bolsheviks solely as scum . . . Mistake Number Three . . . was to show the existing order rushing pell-mell to drink and prostitution . . . If our men and women are no better than Mr Maltby's ladies and gentlemen . . . they are failures and ought to be swept away . . . In effect, the piece is actually pro-Bolshevist.[21]

In the Soviet Union, theatre in the immediately post-revolutionary era had devoted much of its energy to developing new forms of expression, new relationships between stage and audience, and new ways of creating material. It had been recognised that the politics of a performance do not lie solely or primarily in the arguments expressed in its narrative, and that 'ideology is in the form'. The point was understood in the thirties by the theatrical left in Britain, and most of the formal experiments carried out were echoes, if sometimes pale ones, of Soviet experiments from a decade or so earlier. The integration of aesthetic with political radicalism had not been a feature of the twenties, but by the early thirties it was becoming apparent to those who thought about such things that if theatre was to change people's perceptions of the world and retain any importance as a disseminator of ideas, then it needed to find new forms through which to do so.[22]

Leading the assault on the mainstream were such organisations as the Workers' Theatre Movement, Unity Theatre, Left Theatre, Theatre of Action and Group Theatre, and their challenge encompassed a range of areas, including methods of creating theatre, styles of performance, relationships between stage and auditorium, and the search for appropriate audiences and sites for performance. Some of those involved insisted that aesthetics were of no interest, and that everything must serve the political message:

> I don't believe that any of us regarded ourselves as artists or, indeed, as being in any way involved with art. We saw ourselves as guerrillas using the theatre as a weapon . . . to hell with art, let's get on with the job.[23]

In this description, Ewan MacColl, a driving force behind Manchester's Theatre of Action, turns 'art' into something taboo and to be avoided at all costs. But as much of his own work shows, the division was rarely as straightforward as this statement claims, and developing new forms was inseparable from creating new meanings. Montagu Slater, who as editor of *Left Review* helped to develop that journal's political and aesthetic positions, insisted that to value and create art was in and of itself a political act, since to treat as important something which was not justified primarily in terms of profit and economics was a fundamental challenge to the dominant ethics of society:

> Literature concerns human relationships. Capitalism destroyed these
> . . . substituting money or commodity relationships.[24]

Similarly, Terence Gray, the director of the Festival Theatre in Cambridge, argued that a willingness to experiment artistically contains an inherent political dimension, since it becomes impossible as soon as 'art comes under the sway of commerce'.[25]

The Workers' Theatre Movement reached its peak in the early thirties with its staunchly pro-communist and pro-Soviet Union stance, expressed through the agit-prop techniques derived from Soviet, German and American groups. For the WTM, the theatre was a political tool and a means to an end:

> The task of the WTM is the conduct of mass working-class propaganda and agitation through the particular method of dramatic representation.[26]

The WTM saw the form as crucial to the message, and the director Tom Thomas outlined the stages by which a workers' theatre should develop:

> First, the Cultural Theatre for the workers, performing plays from bourgeois sources . . . This grows into the Propaganda Theatre which develops its own revolutionary playwrights within the framework of a naturalistic stage.

In England, said Thomas, both of these forms now belonged to the past since 'in no capitalist country can the naturalistic stage be considered the ideal propaganda weapon of the proletariat'. The final goal, was therefore

> the 'Cabaret' form, for which a stage, curtains and lighting are unnecessary, whose properties can be transported by hand, and a performance of which can be given generally anywhere.[27]

Most of the agit-prop scripts produced by the WTM were choral declamations with simplified images and slogans, which required performers to step only briefly out of a communal chorus to present familiar stereotypes. This had the advantage of demanding little subtlety in terms of acting skills, and of being sufficiently flexible to accommodate a changing cast. However, considering the source of the inspiration, there is an irony in the fact that this form itself came to seem anachronistic after the 1933 Moscow Olympiad, where the British were heavily criticised by international workers' theatre groups for their exclusive emphasis on agit-prop. Just as significantly, the didactic sloganising appeared equally dated following the Communist Party's shift of policy from class-war to the building of a united front to embrace the whole of the anti-fascist movement. Nevertheless, the influence of the formal experiments of the WTM runs through most left-wing theatre which followed it.

Left Theatre was founded in 1934, seeking support from the trade union and Co-operative movements to establish a professional left-wing repertory company. Like the WTM, it aimed for a working-class audience, but its actors, designers and producers were to be drawn from within the professional theatre. An early manifesto stated the company's position and intent:

> The commercial theatre is limited by its dependence on a small section of society which neither desires, nor dares, to face the urgent and vital problems of today . . . The Left Theatre realises that the very class which plays the chief part in contemporary history—the class on which the prevention of war and the defeat of reaction depend—is debarred from expression in the present day theatre. This theatre will perform, mainly in working class districts, plays which express the life and struggles of the workers.

The texts Left Theatre hoped to produce would be political according to a relatively broad definition:

> Politics, in its fullest sense, means the affairs of the people. In this sense the plays done will be political.[28]

The company toured a succession of left-wing plays to London halls, but as the generally sympathetic *Left Review* noted in its analysis of one production, the social background of the performers was in danger of distancing them from audiences:

> In a working-class play like this, something has got to be done about the actors' voices. The Oxford accent may or may not be a thing of beauty; it is certainly not employed by many working men and the sooner it is done away with in productions of this kind the better.[29]

The contrast between this and the amateur performers of Unity Theatre, founded in 1936, was easy to identify:

> The passionate sincerity which the unpaid workers who compose the casts of Unity Theatre productions throw into their acting makes it not acting but living reality.[30]

Working-class actors brought not only conviction, but also an authenticity which Left Theatre's trained actors could not claim:

> There was no shamming . . . all of us believed passionately in what we were doing and what we were saying.[31]

Only workers could be expected 'to give a convincing exposition of the life of workers'.[32] John Allen, one of the directors of Unity's productions, contrasted their actors with professionals who, for the sake of a good part, would 'as cheerfully have given a sympathetic portrayal of a Fascist general as they would have acted the part of Lenin himself'.[33]

In the second half of the decade, Unity built on the discoveries and techniques of both the WTM and Left Theatre. The latter had never established the permanent home of which it had dreamed, but the idea was carried through into the building of Unity's Theatre in St Pancras, proudly identified as 'the first home of drama ever constructed by British workers and professional men in comradeship for themselves and for the movement of which they are part'. Its very construction challenged capitalist ethics as those who worked on it did so voluntarily rather than by hiring out their skills, and the successful completion of the ambitious scheme was compared in the Daily Worker to 'the heroic achievements of the First Five-Year Plan'.[34]

Unity admitted that its non-professional actors were often more suited to chorus work or caricatures than to sustaining major naturalistic characters, and in a direct challenge to the star system, their programmes pointedly refused to identify actors with specific parts. Rather, they were to be seen as workers, representatives of the mass, and therefore nameless. But unlike the WTM, Unity had cultural as well as political aspirations, and was prepared to draw on the expertise of professionals to help challenge the bourgeois theatres. Tom Thomas, a founder of the WTM, had demanded, in a well-known phrase, a 'propertyless theatre for a propertyless class', and Ness Edwards had argued that in a theatre designed for workers

> in contrast with the capitalist drama, the settings and scenic effects have to be entirely subordinated to the theme. No reliance can be placed upon beautiful costumes and sensuous females.[35]

Unity, however, insisted that 'the socialist theatre must be as aesthetically convincing as the theatre it is trying to supplant'.[36] Their official policy included commitments

> To produce and present among as wide an audience as possible stage plays, dealing with social problems and issues of interest to the working class . . .

> To devise, import and experiment with new forms of dramatic art . . .

> To work for the regeneration of the Commercial Theatre along the above lines . . .[37]

Unity did not refer to itself as marxist or communist, preferring to keep the broader term of 'workers' theatre'; indeed John Allen, pointed out that while 'it is not possible to draw many actors together on a pro-Socialist basis, it is possible to get them on an anti-fascist one'.[38] Their material included 'Living Newspapers', mass declamations, and political pantomimes, but they also staged several short plays from America, a full-length Soviet play in the socialist realist genre, and the first British performance of a Brecht play. One of their most striking original successes was *Where's that Bomb?*, a vigorous satire on anti-communist propaganda, written by two London taxi drivers.[39] In this 'cartoon play', Joe Dexter is sacked from his job in a factory for publishing left-wing poems, and in order to pay his bills is reluctantly persuaded to write a romance to be published on toilet-paper, as part of the government's plan to indoctrinate the working classes. However, when he falls asleep his own farcical right-wing propaganda is acted out in front of him in a dream, until eventually the characters reject the stereotypes he has imposed on them—kind boss, tender-hearted daughter, loyal worker and bolshevik striker—and start to subvert his script. When Joe wakes up, he is inspired by their resistance and tears up the story he has written.

The farcical right-wing melodrama within *Where's that Bomb?* is intended to satirise some of the most extreme anti-communist propaganda, especially through the character of Bolshy who wears a sinister cloak and whiskers, slinks furtively around, speaks in a Russian accent, and carries a bomb wherever he goes:

> I'm a Red—I'm a Red.
> An injurious, furious Red.
> I murder and pillage in city and village,
> The world isn't safe till I'm dead,
> For I'm a Red ferocialist, I am,
> A confiscating Socialist, I am;
> With my Russian gold I caper,
> I seduce your wife and rape 'er,
> It's true—It's in the paper!
> I'm a Red.

He blackmails the hero into joining the Communist Party and participating in a strike which calls for double the wages for working half the hours, then threatens to burn the boss's factory and rape his daughter if the demands are not met. By contrast, the loyal worker forms a company union, begs that the men be allowed to work twice the hours for half the money, and rescues the boss's daughter from Bolshy's evil attacks. As well as being a witty attack on government use of the media to prevent people thinking for themselves, the play is also a rousing denunciation of the exploitative nature of capitalism. This is seen most clearly in Joe's dream, when he confronts the character of Moneypower:

MONEYPOWER: If it wasn't for me there'd be no wages, no bosses, no empire, no flags, no glory, no *anything*.
JOE: [*contemptuously*] No! And if it wasn't for you there'd be no

workhouses, no means tests, no wage-slaves, and none of this lousy, lying propaganda!
MONEYPOWER: . . . Capitalism has transformed this world from savagery to civilization.
JOE: Capitalism makes men *prefer* savagery . . .
MONEYPOWER: Ah, but you can't cure anything without Me!
JOE: You can't *cure* anything at all. You can only patch things up. There'll be no real cures until you are smashed.[40]

Yet ultimately the play takes a surprisingly moderate political line when it transpires that all Bolshy and the workers really want is 'another penny an hour'. The only censorship by the Lord Chamberlain focused not on the play's politics but on its references to toilets.[41]

Cultural historians have suggested that the theatre world of the thirties remained little touched by political debate. Yet in 1933, St John Ervine had written that one of the two dangers facing theatre was that it might sacrifice art and become 'a machine for party propaganda'.[42] Ervine attacked plays not only for their ideological content, but also for what he saw as a politicisation of form. In his view, plays which depended on great roles and star-performers had been supplanted by a fashion for collectivity and the depiction of ordinary people. Linking this directly with the world beyond the theatre, he blamed a politically fashionable obsession with equality:

> The authors, either because they were themselves infected with this idea of democracy or were compelled to pay heed to it, began to write plays in which no one 'took the centre of the stage,' and, eventually, to write plays about unheroic characters.[43]

Ervine was right to identify a conscious downgrading of the importance of the individual in the Left's approach to characterisation. In the mid thirties, the playwright Montagu Slater agonised in *Left Review* over the depressing popularity of a film which dramatised the life of Henry VIII. How, he wondered, could a socialist artist create equally inspirational propaganda without pandering to an ideologically unsound cult of the individual as hero:

> What's the opposite of Henry VIII is what I keep asking myself? What is our left to its right? . . . Fables insist on such a ridiculous

spot-lighting of the leading man. What is to be done about it? Can we permit the spot-lighting?[44]

Similarly, in her introduction to the English text of Tretiakov's *Roar China*, the translator, Barbara Nixon, points out that the play breaks fresh ground in focusing on the mass, and in being 'more concerned with the drama of history than with that of individual characters'. She pre-empts criticism of the crudity of the characterisation, by stressing that the Western capitalists have been intentionally created as symbols of imperialism and that the Chinese are important not in their own right but as 'types of the working masses of China'.[45] In fact, the de-centring of the individual in Tretiakov's play can be seen as a direct reflection of its revolutionary thrust, for the narrative concerns the gradual politicisation of a Chinese community and their rebellion against British and American imperialism. Under the colonial system the many are oppressed by the few, and the Stoker repeatedly urges the reluctant boatmen to rebel against their exploiter. The playwright's Brechtian refusal to identify characters by name again illustrates the unimportance of the individual:

STOKER: Why not cut his head off?
1st BOATMAN: Another would grow instead.
STOKER: Cut that off too then.

Society can be changed if people act with and for the whole community rather than as individuals, and the Stoker describes how he has witnessed elsewhere the power of a subjugated group when it has the courage to unite:

STOKER: They were not fighting for themselves.
1st BOATMAN: Who were they fighting for then?
STOKER: For you.
1st BOATMAN: For me?
STOKER: Yes, for you. They want the coolies to be masters over all the world. They starved and fought and died for you, coolies of everywhere. Learn from them. Learn to die for the coolies that are being trampled down by the Imperialists in every country.

He insists they must not rely on individuals or outsiders to liberate them, but trust to their own collective strength:

1st BOATMAN: [*raging*] When—when will they come?
STOKER: Who?
1st BOATMAN: They over there who drove out their masters.
STOKER: They are here.
1st BOATMAN: Show me one of them.
STOKER: [*pointing to the boatmen*] He is one—and he is another
and you are one. We don't need to wait for others. We must fight
ourselves, gun in hand.

In the final scene, the Stoker—now dressed in the uniform of
the Canton Workers' Militia—repeatedly and symbolically appears in
different parts of the crowd, which acts as one entity to shelter and
protect him. Meanwhile, the widow of one of the victims of imperialism
comes face to face with its representative: holding her son up to look
at him, she makes a threatening and prophetic speech which casts them
both as far more than individuals:

> Look into his face. Remember it—remember it for ever. Remember
> his eyes of iron, red cheeks, and the gold in his teeth. He killed
> your father. If ever he asks you for food, don't give it him. If
> he gasps for water, refuse. If he comes to buy, do not sell to him.
> Grow up quickly to kill him. Kill him, and kill his sons and all his
> family.[46]

In the second half of the thirties, several plays reflected the threat of
an approaching clash of extremes which would leave no space for the
liberal to occupy. J.B. Priestley's most outright political play, *Bees on the
Boat Deck*, offers an apocalyptic vision of the future, in which Britain is
symbolised by a once great trading ship, the *SS Gloriana*, now on the
verge of destruction.[47] Abandoned by owners who can no longer afford
to maintain it, and languishing in desperate need of repair, the ship is
looked after by a couple of well-meaning middle-class and very English
do-gooders. These two are visited by a chain of individuals who embody
different and unwelcome contemporary responses to the nation's decline,
and who are motivated by self-interest rather than the needs of the ship.
The owner wants it destroyed so he can claim the insurance; his
daughter takes no interest in it, and prefers going to parties; a scientist
wants to blow it up as a chemical experiment; a communist wants to
blow it up because it is an exploitative capitalist enterprise; a fascist
wants to blow it up and blame the communists. Audience sympathies

are firmly directed to the two caretakers, played in the original production by Olivier and Richardson, who dismiss all the visitors as 'barmy' and insist that the ship could be restored and made to sail again, and who clearly represent the voice of common-sense, assailed by selfishness and extremism. Yet as the communist suggests, their old-fashioned decency and sentiment may ultimately be insufficient to save the ship—and Britain—in the coming battle:

> You're blind, both of you. In the end you will have to come to us
> . . . That Fascist will come again and threaten you with his gun.
> This ship you are so anxious to protect will be taken from you. Then
> there will be nothing left for you but despair and death—or the
> living force of the revolution. Good day, Comrades.
> [*Goes out with dignity. They watch him go, impressed*][48]

In 1938, Spender's *Trial of a Judge* went a stage further in its insistence that the time for moderation had passed.[49] In this abstracted and poetic analysis of the rise of fascism in Germany, liberal humanism, as represented by the Judge, is now a sign of impotence, openly derided by the Fascist Chorus for having failed to prevent them from taking power:

> In our strength lies our seriousness
> As in his weakness lay his irresponsibility.
> For, in refusing to use it, his like secretly destroyed
> The sources of their own power.

The Judge is persuaded to sacrifice his conscience and set free a group of fascist thugs whom he has previously convicted of brutally murdering a helpless Jew. However, in another twist, the last Act specifically refutes his self-martyrdom and his assumption that if he had resisted then the fascists would never have achieved power:

> 3rd RED: No, no, you are neither so wrong
> Nor so responsible as you would like to be.

The Red prisoners point out that even if the Judge had held firm to his principles he would simply have been swept aside, that the role of any individual is irrelevant, and that the future will inevitably be communist. Their vision of future freedom carries the play's rather desperate weight of optimism:

Our world is built upon
The freedom of the peoples, when
Those who dig the minerals for their own fetters . . .
With no nation except their poverty . . .
Will use the mountainous strength of their own arms
Which now pile down against them, to dispossess
Their destructive few oppressors . . .
And in the borderless world of the many
States and separate power melt away.

In the last scene, the walls dividing the cells collapse, and the Red prisoners join hands; finally, their voices are heard from off-stage whispering 'We shall be free. We shall find peace.'[50]

In the same year as Spender's play was performed, Shaw's *Geneva* brought thinly disguised versions of Hitler, Mussolini and Franco before an international court at the Hague where the citizens of Europe can complain about their leaders.[51] The play was particularly hard on the arrogance and prejudices of the British, who all but accept the fascist doctrine that the most advanced race should rule the world. By contrast, although he is satirised for his inability to think for himself without consulting Moscow, it is the Soviet Commissar who comes closest to speaking with the voice of reason, honesty and decency:

> These gentlemen talk of their countries. But they do not own their countries. Their people do not own the land they starve in. Their countries are owned by a handful of landlords and capitalists . . . Russia belongs to the Russians. We shall look on whilst you eat each other up. When you have done that, Russia— Holy Russia—will save the soul of the world by teaching it to feed its people instead of robbing them.[52]

In the world of politics, and contrary to some predictions, only one Communist Party member was elected to the British parliament during the whole of the thirties. Indeed, the prevailing mood has been characterised by historians as one of 'sullen discontent' which remained 'solidly unrevolutionary'.[53] The disappointing failure of the International Brigade against Franco was accompanied by disturbing accounts of communist practice in Spain, while the revelations of the mass trials in the Soviet Union caused further shocks and disillusionment. The signing of the Nazi–Soviet pact in August 1939, the Soviet invasion of Poland, and the volte-face of the CPGB—which initially supported the war against fascism and then denounced it as an imperialist war—meant that the decade ended with no broad sympathy in Britain for either the Communist Party or the Soviet Union. In November 1937, *Left Review* had published in a pamphlet called 'Authors Take Sides' what it claimed to be proof of the broad left-wing commitment among writers; yet by the following spring, *Left Review* itself was closing down. In its first issue of January 1940, *Horizon* clearly signalled a retreat from the political involvement of the artist:

> The impetus given by Left Wing politics is for the time exhausted
> ... our standards are aesthetic, and our politics are in abeyance.[54]

Yet the extent to which left-wing thinking dominated culture in the thirties should not be exaggerated. In 1939, a typically vitriolic but lucidly argued collection of essays was published under the title *The Left Heresy in Literature and Life*. Among a host of charges, this asserted that 'only irritable people read Left novels with any enjoyment', and accused communists of immorality and of perversely surrounding themselves with gloom while 'dwelling unnaturally on physical suffering'.[55] Even if the communists could be said to have briefly enjoyed an element of control over the mainstream of English literature, by the end of the decade that control had dissipated.[56]

I want to end this chapter by looking at two French plays about the Soviet Union which were performed in London during the thirties. The first, *Tsar Lénine*, was arguably one of the most strikingly innovative and theatrically exciting plays presented in London during the entire decade. However, labelled and dismissed by reviewers as 'expressionist', it suffered from the assumption that naturalism and a psychological approach to characterisation were the essential basis for contemporary plays. The second play, the trite and sentimental *Tovarich*, was one of the most popular plays of the decade, not only in London, but through much of Europe and in America.

Ervine had specifically criticised the 'vogue of Expressionism' for its refusal to concentrate on psychology and great individuals, and though rarely defined as a term, expressionism was used by critics to damn almost anything which dared to challenge the dominant theatrical form. François Porché's *Tsar Lénine* approaches the Soviet revolution not through a detailed and linear dramatisation of events but by distilling them into metaphors.[57] The most obvious theatrical device which runs throughout the play is the simultaneous use of two stages; in the first

Act, the characters who appear on the central stage are individuals, and the events which occur do so in real time and space—namely, Paris in 1910. But on a peripheral stage which surrounds this, Porché places symbolic characters who represent different sections of Russian society —an aristocrat, a bolshevik workman, a poor peasant, a monk, and a general; these characters exist outside time and space, able to observe and discuss the main action, irrespective of whether in real life they would have been present or would have met each other. They function partly as a chorus, though Porché points out that, by contrast with Greek theatre, his chorus is composed of people with differing perspectives and identities. Porché also justifies his use of stereotypes defined by class and social identity, rather than psychologically based characters, on the grounds that this represents the way in which his central character viewed people. Since no-one on the main stage other than Lenin is able to see or relate to these characters, the audience sees them as if through his mind.

The first Act of *Tsar Lénine* shows Lenin welding together an effective revolutionary force out of squabbling factions; the second culminates in the moment when he seizes power; the third concentrates on his struggles to prevent a counter-revolution, and an Epilogue deals with his death, his refusal to repent and his concern about his successor. None of this was written to be staged according to the conventions of naturalism. The play's title provides an obvious clue to the overall perspective on its central figure, yet its politics are more complex than this might suggest. Porché had lived in Russia immediately after the events of 1905, and he shows no sympathy for the old regime. Yet he conceives of the revolution as a tragedy and blames Lenin for having undermined fundamental moral values. Though inspired by positive motives, Lenin's ruthlessness and willingness to permit human atrocities for the sake of an abstract ideal lead to the revelation in the final images of the play that he is an unconscious servant of Death itself. One of the things which clearly fascinates the playwright is the extent to which power is embodied in an apparently unexceptional individual, and the way in which this contradicts Lenin's own fundamental beliefs regarding the irrelevance of individuals to world movements and events.

Lenin is shown as an avid chess player, able to carry his skills into dealing with real people; at the end of the first Act, he sweeps the symbolic characters from the board as he counters their arguments and temptations. The second Act uses a grotesque dance sequence to trace the events leading to the March Revolution and the bolsheviks' rise to power. At the climax of this Act, Lenin stands directly in front of the figure of Death to proclaim the inauguration of the socialist order, and to institute the Terror:

> Don't worry yourselves about subtle distinctions between Justice and Injustice. Our symbol is not the scales but the pistol . . . If it is a question of stamping out entire classes in order to bring about the New Russia, then let's do it . . . without remorse.

The figure of Death raises his arms, signalling the start of a frenetic dance by the prisoners as the curtain falls.

The third Act begins with the bolsheviks apparently on the point of defeat. Porché depicts a society dominated by secret police, spies and queues for non-existent supplies; the carillons which formerly pealed out 'God Save the Tsar' now chime 'The Internationale', and the Tcheka has adopted the methods and even the officers of the Czar's secret police. Yet we are shown that Lenin gives himself no special treatment and chooses to suffer the same deprivations as all fellow-workers. When he is visited by the ghost of a former colleague, Lenin refuses to recant and produces logical answers against the charges of tyranny: namely, that the Soviet Union has been bitterly opposed by foreign powers, that terror is a legitimate weapon until the revolution is international, and that nothing is immoral if it serves the Party. In the Epilogue, Lenin is a helpless invalid, and the figure of Death forces him to confront the groans and sighs of his victims, who are ushered in to see him. Even now, Lenin defends himself against their accusations, identifying the goal for which he has been striving:

> Fraternity is only a word. Liberty an idle fantasy; from the age of sixteen I have had only one thought, one care, to bring about the triumph of Equality.

It is at this moment that Death places his hands on Lenin's forehead and chillingly reveals that equality is also his great law:

> DEATH: You have served me superbly! I salute you, Tsar Lénine, peerless gravemaker!

In the final image, Lenin's dead face is faintly seen in near darkness, as the echoes of bells and cannons gradually fill the stage.[58]

In its theatrical language, *Tsar Lénine* broke many conventions and consciously drew on elements of film vocabulary. In showing the events between December 1916 and October 1917 as one continuous and uninterrupted action, Porché cites the influence of films which compress time to show the germination of a plant or the metamorphosis of a chrysalis into a butterfly. Such compression, argues Porché, *reveals* rather than *alters* reality, and is closer to the selective way in which our own memories and perceptions work. Yet he felt it necessary to justify his adaptation of cinematic language and insist on the fundamentally theatrical conception of his play:

> Tous ces moyens . . . sont du théâtre pur, rien que du théâtre.

Porché maintained that while theatre must develop by discovering the essence of the theatrical and not by competing on cinema's terms, there are effects that each medium can adapt from the other. Crucially, however:

> il devra les transposer sur son terrain propre, les adapter à son usage.

In fact, in its stage techniques *Tsar Lénine* also refers to Greek, to medieval, and—in its use of a ghost as a conscience to haunt Lenin—to Elizabethan conventions. The scene in which the approach of the revolution is shown through a 'danse macabre' is reminiscent of medieval allegory, as a nightmarish orchestra plays disturbingly bizarre music while a valet in funeral dress hands glasses of champagne to symbolic characters. The image is specifically derived from the paintings of Holbein and Dürer, and Porché described the second Act as 'la peinture stylisée d'une grande période historique'.[59] The experiments with form, though they antagonised the British critics, were integral to the play's content. It is no empty sign to represent the pre-revolutionary government with a set of wax mannequins, or Kerensky's taking of power by the substitution of an identical set. Yet Porché was typically and lazily accused of having

> taken the easy line of the very modern dramatist who, unable to build a scene, does not try to do so, but simply bombards his audience with a volley of bits and pieces and knows that his

audience, being used to films, will not notice his slackness or incompetence.[60]

Tsar Lénine had to wait until 1937 for its single Sunday night performance in London. By contrast, Jacques Deval's *Tovarich* was one of the most commercially successful plays of the decade. At first sight, the most extraordinary thing about this romantic fantasy in which two former Russian aristocrats are living as servants in France, is its immense international popularity. Opening in Paris, where it ran for over 800 performances, it was subsequently performed, according to Robert Sherwood, its English translator, 'in virtually every city and town in Europe'—with the exception of the Soviet Union. It reached London in 1935, where its audience included royalty, the Soviet Ambassador and Prince and Princess Yussupoff.[61] In Berlin, Hitler supposedly saw it four times; 'it tickled him', wrote Sherwood.[62]

The plot of *Tovarich* centres on the fact that the exiled aristocrats are faithfully looking after a large sum of money entrusted to them by the Czar before the revolution; so seriously do they take their charge that they refuse to invest the money in French banks or, more surprisingly perhaps, in a claimant to the Russian throne who wishes to start a counter-revolution against the bolsheviks. Unlike the deposed aristocrats in the melodramas of the twenties, they seem more or less happy in their new positions, and beg to be allowed to stay even when their employers discover their true identities. Even the Lord Chamberlain's report doubted the plausibility of this:

> Whether people with their antecedents could really have been so happy as valet and maid, even after their hardships, is doubtful.[63]

However, the real surprise on which the narrative hinges occurs when the two exiles finally allow themselves to be persuaded into giving the Czar's money to the desperate Soviet government, so that Russian oilfields will not have to be sold to foreign investors. The magnanimity of this act shows that love of country and national identity outweigh political considerations, as they rise above the desire for revenge or the wish to restore the old order. As the title suggests, they too have become Comrades, even while remaining loyal to the Czar.

Writing in 1937, Sherwood drew a strange parallel between the success of *Tovarich* and that of the arms industry:

> Those who have travelled over the scarred face of Europe in
> recent years have noticed that a certain lack of harmony prevails
> . . . But while observing chaotic differences between the European
> state, you will also notice that the nations have retained resemblance
> to each other in two respects: in all of them the munitions plants
> have been doing capacity business, and so has a comedy called
> *Tovarich*.

He attributes the play's success to the reassertion of a common, shared
humanity at a time when threatening international conflicts and
confrontations in Europe suggested that 'all biological laws which seek
to establish an essential similarity between one human being and another
have evidently been repealed'. *Tovarich* offered the welcome possibility
of universal brotherhood and reconciliation:

> Two people, whom you can't help liking, get together with their
> worst enemy and make peace with him and give him all they possess
> and call him 'Comrade' and then go out to get good and drunk . . .
> It may well be that the universal popularity of *Tovarich* is entirely
> due to the fact that it tells the meaning of the unpronounceable
> word which is its title—'Comrade.' Perhaps, inadvertently, M. Deval
> has proved that those biological laws have not been repealed, after
> all.[64]

It is not hard to understand the desire in the thirties for art to reveal
laws which would transcend political differences and unite enemies as
comrades together.

In 1938, an International Theatre Congress at Stratford-upon-Avon
discussed propaganda in the theatre. One of the main speeches
was given by another French playwright H.R. Lenormand, who told
his audience that the French delegation 'views with anxiety every
attempt to place dramatic art at the service of a cause alien to its
spirit'. Art should not to be used 'for definite ends', and though the
dramatist 'should bear witness to his own times', Lenormand insists
that 'a writer is not a soldier' and that it is not his duty to serve the
public:

> At a time like this, when in every corner of the earth opposing
> ideologies confront us, there is a great temptation for governments
> and politicians to look upon our art as an auxiliary force to subdue
> and bend to its own purpose. It cannot be denied that the theatre

exercises a powerful influence over the people. More effectively than books, articles in the press, pamphlets and speeches, it can engender enthusiasm, hatred, impassioned support for a set of ideas. The leaders of nations recognise the power it possesses to direct, to sway or to overthrow.[65]

During the next few years, the British government would seek to control that influence more directly than ever, not merely by preventing the expression of certain views but by actively encouraging and instigating the performance of its own political propaganda.

6

The Land of the Free

RUSSIAN WOMAN: His name was Vladimir Ilyich Ulyanov—
RUSSIAN MAN: Otherwise called Lenin.
RUSSIAN WOMAN: And Petrograd is now called Leningrad.
RUSSIAN MAN: And Leningrad today is a bulwark of freedom.
RUSSIAN WOMAN: Just as the whole of this country is one great
arsenal of freedom.[1]

When Stalin invaded Finland in 1939, Churchill interpreted the Red
Army's inability to defeat a minor power as proof of the inadequacies
of the Soviet system: 'Everyone can see', he claimed, 'how Communism
rots the soul of a nation', and the British media duly portrayed the Finns
as gallant heroes resisting expansionist aggression. By 1941, when
Germany broke its pact of non-aggression and invaded the Soviet Union,
Churchill had reluctantly reconciled himself to fighting alongside
Stalin, excusing himself in Parliament with the announcement that 'if
Hitler invaded Hell I would make at least a favourable reference to the
Devil'.[2] Following the Anglo–Soviet alliance, signed in June of that year,
the British government suddenly found it necessary to demonstrate its
active support for a new ally, without encouraging support for that ally's
political structures and philosophy. Such a balance was not easy to
achieve, even though the government could now take a much more
direct control of the media and harness it for war-time propaganda. The
main focus of this chapter will therefore be on performances staged at
a time of official co-operation and friendship between Britain and the
Communists.

In March 1940, well before the new alliance had been created, Unity
Theatre staged the first production of Sean O'Casey's most explicitly
communist play, *The Star Turns Red*. They were never allowed to
perform it publicly.[3] Presumably thinking of the adverse publicity which

would be caused by censoring a well-known writer, the Reader's Report for the Lord Chamberlain's Office noted that it was a play which 'in normal times it would be unwise to ban', but found it 'at the present juncture to be somewhat subversive' and therefore not permissible. The Report suggested consulting the Home Office, but the Lord Chamberlain himself decided that 'in view of the necessity of preventing anything of this nature in these dangerous times I cannot grant a licence'.[4] *The Star Turns Red* had been written between 1937 and 1939, but by the time it opened at Unity Theatre, the political context was less favourable for a play which advocated proletarian revolution. O'Casey himself described the Soviet–Nazi pact as 'inevitable', insisting that Britain should have formed an alliance with the Soviet Union during the thirties, and in an observation which also made clear his own political allegiance, he explained that 'people make the mistake of thinking that Communists are idealists. On the contrary, we are realists.'[5] Despite the timing, which made a professional production unlikely and caused O'Casey's American publishers to withhold publication, the play became one of Unity's most committed and widely discussed productions.

The events of the play take place in Ireland 'to-morrow, or the next day', and build to a climactic confrontation between the Communists and the Fascists in which O'Casey endorses a Soviet-style revolution, as the soldiers refuse to fire on the workers.[6] In the final moments, music is used non-naturalistically to represent the violent battle, mixing with the sounds of workers and soldiers cheering and singing 'The Internationale', while, according to a stage direction, 'the Red Star glows, and seems to grow bigger as the curtain falls'.[7]

O'Casey himself called the play 'a confession of faith', and he employed heavily symbolic imagery and a highly poetic and often religious language to encapsulate the polarisation of issues and conflicting stances.[8] The parental home of the first Act has two sketches on the wall, one of a mitred bishop and the other of Lenin; the communist son haltingly plays 'The Internationale' on his cornet, in competition with the sound of 'Come All Ye Faithful' from carol singers, and his brother enters with a Fascist salute and goose-steps across the living room. The action is concentrated into a Christmas Eve, so the beckoning star of salvation and the coming of a Messiah are recurring images, especially as the star remains visible throughout:

JACK: How does the star shine, Mother?
OLD WOMAN: It shines as purest silver shines, all brightened by
a useful and a loving hand.
JACK: So it shone when it led the kings. So shall it not shine when
it leads the people. It leads no more, and never shall till its silver
turns to red.

In part, the play is a searing attack on a Church which has become an
instrument of repression in its rejection of communism and its support
for fascism. This is embodied in the threateningly powerful figure of
the Purple Priest, who identifies what he calls the 'restless red rats' with
the 'powers of darkness'. Red Jim, the leader of the revolutionaries whose
character was based on the actual union leader Jim Larkin, forthrightly
condemns such religious attitudes:

> If your God stands for one child to be born in a hovel and another
> in a palace, then we declare against him. If your God declares that
> one child shall be clad in silks and another in sores, then we declare
> against him . . . once and for all and for ever we declare against your
> God, who hath filled the wealthy with good things and hath sent
> the poor empty away.[9]

But O'Casey constantly superimposes Christian imagery, language and
principles on the communist stance which he is advocating. The star
itself is only the most obvious visual symbol of this, heralding a
revolution which is to be proclaimed by 'the trumpet of God'.

A number of critics saw *The Star Turns Red* as adopting the allegorical
approach of a medieval morality play, and several of the characters'
names actually derive from Gaelic words which express their personalities.[10] Seen in this context, the critical attack on O'Casey for dividing
the characters and the issues so starkly loses some of its force, and Shaw
praised O'Casey for having 'brought the language of the Authorised
Version back to life'.[11] On the other hand, in a swift reaction against
his own former acceptance of communist dogma, Spender wrote
disparagingly of 'characters who exist only as symbols', and under the
headline 'A Morality Play with No Morals', patronisingly mocked the
visual imagery, in which the silver star of Bethlehem 'turns an em-
barrassed pink', and especially the committed physicality of the actors:

> The symbolism of the clenched fist and the even more firmly
> clenched jaw which the Communist actors manage marvellously to

sustain for two and a half hours (substituting a gymnastic feat for the usual play of countenance which bourgeois actors indulge in), seems curiously ineffective.[12]

Spender was not alone in turning violently against the Communist Party, and this was an uncomfortable time to be a member of the Party in Britain as its policy echoed Moscow's insistence that the international conflict was an imperialist war. According to this official line, critics of the capitalist system should refuse to fight against the Germans, and wait instead for the opportunity to attack their real enemy, the British ruling class. It is true, of course, that the Germans had had friends in high places within the British political Establishment, and Unity Theatre's *Launcelot's Dream*, written in the form of a fairy tale because 'the events of that time are so completely fantastic', set out to highlight the sympathy for Hitler which had existed in British ruling circles since the early thirties.[13] In one scene, Launcelot is shown literally fishing for allies—Chamberlain was, of course, well known as an enthusiastic fisherman—and baiting his hook with tasty morsels to try and attract the big black fish, while turning away the one with red scales. In another scene Chamberlain himself is seen asking Hitler to deal with 'those frightful Russians', and promising in return to allow him to annex Czechoslovakia. A third scene has a particularly provocative climax:

> HITLER: Russia will be dealt her death blow by the hand of National Socialism. The Asiatic Monsters in the pay of International Jewry shall cringe before the Nordic Legions of the Reich . . . The word 'Bolshevism' will disappear from the dictionaries of the world.
> CHAMBERLAIN: Sieg Heil! Sieg Heil! Sieg Heil![14]

In Unity's political pantomime of 1940, *Jack and the Beanstalk*, the supposedly evil giant stands for the Soviet Union, but turns out to be merely an invention of the authorities—an external threat created to distract and displace people's anger from the injustices of their own societies. Nevertheless, during the German–Soviet pact of non-aggression, support in Britain for the Communist Party had collapsed, since their position appeared tantamount to supporting Hitler. The sudden German attacks on the Soviet Union not only changed the Party's line, but also brought to the people of Britain a welcome respite from extensive aerial bombardments. Immense gratitude was immediately directed towards Hitler's new enemy, and when the Soviet Union defied predictions that it would be easily overrun, many people in Britain began to question the assumptions of those who had dismissed the communist system as fundamentally incompetent and incapable of producing effective organisation. *Our Time*, the leading cultural journal for Party activists and sympathisers, crowed delightedly:

> Imagine it! Those bootless, feckless Russians, overcrowded, underfed, without plugs in their lavatory basins, have actually proved able to manage what Lord Blimp and Cost Plus Contracts Ltd. could not. It is not only the Fuehrer that has a headache.[15]

Widespread public support for the Soviet Union was symbolically expressed in the wearing of hammer and sickle badges, and above all in efforts to raise aid for Russia and in the persistent calls for Britain to open a second Front against the Germans in order to relieve the Red Army. This last demand was the focus of a demonstration by 50,000 people in Trafalgar Square in May 1942, and of a song regularly performed by the outdoor section of Unity Theatre, with a chorus which encouraged the audience to join in:

> The Germans are fighting the Russians,
> The Russians are rather hard pressed.
> The Germans are fighting the Russians,
> So Why Don't We Strike In The West?[16]

A Living Newspaper submitted for licensing in September 1941, bitterly and ironically titled *The Spectre that Haunts Europe*, went on the attack, directly suggesting that the Anglo–Soviet alliance was threatened by members and friends of the British government, who were even now secretly maintaining their preference for the Fascists. The Lord Chamberlain refused to pass the script for public performance.[17] *The Spectre* . . . took the form of a revue, and was sometimes savage in its criticisms, but it was also cleverly theatrical. The first scene opens with an actor on stage and a plant in the audience agreeing how much they would like to see a production which showed the English and Russian peoples uniting to destroy Fascism. The actor then explains that since this has not yet occurred, the performance will concentrate instead on those in England who do not want such an event to take place. A stranger arrives, arguing that Britain has made 'a very grave mistake' in allying itself with Bolshevism, since the Soviet Union stands for 'all that is most barbarian, most evil, most primitive in the modern world'. He proudly admits that Britain has supported Hitler against the communists, 'built him up, financed his storm troops, helped him to create his army and his fleet'. The actor then shoots the stranger, but the performance plays on theatrical convention to accuse the audience of complacency and naïvety:

> Easy, wasn't it? [*The Stranger rises and dusts his clothes*]
> It was too easy. The cartridge was a blank, but it took you in didn't it? . . You were fooled in just the same way after Munich. The men who made Hitler strong are still at large, they occupy high positions of power.

The scene then employs direct quotations from British newspapers and political speeches to expose compliance with Germany, and the theme is continued into the second sketch, in which three Fascists are depicted as dancing vultures, perching to read aloud extracts from *Mein Kampf*. Unity Mitford, portrayed as a crow, sings a duet with them, based on a popular song of the period:

> CROW: Poppa, may I join the Führer?
> VULTURES: Yes, my darling daughter.
> CROW: Help him to make Europe purer.
> VULTURES: Yes, my darling daughter.
> CROW: There are many Reds, Poppa darling,
> Doing things they didn't ought ter
> Who'll you get to keep 'em down sir?
> VULTURES: Hess, my darling daughter.[18]

Chamberlain's betrayal of Czechoslovakia is dramatised in the style of a Hollywood gangster film, with the gang's leader meeting Chamberlain in a speakeasy—('siddown punk')—and arranging a deal in which he is allowed to take over 'Johnny the Czeck's joint' in return for destroying 'Joe the Red'. Meanwhile, anti-Soviet propaganda in the media is satirised in a scene based on *Macbeth*:

> 1st WITCH: Thrice the Daily Mail hath warned
> 2nd WITCH: Thrice and once, the Link hath whined
> 3rd WITCH: Goebbels cries 'Tis time, 'Tis time.
> 1st WITCH: Round about the cauldron go
>   In the propaganda throw . . .

> Russian horror, Clergy shot.
> Boil them first in the charmed pot . . .
> 2nd WITCH: Virgins twelve and babies six
> Ravished by the Bolsheviks.
> 'Russian peasants Starving' tale
> Five Year Plan is bound to fail . . .
> 3rd WITCH: Tongue of liar, hand and wrist of
> Anti-Soviet Journalist,
> Spittle of Gestapo Nark
> Red letter forged in the dark.
> Liver of a Marxist Jew
> False facts to make the news seem true.

In another sketch, Chamberlain is presented as the Ghost of Hamlet, greeting Hess in Scotland and advising him on how to call up Germany's many friends within England:

> If you would summon aid to the Führer's cause just say 'We must rid the world of Bolshevism' and your friends will rise and march with you . . . Adieu! Adieu! Adieu! Remember me.[19]

In banning it from public performance, the Lord Chamberlain's report described *The Spectre that Haunts Europe* as 'full of the usual misleading historical half-truths', and insisted it threatened the nation's unity:

> Does the pillorying of a number of probably quite harmless old gentlemen, and the misrepresentation of the characters and aims of a deceased statesman, really strengthen our determination to win the war? I think not, but rather that it is more likely to cause despondency and alarm—and class-hatred, which is no doubt the author's chief aim.

The typically disingenuous instructions with which the Report concludes reveal a careful manipulation of the truth:

> I should tell these people that we recognize the patriotic purpose of their play (for no doubt it has certain good points as propaganda), but that as we do not allow offensive personalities we cannot pass it.[20]

By 1942, even Conservatives were beginning to acknowledge the need to look forwards rather than backwards, realising that only the promise of social and economic reforms could raise public morale and support for the war-effort against Germany. *The Times* argued that

> the new order cannot be based on the preservation of privilege, whether the privilege be that of a country, of a class, or of an individual.[21]

Peter Ustinov's *House of Regrets*, which was staged in London in October of that year, focuses on a group of Russians who have been living in Kensington in self-imposed exile since 1917.[22] The central conflict is between those who are indeed looking back, trying to preserve their national traditions at all costs, and those, mainly the younger generation, who wish to abandon the archaic values and practices of a vanished culture. The polarisation is dramatised through an elderly General, who still believes he can restore the pre-revolutionary regime, and his eighteen-year-old grand-daughter, Marina, who calls herself a communist. Marina outrages her family by announcing her intention to emigrate to the Soviet Union—'the land of the free'—where she and her English boyfriend will discover 'Socialistic Love' together, and will be able to 'work and sing the songs of the people'. Though gently mocked for parroting trite phrases and idolising the Soviet Union, Marina's innocent idealism is shown to be both more attractive and, crucially, less implausible than the General's ridiculous plan to retake Moscow on horseback, especially since in order to achieve this, he is equally prepared to support the British or the Nazis. Even the General's elderly companion admits the superiority of Marina's ambitions, and acknowledges the Soviet Union's potential to become the model and symbol of a better world:

> ADMIRAL: She deserves a life which is not for us, which we do not understand, and which many of us hate blindly, for no reason other than self-pity . . . there is something new in the world which automatically makes us museum pieces . . . a new religion . . . a new faith . . . in simple things . . . in the brotherhood of man . . . in the soil . . . in the songs of people at work.[23]

Ustinov was hardly a communist, but the British government was increasingly worried that war-time support for the Soviet Union could be translated into subsequent sympathy for its political system. To some, the active Party member was a 'red-clad Pied Piper intent on leading a gullible populace towards Bolshevism'.[24] Indeed, *Our Time* repeatedly argued that the Red Army was strong because, by contrast with the British army, it had something definite to fight for and something positive to defend. Even a British Home Intelligence report of 1942 conceded that this was a widely held perception:

> The public has no clearly worked out conception of the purpose of the war. The Russians have a clear cut purpose: they have a way of living that they think worth fighting for and which enables them to fight well. The Germans are believed to have a purpose. We have only vague conceptions.[25]

As a result of this, Churchill requested the Ministry of Information

> to consider what action was required to counter the present tendency of the British Public to forget the dangers of Communism in their enthusiasm over the resistance of Russia.[26]

The Ministry had already identified the problem, noting that the growing popularity of the Soviet Union 'must, if it is not interfered with, equally popularise Communism as a method of political living.' However, the government had every intention of interfering, cynically judging the average British person to be more concerned with home comforts than with the possibility of improving society:

> He hates Nazism and can be brought to hate Communism . . . So long as there is a chicken in the pot there is no revolution in the State: and a man who is sure of a chicken next Sunday, and all Sundays, will not raise the Red Flag to make the chicken a turkey.[27]

There were two strands to the strategy devised by the British government to prevent the Left from taking advantage of the situation. First, the public enthusiasm for the Soviet Union must be depoliticised by separating the military success from the political system: it was to be emphasised that the Russians were fighting not on ideological grounds to defend a way of life, but on nationalistic ones to defend land and property:

It would be well to suggest that Russia is a Communist country only in name; and that it is, essentially, a Russian patriotic, nationalist country . . . the British worker could be made to understand that his Russian counterpart was fighting not to preserve the regime but to prevent a German conquest of his soil.[28]

Second, the government decided to pre-empt any plans the Communist Party might have to take advantage of the situation by themselves leading the way in honouring the Soviet Union, so that the support could be directed into acceptable channels. Suddenly, public criticism of the Soviet Union or Stalin became heretical. Lord Beaverbrook praised communism and Stalin for having produced unequalled patriotism and the best armies of Europe, while the Soviet Ambassador in London was told by a British general who had always previously appeared to detest the Soviet Union that the Bolsheviks had saved civilisation, and that their efforts indicated that 'there is something healthy in your system'.[29] Anti-Bolshevists were banned from lecturing to the British armed forces; Orwell's *Animal Farm* was rejected for publication because its thesis was not 'the right point of view from which to criticize the political situation at the present time'; Churchill sacked a minister who dared to suggest that the ideal solution for Europe would be if the Soviet Union and Germany were to destroy each other.

The Government's strategy was not without danger. Anthony Eden, the Foreign Secretary, pointed out that

nothing could be more unfortunate than if the impression was ever to get abroad that in a desire to promote better Anglo–Russian understanding . . . H.M. Government were lending itself to the popularising of Communist creeds.[30]

Other ministers also queried whether it was possible to praise Russia 'without implying some approval of the experiment that has been going on there for these last 24 years', and the right-wing *National Review* expressed the fear that the government was 'ready to alter our political system and to rush into Bolshevism at all costs'.[31]

Meanwhile, the Left assiduously drew direct connections between cultural ideology and nationalism. *Our Time* was in the forefront of the movement, reprinting Gorky's 1928 assessment of the Red Army which had insisted that it was far more than a military force, and marched 'with poetry in its knapsacks, music in its lorries, art in its ammunition cases'.[32] On another occasion they published an account by a soldier describing a British army audience seeing Russian films for the first time:

> The first and greatest reaction is an immediate and often blasphemous denunciation of the anti-Soviet propaganda of the past . . . Next comes the admiration for the Red Army . . . and last but not least, they discuss—'Joe' . . . his quiet and unassuming manner is so different from that of the blustering dressed-up leaders of the axis . . . from the realisation that the Soviet Union is a bulwark against Fascism comes a more positive outlook. They realise why the Soviet Union is so strong . . . As one soldier said 'After seeing those films I think what we need is twenty-five years of b—— Communism!'[33]

In practice, it was not always easy to praise the Soviet Union without appearing to commend its political system. In November 1943, the BBC broadcast an entire evening of programmes 'In Honour of Russia'. As well as two renderings of 'The Internationale'—which Churchill had previously banned from being broadcast—this included a programme of Soviet War Songs, an account of the birth and growth of the Red Army, descriptions of Moscow's celebrations of its National Day, and discussions about life in the Soviet Union. On another occasion, to accompany the broadcast of Shostakovich's Leningrad Symphony, the *Radio Times* published an article about music in the USSR which declared that 'never in the history of the world has any government placed so highly the cultural importance of art'. The magazine's celebration came close to official Soviet propaganda in offering a coded defence of Stalin's fascistic control of artistic communication:

> Certain technical and aesthetic restraints are imposed on the Soviet composer because his first concern is to write music that will be understood by the people and inspire them to greater effort.[34]

The BBC also made a series of radio dramas with Russian themes, a number of which were contributed by Louis MacNeice, who had joined the Features section of the BBC in May 1941. His epic version of *Alexander Nevsky*, based on Eisenstein's film, was broadcast in the following year, with modern parallels and allusions abounding as the outnumbered Russian people defeat the cruel and barbaric Germans. In his victory speech, Nevsky promises that 'every invader is doomed'; while hoping the Germans will realise once and for all their mistake in imagining 'that their brute strength would conquer the Russian soul', he predicts that freedom will have to be fought for again by future generations.[35] MacNeice's script—which was actually written as the direct result of a suggestion by the Foreign Office—stresses that it is nationalism and land rather than ideological beliefs which motivate the heroic Russian resistance.[36]

In April 1942 the BBC broadcast MacNeice's *Salute to the U.S.S.R.*, in which explicit parallels are again drawn between the present and the past. The play opens with a voice admitting to the 'mistake' that has been made in invading Russia; the speaker proves to be Napoleon, but though Hitler is immediately heard denying the validity of any comparison with his own invasion, the collapsing of time, the textual intercutting, and the use of linguistic repetition all assert a direct connection between France's historical defeat, and the fate awaiting the Germans:

> NAPOLEON: These Russians will collapse at once.
> 1st NAZI: Six weeks and all will be over . . .
> HITLER: I have made my plans with the utmost care. My time-table is perfect.
> NAPOLEON: I had made my plans but the Russians baulked them. My time-table fell to pieces.

Sometimes MacNeice's carefully constructed montage deliberately obscures from the listener which of the two dictators is speaking:

> HITLER: The advance of the German armies is rapid and over-whelming.
> NAPOLEON: They burned their towns before me. The deeper I went into Russia the darker my prospects.
> 1st NAZI: (*whispering*) The darker our prospects.

Eventually the focus shifts to the present, striking a style reminiscent in its simplicity and directness of the agit-prop form developed by the Workers' Theatre Movement a decade or so earlier:

> 2 BRITISH SPOKESMAN: Salute to the City of Moscow!
> 1 BRITISH SPOKESMAN: Salute to the City of Moscow!
> VOICES IN UNISON: Salute to the City of Moscow! . . .

2 BRITISH SPOKESMAN: Salute to the People of The Soviet Union!
1 BRITISH SPOKESMAN: Salute to the People of The Soviet Union!
VOICES IN UNISON: Salute to the People of The Soviet Union![37]

Probably such messages were considered too explicit. In December 1942, MacNeice outlined proposals for a series of features to be broadcast under the general heading of 'The Four Freedoms'; the series would consist of programmes covering the French Revolution, the Early Christians, Pericles, the Renaissance, Milton and Lenin, and the programmes were all duly accepted, written and broadcast early in 1943, with the single exception of the one about Lenin, which was never made. Instead, the BBC broadcast *The Spirit of Russia*, a tribute by MacNeice which drew on Ukrainian dancing, folk tales and timeless tradition, rather than on contemporary associations:

> Russia is the cry of quails and the cornflowers in the corn,
> Russia is a wooden hut with a roof of straw and with red
> shutters . . .
> From pine-tree to palm-tree, from vineyard to tundra.[38]

Several plays by Soviet writers were produced for radio at this time, and others were published for the benefit of amateur groups seeking topical material to perform. *Our Time* and Unity Theatre's publishing arm each made several scripts available, while the publishing firm of Hutchinson—which had already launched a Library of Soviet Novels under the slogan 'understanding our allies'—produced a collection of full-length texts under the title *Four Soviet War Plays*.[39] Most of the Soviet plays made available at this time were set against the backdrop of the current war, and celebrated, often rather crudely, the heroism of ordinary Soviet people against evil Germans. However, they sometimes contained broader ideological implications. In *According to Plan*, for example, the arrogant dismissal of the communists by the Nazis may well have reminded some people of statements made by certain British politicians:

> The Bolsheviks will crumple . . . It stands to reason that the Reds
> will crumple. They've got no morale, they're not civilised, living their
> beastly collective lives.[40]

Occasionally, the theme went beyond the war against Fascism into a comparison of communist and capitalist values. In *The Ocean*, an American seeking to make money for himself is contrasted with a Russian committed to working for the benefit of all. Having scientifically developed a beautiful blue rose, the latter is briefly tempted by the American's promise that in his country the discovery could make her rich:

> Tens of hundreds of thousands will want just to look at the rose. But individuals, only a few particular people, will dare to aspire to own one. That is where you dictate your own terms. And however high they are, they will be accepted. No price is too high to pay to possess something that others are unable to have. For your rose will belong only to the chosen few.

He laughingly dismisses her wish that the flower must 'bloom for everyone', but her continued assertion of this principle becomes not only a demonstration of the moral superiority of communism over capitalism, but also a metaphor for the inevitable spread of communism throughout the world:

> But that's exactly what it must—for everyone! So far I've only succeeded in cultivating one bush, but in a few years' time my rose will be capable of blooming in any climate. We shall make it strong, able to withstand the north wind and cold. Blue roses will bloom everywhere for everyone.[41]

Several full-length Soviet dramas were also presented on the London stage. Unity produced Gorky's *Dostiageff and the Others*, revived Hubert Griffith's translation of Afinogenev's *Distant Point*, and also staged a new play called *Comrade Detective*.[42] This was a rather clumsily written war-time spy story set in the not too distant utopian future, when all crime will apparently have become a thing of the past:

> What cases will there be under communism, in that happy era when smiling militia-men at crossroads will be handing out tulips to passers-by, free of charge?

The real point of the narrative, though, is the way in which Soviet citizens are able to act as one to foil those who would destroy their country, because they all own and share that country equally. In Germany, by contrast, even those who sincerely believe they are serving their country are really stooges for the business men who run it. The experienced German spy is trapped because he assumes Soviet citizens must be as corrupt and bribeable as those who live under capitalism:

> TOLSTOY: I looked at him and thought, 'Huh, it's a long time since you've been to the country, if you think you can buy us with money'.

He also fails to allow for the fact that while his country may have up to 10,000 secret agents, the Soviet Union has '170,000,000 open agents'. When captured, the German spy eventually admits that his reasons for opposing the Soviet Union have always been negative and based on jealousy:

> I lived for hate . . . Hate for you, for your country. All my life I lived in Russia. All my life I hated it . . . I hate your self-confident youth, infecting the whole world with the poison of your teachings . . . I hate even your very earth, because it belongs to you![43]

The naïvety of *Comrade Detective* was mirrored in the critics' exaggerated enthusiasm for another Soviet play, Simonov's *The Russians*.[44] Essentially, this was an equally simplistic fable in which Germans are brutally sadistic but cowardly, and, apart from the occasional traitor, Russians are heroes who never submit to threats or torture. Yet the responses to Tyrone Guthrie's Old Vic production in 1943 were almost ecstatic, with critics rejoicing in its 'thundering melodrama', while insisting that the story was not only factual, but encapsulated 'an ancient truth'.[45] Ivor Brown's review in the *Observer* was typical:

> There are no fine shades, no reticences, just glorious Russian courage, a little Russian treachery, filthy German brutality, desperate doings, and the deuce of a din . . . this mixture of old melodrama and new history seems crude. But war is crude. If you like bare fact, here it is, and through the force of actuality rather than of art, it drives so lavishly at the heart as nearly to turn the stomach. The author writes from front-line knowledge and his truth is stronger than fiction.[46]

A programme note for *The Russians* once again suggested that the play contained a far-reaching significance:

> We hope that the English audience will feel that in this play, they see the struggle and share the victory, not only of their brothers in arms, but their brothers indeed.[47]

Some of the spectacular theatrical pageants of this period, which were officially designed only to cement a war-time alliance, conveyed a similar message of international solidarity and unity, and it is the content of these pageants, and the circumstances surrounding their presentation, that reveal most about the performance of politics within British society at this time. In June 1942, for example, an event was held at Earl's Court to mark the first anniversary of the Anglo–Soviet alliance. It was chaired by the Bishop of Chelmsford, who invited God to bless Russia, and the spectacular action consisted of military groups and workers displaying their contributions to the war effort. It included not only demonstrations by first-aid and fire-fighting units, but also music, sound effects of guns, aeroplanes and sirens, smoke, military manoeuvres, mime, Russian clowning, ballet, poetry, newspaper reports and physical acrobatics, all of which were integrated to embody the unity and determination of the British and Russian peoples. Though the main speaker was a government minister, the performance was largely organised by committed communists and was based around a script by Montagu Slater, now editing *Our Time*, entitled *An Agreement Of The Peoples*.[48] This repeatedly reminded the audience of the bravery of the Russian people: 'Can flesh and blood stand what they stand?' asked the narrator, pointing out that Soviet cities had already suffered 'the deaths of Coventry, Plymouth, Southampton, Bristol, London multiplied by a hundred'. At the climax, the entire cast fills the arena, and a formal and weighty pledge is made to the Soviet Union and to 'all the oppressed people of Europe' that the two countries will 'maintain this Alliance and build on it'.

The narrative hinged on a device familiar from Living Newspapers during the thirties in which an outsider provides a link between stage and auditorium, continually asking questions about what is going on. Here, the outsider is Jonathan Swift's Gulliver, dressed in eighteenth-century costume, and ignorant of what is happening in twentieth-century Britain:

They tell me that for a year now much of its life and expectations have turned on its alliance with a certain Union of Socialist Soviet Republics. I am interested in that.

Gulliver's probing allows an English worker to explain the significance of everything the audience sees and hears, and to provide a historical and political context. The spectacular physical sections of the pageant are punctuated by questions and answers:

> GULLIVER: I've seen the Lilliputians, the Brobdingnagians, the Houyhnhnms, the Yahoos. What is there so remarkable about these Republicans of yours on the other side of the world? . . .
> SPOTTER: What is there wonderful about them? They built Dneiperstroy . . . and blew it up. They fought on a two thousand mile front from the Arctic to the Black Sea. They died in legions. They killed millions. Falling back they scorched the earth foot by foot. They fought through the summer. They went on fighting through the Russian winter. There was no limit to what they would sacrifice.

The text leaves no room for doubt that the Soviet Union's success in resisting Germany is the direct result of having built a society which all its citizens have an interest in maintaining. Unlike Britain, the Soviet Union is fighting not just *against* but also *for*, and the writer and broadcaster C.E.M. Joad illustrated this through the part of the Philosopher, for which he wrote his own speech:

> PHILOSOPHER: Suppose your soldier says to himself, Life is so good, what I've lived through and the prospects I've seen just ahead are so good, that at all costs this life has to be fought for and defended. This is the Russian feeling . . . Philosophers have asked each other for centuries, What is the good life? And here are millions of people answering, if not in so many words, 'We've got a fair idea what it is in practice'.[49]

In May 1943, the National Council for British–Soviet Unity produced another so-called Living Newspaper script, which was intended for performance throughout the country to commemorate the Soviet entry to the war and to celebrate the alliance. *Alliance For Victory* opens at a Moscow Festival of Youth, with a utopian vision of a land at peace:

NARRATOR 1: Every street, every square and park is thronged with happy crowds. Soviet Youth is on holiday, celebrating the new life with singing, dancing and music. They march through the Red Square to salute their great leaders . . .

The achievements of the Soviet Union are glorified in speeches of unadulterated, if awkwardly written, triumphalism:

NARRATOR 2: New generations are reaching manhood. Behind them are two decades of ceaseless endeavour, crowned by un-paralleled achievement. A new and mighty nation has risen out of the darkness of the past. Freedom has triumphed over tyranny and superstition. In a land of promise and unbridled opportunity Soviet Youth rejoices.

Then an ordinary working woman describes the contentment and prosperity her town enjoyed before the arrival of the fascists:

Our children were cared for and happy. They sang as the birds sang, and grew strong and wise in their creches, kindergartens and new schools. The fields yielded fine crops, the factories grew, and we lived a full life.

The performance also employed vast choruses of British and Soviet workers, presenting a mass declamation which incorporated music and dance, while British workers and seamen express their total commitment to supplying their Soviet ally. Russian workers describe their heroic and crucial defence of Stalingrad—a name 'written in the heart of all free peoples'—and alternately identifying allied victories over the fascists, British and Soviet workers hold hands to symbolise their pledge to continue working together:

Long live the Alliance of the British and Soviet peoples.
Long live the unity of the free peoples of the world.[50]

Possibly the most striking thing about this eulogising is the ease with which the Lord Chamberlain licensed the script for performance, quite inaccurately describing it as 'merely a review of the salient events in the struggle between Russia and Germany'.[51]

In many ways, *Alliance For Victory* was simply a milder version of the most public and controversial pageant of all, which was performed at the Royal Albert Hall in February 1943 to commemorate the twenty-fifth anniversary of the founding of the Red Army. The arguments and embarrassment which emerged in the Cabinet over Louis MacNeice's script for this clearly demonstrate the difficulties for the British government in separating support for a war-time ally from enthusiasm for its political system. *Salute to the Red Army* was intended to be an elaborate spectacle, endorsed and controlled by the government:

> The performance will be martial in character, with a strong vibrant note throughout. At the same time, it must be extremely dignified, without a trace of theatricality—a sort of 'neo-classicism' will be aimed at.[52]

It was to be produced by Basil Dean, the director of National Service Entertainment, and was planned to involve two orchestras, three hundred choristers, two regimental bands, trumpeters and drummers from the King's household cavalry, and a parade of men and women representing groups from nurses and miners to the merchant navy. The draft programme indicated that the production would 'be speaking to the Russian Army through the universal language of music', and would combine this with a narration describing 'typical acts of heroism by the Red Army', in a script to be written by MacNeice. The two-hour presentation was to begin with the British National Anthem and end with 'The Internationale', though the highlight would supposedly be the minister's speech and a march past by uniformed services. The whole event was to be recorded on film, which would then be sent to the Soviet Union.

The government had at least two hidden motives for sponsoring the event, and these were specified in a letter sent by Brendon Bracken, the Minister of Information, to the Foreign Secretary, Anthony Eden, inviting him to speak during the pageant. Bracken anticipated Eden's reluctance to express support for a communist power in public, and carefully explained the two functions:

> First, to show the Russians that all sections of political opinion are genuinely behind our Alliance with Russia; second, to get in ahead of the Communist Party in organising authoritative and impressive demonstrations in the main centres of population.

The political effect was paramount:

> Above all things, the total effect of the Salute must be of a sincere
> and convincing gesture, if its political objects are to be achieved.

However, problems emerged when the Foreign Office received
MacNeice's script from the Ministry of Information just over a week
before the performance, with an accompanying letter which asked that
the matter be considered urgently for the sake of the actors, since 'we
are naturally most anxious that there should be no "author's corrections"
imposed on them once they have started to memorise the script'. A
less formal note hinted at the Ministry of Information's extensive
reservations, and near panic:

> There has been a frightful muddle in the Ministry over this script
> . . . one Department in the Ministry has gone ahead without
> consulting any of the others concerned with the political aspect and
> without referring the matter to higher authorities in the Ministry.

The only specific objection recorded is the script's requirement that 'The
Internationale' be sung as well as played, the Ministry of Information
disingenuously suggesting that most Russians would probably prefer the
music to be performed without words. But more extensive concerns were
implied, and while acknowledging that, unfortunately, there was now
'no time to get a completely new programme thought out', officials
strongly hinted that certain sections should be removed. Foreign Office
staff added their responses on the letter. 'This is sorry stuff', remarked
Sir Alexander Cadogan; he insisted that 'section 10 is pernicious and
must be cut out or drastically altered', while another official queried
'What has happened to the people of England if they can really stomach
this?'. The formal response confirmed the Foreign Office's demands:

> We feel that section 10 of the script should be omitted or so radically
> altered that it does not, as at present, imply that the 'upper class
> man and woman' took a very poor view of Russia's chances in 1941,
> whereas the working class men and women did not do so. My
> Secretary of State also thinks that the Internationale should not be
> sung at the end of the programme as proposed in Section 27 but
> that it should only be played.

MacNeice's script was duly modified, despite the attempts he had made to preclude censorship by categorically stating on the title page that 'the removal of any part . . . will dissipate the total effect'.

The Albert Hall performance relied partly on visual effects and images. Masking the organ pipes of the Hall was a 'large perspective stylised view of Stalingrad', with elevated platforms at the front of the stage for the two narrators; the performance space itself was extended throughout the length of the hall, with trumpeters and drummers in the gallery above. According to *The Times*, which reviewed the performance with considerable enthusiasm, the producer used the arena 'as an artist uses a canvas', and the stage resembled 'an impressionist design in cubism'. The vast number of performers was crucial to the impact, as the arena was filled with military contingents and crowds of workers paying tribute to the Red Army, while Ralph Richardson and Sybil Thorndike were dressed in gold cloth and helmets, and placed in pulpits painted battleship grey to play the narrators. These 'erect, heroic beings', were contrasted with the evil enemy:

> Beneath and between them gesticulated the Nazi (Mr Marius Goring), a dark menace, moving and crouching in his own shadow.[53]

As in his radio features, sections of MacNeice's script were historical, with a modern parallel always implicit. For example, Nevsky describes his victory over the Germans:

> The Germans . . . thought that Russia was an easy prey, they thought to pick off our cities one by one . . . they made a grave mistake.

Other early sections create pre-war images of the Soviet Union and Britain at peace, as the chorus sings 'The Volga Boat Song' and a group of Welsh factory workers replies with 'All Through the Night'. The idealised picture of the Soviet Union is reinforced by a series of poetic images, spoken in darkness by the narrators:

> SPOKESMAN: Plan and plant, build and dig;
>   The chimneys rise and the deserts bloom . . .
> SPOKESWOMAN: A new life in an ancient land—
> SPOKESMAN: New oil for the lamps of Russia—
> SPOKESWOMAN: New schools—
> SPOKESMAN: New factories—
> SPOKESWOMAN: New mines—

SPOKESMAN: New Dynamos—
SPOKESWOMAN: New farms—
SPOKESMAN: New songs.

This idyllic world is threatened by the Nazis, even though they cannot help acknowledging the contentment of those whom they attack:

NAZI FIGURE: Listen, you people of Russia.
  You who are working and laughing,
  You who are singing and dancing—
SPOKESWOMAN: Working in collective farms—
SPOKESMAN: Handling hammer and sickle—
SPOKESWOMAN: Dancing to the tambourine—
NAZI FIGURE: Dance away! It will all be over soon.

The main grievance of the Foreign Office had concerned a section which suggested that the British working class had shown more faith than the upper classes in the Red Army, but the removal of that one scene scarcely changed the overall tone of the performance or its near idolisation of the Soviet Union:

SPOKESWOMAN: What is that moving in the pine-tree?
SPOKESMAN: That is a Red Sniper.
SPOKESWOMAN: What are those mounds of snow?
SPOKESMAN: Those are camouflaged tanks.
SPOKESWOMAN: What is that whistling in the wind?
SPOKESMAN: That is the charge of the Cossacks.
SPOKESWOMAN: What are those white ghosts gliding down from the hill?
SPOKESMAN: Those are the Russian ski-troops . . .
SPOKESWOMAN: What is that star rising over the steppes?
SPOKESMAN: That is the Red Star . . . Red Star over Russia!
SPOKESWOMAN: Red Star over Russia!
SPOKESMAN: Red Star over Russia!

Even where the explicit message of the script differed little from official policy, the emotional rhetoric of the language and performance inevitably seduced the audience into a much more empathetic relationship than was encouraged by the unadorned statements of ministers. Thus Eden's official address prosaically declared that

His Majesty's Government have asked me to come to this celebration
to pay their tribute and also, I know, the tribute of British people
everywhere to the valour of the Red Army.

By contrast, MacNeice's expression of what is essentially the same point
has almost the evangelical tone of a revivalist meeting:

> SPOKESWOMAN: Shall we call on the British people?
> SPOKESMAN: They know what they owe to Russia.
> SPOKESWOMAN: They trust in the Red Army.
> SPOKESMAN: The Russian Front is their front too.
> SPOKESWOMAN: They are glad to salute the Red Army.
> SPOKESMAN: Let us call on the British people.
> SPOKESWOMAN: Men and Women of Britain,
> SPOKESMAN: Working people of Britain,
> SPOKESWOMAN: Come and salute the Red Army.

From the perspective of Her Majesty's Government, the climax was
intended to be Eden's twelve-minute speech, but even this would have
been crucially mediated by the fact that Eden spoke in front of a huge
red flag and with a Russian soldier elevated high above him on a plinth.
In this image, the implicit metaphor at the root of the whole performance became physicalised, as the Soviet Union was actually located on
a pedestal. Eden's speech was followed by 'The Internationale', and
though the government had insisted that this should be only orchestral,
members of the audience sang the words. Moreover, the anthem was
coupled with a powerful visual image:

> *On the first note of this the Red Army flag is broken at the rear of the
> stage in front of the organ, and in front of it is the figure of the Red
> Army Man with rifle and bayonet fixed.*

The Red Army was truly centre stage at the heart of the British
Establishment.

Whatever the authorities' reservations, they could not be admitted in
public, and *The Times*, focusing on the aesthetics of the performance,
pronounced it 'a triumph' and the first expression of 'a new art form'.[54]
The Cabinet, gritting its collective teeth, claimed that the event had
been successful propaganda, having,

helped to dispel the idea, which was at that time being fomented
by the Communist Party in this country, that His Majesty's
Government was insincere in its professions of friendship for its
Soviet Ally.[55]

Yet one might question whether it was it worth the price they had to
pay, given that the context of the performance necessarily suggested
that the government endorsed everything in the script. It was staged in
the presence of senior ministers and military commanders, prime
ministers and senior figures from the allied nations—including
the Russian Ambassador, representatives from the nations of the
Commonwealth, all the mayors of London, and Churchill's family.
What these people witnessed was the British Foreign Secretary, dwarfed
in the Royal Albert Hall by a Soviet flag and soldier, paying fulsome
tributes to Stalin and categorically declaring that Britain and Russia
would work together in peace as well as war to create a new world order.

Though never committing their reservations fully to paper, the scale
of the Cabinet's unease is hinted at by minuted discussions about
whether the event should be replicated the following year. While feeling
obliged to do something—'failure to repeat our tribute . . . may give
rise to unfavourable comment'— they determined that future ceremonies
must not be 'of the appalling character staged last year'. Eventually, the
Ministry of Information decided on an annual celebration which 'could
very easily be terminated with the end of the war'. The policy was
motivated by the determination to prevent 'Communist inspired bodies'
from taking over such celebrations:

> If on one such occasion in the year H.M.G. is to take the wind out
> of the sails of these bodies, Red Army day seems much the best, as
> being non-political.

In cultural terms, the war years have often been seen as marking an
artistic withdrawal from politics, when compared with the direct
involvement of the thirties. Of course, some writers did retreat from
their belief in positive political action: Spender, for example, now
compared the intellectual of the thirties to an Orestes, 'pursued by Furies
of Ends and Means, Propaganda and Necessity'.[56] But to see culture as
having become separated from politics is an over-simplification. Orwell
edited a new series of books which aimed to 'criticize and kill what is

rotten in Western Civilization';[57] Grierson's documentary unit of the thirties became the Ministry of Information's Crown Film Unit; Olivier's *Henry V* made Shakespeare as political a writer as he had ever been. Meanwhile, outdoor sections of London's Unity Theatre found a wider audience, and Glasgow's Unity, formed in 1941, quickly produced two full-length Russian plays and a compilation of poems and sketches about life in the Soviet Union; ENSA developed the drama documentary specifically to discuss political issues, and in June 1944 the ABCA Play Unit was created—with André Van Gyseghem, Jack Lindsay and Ted Willis amongst its active members—to devise lively ways of stimulating discussion and teaching factual information to audiences.

Despite the restraining efforts of the government, the public's empathy with the Soviet ally was stimulated through pageants, and increasingly linked with the feeling that its political system was not a handicap or an irrelevance to its military campaigns, but a huge asset which might offer a valuable model for post-war reconstruction. The war also provided an opportunity for several left-wing artists to invade and occupy the Establishment, though it is arguable that they were neutralised and absorbed within the spirit of national unity against a foreign enemy.

Writing in 1941 under the slogan 'The Theatre is our Weapon', André Van Gyseghem had recognised an urgent and increased responsibility for a war-time theatre which would 'cease to follow limply in the wake of crises and march side by side with the vanguard'. In such critical times, he had argued, people live at a heightened level of awareness, and are more ready to be influenced by the entertainment they see:

> Now, minds are open to new viewpoints; now there is an eager interchange of ideas and a much greater willingness to absorb new ones.[58]

If the landslide victory of the Labour Party in 1945 marked a wish to break with free-market capitalism and a belief in a more equitable and planned society, then the changing representations of the Soviet Union in war-time performances must surely have contributed to the changing consciousness and climate.

Afterword

MARXIST: Comrades! Take him to the wall. Liquidate this hare.
He's a Trotskyist . . .
HARE: Put me against the wall; I have nothing to lose but
my brains.[1]

The use of Soviet history and ideology for theatrical source material did
not come to an end in 1945. The following year, the BBC broadcast
Salute To All Fools, a radio play by Louis MacNeice about a March Hare
who pretends to be a Marx Hare in order to avoid being shot, and who
is seeking to make Truth his bride. 'Follow me if you dare', he invites
the audience, as he escapes from the chains of Marxist, for whom 'Truth
is what we decide at our next meeting'.[2]

Some thirty years later, Robert Bolt's epic drama, *State of Revolution*,
was performed on the stage of the National Theatre, and he explained
why in his view the subject still demanded attention:

> The Russian Revolution is so fraught with urgent implications
> for ourselves that it is hard to see it at dramatic distance. But
> perhaps for that same reason the idea won't go away. And then,
> the event was so terrible . . . the endeavour so total and the out-
> come so tragically far short of what they had intended that merely
> to think about it steadily is to be overwhelmed by primitive pity
> and awe.[3]

There are plenty of more recent dramatists who have felt the need to
revisit the history of the Soviet Union and of communism, though it
has generally been playwrights of the Left rather than of the Right who
have done so. Such visits have often been more in the nature of inquests
to examine what went wrong than in order to celebrate. Howard

Brenton's *Thirteenth Night*, for example, was written at the start of the eighties as a conscious warning to fellow-travellers:

> I became fed-up with the unreality of some of us on the left, who would not address the Stalinist horrors, the repression in what were called 'socialist countries' in Eastern Europe.[4]

In this 'dream play', loosely derived from *Macbeth*, Britain is ruled by an increasingly tyrannical communist dictatorship, which starts with high ideals but soon transforms the country into a hell riddled with barbed wire, corruption and secret police, where all opposition is brutally murdered. The ghost of Stalinism haunts the background—literally so towards the end—and after the dictators have eventually been over-thrown, the epitaph to their regime is only too apposite to the actual fall of the leaders in the Eastern European bloc a decade later:

> You were socialists and dreamt up tyranny. More dangerous than atomic waste. Better you be buried in glass. Deep. And pray the glass never cracks for twenty thousand years.[5]

There is doubtless another book to be written about the portrayal of the Soviet Union and communism in post-1945 British theatre, though it would presumably start by acknowledging that theatre itself—at least in terms of plays performed inside buildings—would generally be recognised to be a less dangerous and significant medium for ideological communication and propaganda.

I began by pointing out that in the twenties and thirties, mainstream theatre is often seen as political only in its supposed resistance to the intrusion of political subject matter into the realm of entertainment. A Workers' Theatre Movement sketch performed in the early thirties nicely, if unsubtly, satirised some of the principal strategies by which those in power ensured the preservation of the status quo:

> 1st: The press
> 2nd: The schools
> 3rd: The theatres
> 4th: The cinemas
> ALL: Are controlled by the capitalist class.
> 2nd: When things get bad they sing to you at the pictures . . . And that's how they do it on you. There's always a good time coming—but the workers never get it.[6]

At the end of the twentieth century one might argue that distracting people from social injustice by providing escapist entertainment through the media is still, in part, 'how they do it on you'. Explicitly right-wing plays continue to be hard to find, and the very term 'political theatre' is still often taken as a synonym for left-wing theatre.

Yet in a period when socialist or communist revolution appeared to many to be a plausible threat, a besieged Establishment was not infrequently driven to wear its brains and its heart more openly on its sleeve than it has needed to in recent times. What particularly focused the minds of participants on both sides of the ideological divide was the existence of the Soviet Union and the profound shock which the 1917 revolution caused throughout Europe, and the subsequent formation of the Communist Party of Great Britain which brought that threat closer to home.

All wars, especially cold ones, are fought in part through the media. While we know that many on the Left were tragically naïve in their refusal to face up to the horrors of Stalinism, this was at least partly due to the extreme venom habitually directed against all things Soviet, which itself rendered media evidence suspect. In *The Russians are Coming*, an analysis of what he describes as 'the politics of anti-Sovietism', Vic Allen examines how Britain and America employed explicit and implicit propaganda over a prolonged period of time in order to instil in the public mind a one-sided view of the communist regime:

> From early in 1918 fear generated hostility and hostility legitimized the perversion of the truth . . . Horror stories appeared in the press claiming that Bolshevik rule was a compound of slaughter, confiscation, anarchy and universal disorder and describing Bolshevik leaders as 'assassins and madmen', 'human scum', 'crime mad' and 'beasts'.[7]

Theatre, too, played its part in defining the changing perspectives from which the Soviet Union and communism could be viewed.

Notes

Preface and Acknowledgements

1. J.C. Trewin, *The Turbulent Thirties—A Further Decade of the Theatre* (London: Macdonald, 1960), p. 17.
2. Ronald Blythe, *The Age of Illusion: England in the Twenties and Thirties, 1919–1940* (London: Hamish Hamilton, 1963), p. 117.

Chapter One

1. *Reparation* is an unpublished one-Act play by Robert Hutchinson, first performed at The Grand Theatre, Lancaster in March 1918. Quotations are from the manuscript in the Lord Chamberlain's Collection of Licensed Plays.
2. The first remark, by E.F. Smythe Pigott is cited in James Woodfield, *English Theatre in Transition 1881–1914* (Beckenham: Croom Helm, 1984, p. 113). The second, by G.A. Redford, is also in Woodfield (p. 259) but can be found more fully in context in the *Report from the Joint Select Committee of the House of Lords and the House of Commons on the Stage Plays (Censorship) Together with the Proceedings of the Committee, Minutes and Appendices* (London: Government Publication, 1909).
3. For the Workers' Theatre Movement, see especially Richard Stourac and Kathleen McCreery, *Theatre as a Weapon: Workers Theatre in the Soviet Union, Germany and Britain 1917–1934* (London: Routledge and Kegan Paul, 1986. Also an unpublished Ph.D. thesis by Ian Saville, *Ideas, forms and developments in the British workers' theatre, 1925–1935*, The City University, 1990. For Unity, see Colin Chambers, *The Story of Unity Theatre* (London: Lawrence and Wishart, 1989). For Group Theatre see Michael Sidnell, *Dances of Death* (London: Faber, 1984). For Theatre of Action see Howard Goorney and Ewan MacColl, eds, *Agit-Prop to Theatre Workshop* (Manchester: Manchester University Press, 1986). See also, more generally, Raphael Samuel, Ewan MacColl and Stuart Cosgrove, *Theatres of the Left 1880–1935* (London: Routledge and Kegan Paul, 1985).

4. Hubert Griffith, 'Introduction' to *Red Sunday* (London: Cayme Press, 1929), p. xi.

5. John Johnston, *The Lord Chamberlain's Blue Pencil* (London: Methuen, 1990), pp. 46–7.

6. Dorothy Knowles, *The Censor, the Drama and the Film 1900–1934* (London: G. Allen and Unwin, 1934), p. 122.

7. Cited in Knowles, p. 122.

8. Introduction to Knowles, p. 4.

9. Knowles, p. 162.

10. G.B. Shaw, *Agitations: Letters to the Press 1875–1950*, ed. Dan H. Laurence and James Rambeau. (New York: Frederick Ungar, 1985), pp. 100–101. Although Shaw's remark had been written in 1907, it was cited in Knowles, p. 79.

11. Victor L. Allen, *The Russians Are Coming: The Politics of Anti-Sovietism* (Shipley: Moor Press, 1987), p. 308.

12. *The Bolshevik* was an unpublished play by A. Edward Brooke, first licensed for performance in Reptford in December 1919. The quotation is from the manuscript in the Lord Chamberlain's Collection of Licensed Plays.

13. *Red Nights of the Tcheka*, subtitled 'A Melodrama of the Russian Revolution', was translated by Terence Gray of the Festival Theatre, Cambridge, from the French of de Lorde and Bauche, and presented there in May, 1927. Quotations are from the manuscript in the Lord Chamberlain's Collection of Licensed Plays, and the play is further discussed in Chapter Four.

14. Frank Swinnerton, writing in the *Nation*, 23 October 1920, p. 130. He claimed that 'the only story that anybody has ever wanted to see or to read or to write has been a love story'.

15. See *Theatre World*, January 1929. It is even tempting to see a parallel between the erosion of the pits in theatre auditoria and the shift to all-seater stadiums at football grounds.

16. According to the play's producer and star, Leon Lion, he was repeatedly questioned by the King, who showed 'an avid interest in the play and why it had been taken off'. See Leon M. Lion, *The Surprise of My Life* (London: Hutchinson, 1948), p. 90.

17. *Reparation*.

Chapter Two

1. Hubert Griffith's sarcastic and cynical assessment of the censor's attitude is in his 'Introduction' to the published text of his play *Red Sunday* (London: Cayme Press, 1929), p. x.

2. The play was submitted on 20 February 1918; the letter refusing the licence was sent to DeGray on 30 March. DeGray wrote again on 4 April, pointing

out that the decision 'has been a great inconvenience, and loss to me, as my bookings included some of the best Provincial Theatre's [sic], and ran well into autumn'. He also queried the decision as 'all the more unexpected, as I notice there is a picture, on the same subject—a bill of which I enclose—touring the country in the Cinema Houses'. For all material relating to the play and its censorship see the Lord Chamberlain's Correspondence Files: *The Russian Monk*.

3. *Observer*, 12 November 1922.
4. John Johnston, *The Lord Chamberlain's Blue Pencil* (London: Methuen, 1990), p. 28.
5. Cited in, for example, James Woodfield, *English Theatre in Transition 1881–1914* (Beckenham: Croom Helm, 1984), p. 109.
6. See the *Report from the Joint Select Committee on the House of Lords and the House of Commons on the Stage Plays (Censorship) Together with the Proceedings of the Committee, Minutes and Appendices* (London: Government Publication, 1909), p. iii. This contains the full text of the official proceedings.
7. The report was published in November 1909. The other things forbidden to a play seeking a licence were:
   'To be indecent;
   To contain offensive personalities;
   To do violence to the sentiment of religious reverence;
   To be calculated to conduce to crime or vice.'
8. From Shaw's 'Preface' to *The Shewing-Up of Blanco Posnet*. See G.B. Shaw, *The Prefaces* (London: Constable, 1934), p. 401.
9. Johnston, p. 20.
10. The phrase appears on headed notepaper used by DeGray for a letter he sent to the Lord Chamberlain in March 1921. See the Lord Chamberlain's Correspondence Files: *The Russian Monk*.
11. All quotations from the unpublished text of *The Russian Monk*, which is in the Lord Chamberlain's Collection of Unlicensed Plays.
12. See the Lord Chamberlain's Correspondence Files: *The Russian Monk*.
13. The play itself is discussed in Chapter Four.
14. Griffith, 'Introduction' to *Red Sunday*, pp. xv–xvi.
15. *The Times*, 1 July 1929, p. 15.
16. The original letter was from Peter (later Sir Peter) Bark, Hon. GCVO, the Russian Finance Minister from 1914 to 1917. The Keeper of the Privy Purse sent an unsigned memorandum to the Lord Chamberlain on 3 July 1929. These and all documents subsequently referred to in connection with the censorship of this play—unless otherwise indicated—are in the Lord Chamberlain's Correspondence Files: *Red Sunday*.
17. Griffith, 'Introduction' to *Red Sunday*, p. xiv. Elsewhere, Griffith reports the Lord Chamberlain as having said: 'I know what the play is about. I

will save you your two guineas reading-fee by refusing even to read it. I know in advance that I will not license it.' See Hubert Griffith, *Seeing Soviet Russia* (London: John Lane, 1932), p. 5.

18. Griffith, *Seeing Soviet Russia*, p. 5.
19. See the Lord Chamberlain's Correspondence File for *Hoppla!* by Ernst Toller. Gray's comment came in *the festival theatre review* 3 (23 February 1929), p. 8. For a fuller discussion of the battles between Gray and the Lord Chamberlain see Steve Nicholson, ' "Nobody Was Ready for That": The Gross Impertinence of Terence Gray and the Degradation of Drama', *Theatre Research International* 1996 (xxi, no. 2), pp. 121—31.
20. See *the festival theatre review* 4 (18 April 1931), p. 9.
21. For this and subsequent references, see the Lord Chamberlain's Correspondence Files: *Roar China*.
22. The production had been seen in Frankfurt in November 1929.
23. Gray's comment came in *the festival theatre review* 4 (9 May 1931), p. 7.
24. The Manchester production had been directed by Sladen-Smith in November 1931.
25. Manchester Repertory Theatre enquired about a possible production in 1936, but abandoned the idea when informed by the Lord Chamberlain that the play was unlicensed. Gray had created the Festival Theatre in Cambridge in 1926, and ran it for seven years as one of the more exciting and progressive theatres in Britain until he could no longer stand the battles with the authorities and, especially, with the Lord Chamberlain. He spent most of the rest of his life in France.
26. The play was *Rasputin* by A.N. Tolstoy and P.E. Shchegoleff, produced in a translation by Clifford Bax in club conditions in London in 1928. See the Lord Chamberlain's Correspondence Files: *Rasputin*. The play is discussed in Chapter Four.
27. See Dorothy Knowles, *The Censor, the Drama and the Film 1900–1934* (London: G. Allen and Unwin, 1934), pp. 154–5.
28. Griffith, 'Introduction' to *Red Sunday*, p. viii.
29. See *the festival theatre review* 4 (9 May 1931), p. 7.

Chapter Three

1. From the unpublished manuscript of *The Bolshevik Peril* in the Lord Chamberlain's Collection of Licensed Plays.
2. For discussion of this and further examples see R. Page Arnot, *The Impact of the Russian Revolution in Britain* (London: Lawrence and Wishart, 1967) and Phillip Knightley, *The First Casualty* (London: Deutsch, 1975). The article entitled 'Bolshevist Marriage' was published in *The Times*, 11 February 1919.
3. See Knightley, p. 149.

4. G. E. Rain and E. Luboff, *Bolshevik Russia* (London: Nisbit, 1920), p. 48.
5. Victor L. Allen, *The Russians Are Coming: The Politics of Anti-Sovietism* (Shipley: Moor Press, 1987), pp. 13–14.
6. Facts which contradicted the version of events which the newspaper chose to project were largely unreported in Britain, where any story defending the Red Army or criticising the Allies was liable to be banned as 'Bolshevik Propaganda'. In writing its own history, *The Times* admitted that 'British public opinion had been roused, very largely by The Times, into active animosity to [the Bolsheviks] who were regarded as conspirators with but a short expectation of power'. See *The History of The Times: The 150th Anniversary and Beyond, 1912–1948* (London: The Times, 1952), p. 247. See also Kenneth O'Reilly, 'The Times of London and the Bolshevik Revolution', *Journalism Quarterly*, (Part 56, 1979), pp. 69–76, and Knightley, p. 149.
7. Dr C. Hagberg Wright, 'Bolshevism in England', *The Times*, 8 November 1919.
8. See *The Times*, 15 February 1919, p. 8.
9. See Michael Sayers and Albert E. Khan, *The Great Conspiracy against Russia* (New York: Boni and Gaer, 1946), pp. 154–5.
10. *The Times*, 1 February 1919, p. 9.
11. Horace Wykeham Can Newte, *The Red Fury: Britain under Bolshevism* (London: Holden and Hardingham, 1919). John Cournos, *London under the Bolsheviks* (London: Russian Liberation Committee, 1920). Charles Ross, *The Fly-by-nights* (London: Murray, 1921). Edgar Alfred Jepson, *A Prince in Petrograd* (London: Odhams, 1921). John Buchan, *Huntingtower* (London: Hodder and Stoughton, 1922). Martin Hussingtree, *Konyetz* (London: Hodder and Stoughton, 1924). For a fuller listing, see Anthony G. Cross, *The Russian Theme in English Literature* (Oxford: Oxford University Press, 1985).
12. *Stage*, 16 December 1920, p. 16.
13. *It's All Wrong*, subtitled 'A Musical Complaint', was written by Elsie Janis, and ran at the Queen's Theatre in London for 112 performances between December 1920 and March 1921. The unpublished script, from which all quotations are taken, is in the Lord Chamberlain's Collection of Licensed Plays.
14. *The Bolshevik Peril*, by R. Grahame, was first performed in Tredegar in March 1919. All quotations are taken from the unpublished script, which is in the Lord Chamberlain's Collection of Licensed Plays.
15. From the 'Reader's Report' on *The Bolshevik Peril*, filed with the manuscript.
16. *The Right to Strike* by H. Ernest Hutchinson ran for 82 performances at the Garrick, Lyric and Queen's Theatres between September and December 1920. All play quotations are taken from the text in the Lord

Chamberlain's Collection of Licensed Plays. The play was never published, but a novel co-written by Hutchinson came out under the same title in 1921.

17. See Leon M. Lion, *The Surprise of My Life* (London: Hutchinson, 1948), p. 90.
18. *Stage*, 30 September 1920, p. 16.
19. *Nation*, 23 October 1920, pp. 129–30.
20. Lion, p. 90.
21. *Sunday Times*, 3 October 1920, p. 6.
22. *Saturday Review*, 9 October 1920, pp. 292–3.
23. *Spectator*, 16 October 1920, p. 500.
24. It is the basis, for example, of a number of Trevor Griffith's plays of the seventies and early eighties.
25. *The Times*, 29 September 1920, p. 8.
26. Letter from Charles Kenyon of the Garrick Theatre to the Reader of Plays, dated 21 September 1920. The only threat of direct censorship concerned the use of the word 'bloody', but Kenyon claimed that 'by making us alter this particular word, you are weakening the strongest situation in the Play'. He invited the Lord Chamberlain to the first performance to 'see if he does not agree with our views', and the objection was officially withdrawn. See the Lord Chamberlain's Correspondence Files: *The Right to Strike*.
27. *First Blood* was performed in northern venues, including Stockport and Leeds, from 1925 onwards. It was produced at the Gate Theatre in London in December 1926.
28. See Swinnerton's review of *The Right to Strike*, in *The Nation*, 23 October 1920, p. 130.
29. All quotations taken from Allan Monkhouse, *First Blood* (London: Benn, 1924).
30. *Labour On Top* by C.T. Podmore was licensed for performance at the Hippodrome, Hulme, in May 1926. Quotations and references are from the unpublished script, which is in the Lord Chamberlain's Collection of Licensed Plays.
31. *What Might Happen: A Piece of Extravagance in Three Acts* opened at the Savoy Theatre in June 1926. The script was published in 1927 by the Stage Play Publishing Bureau. Maltby subsequently co-wrote *The Red Light*, performed in 1931, which offered a similar but darker and more exhaustive warning of the future facing Britain if the communists were allowed to take power. *The Red Light* is discussed in Chapter Five.
32. See the Lord Chamberlain's Correspondence Files: *What Might Happen*.
33. Quotations taken from the manuscript version of *What Might Happen* in the Lord Chamberlain's Collection of Licensed Plays.
34. Maltby accused Mrs Patrick Campbell of sabotaging a play which would otherwise have been a great success: 'she just sulked, lost all interest in

the production, made no attempt to learn her lines and deliberately went out to wreck the whole show.' See H.F. Maltby, *Ring Up The Curtain* (London: Hutchinson & Co., 1950).

35. *Shadows of Strife* was performed in Sheffield in March 1928, and reached London in a production presented by Sir Barry Jackson at the Arts Theatre in December 1929.

36. *Saturday Review*, 14 December 1929, pp. 722–3.

37. All quotations from John Davison, *Shadows of Strife* (London: J.M. Dent and Sons, 1929).

38. *Yellow Sands* opened on 3 November 1926 and closed on 25 February 1928. It was featured with extensive photographs in *Theatre World, The Play Pictorial* and *The Sketch*, and was subsequently made into a feature film.

39. Quotations from Eden and Adelaide Phillpotts, *Yellow Sands* (London: Duckworth, 1926).

40. *Nation and Athenaeum*, 13 November 1926, p. 217. However, the reviewer noted that he 'would have preferred something a little more "morbid" ', but was in a minority in being 'too exasperated by life . . . to appreciate what is known as "harmless fun" '.

41. *Sunday Times*, 7 November 1926, p. 6.

42. Strindberg's play had been dismissed by the Lord Chamberlain's Office as 'a morbid and thoroughly disagreeable play' and refused a licence in September 1925. It was not only the supposed sexual immorality which had worried the censors, but also the political and class implications of the central relationship. For discussion of this see also Steve Nicholson, ' "Unnecessary Plays": European drama and the British censor', *Theatre Research International*, Vol. 20, No. 1 (Spring 1995), pp. 30–6.

43. From Ivor Brown's review in the *Saturday Review*, 13 November 1926, p. 583.

44. *Spectator*, 13 November 1926, p. 853.

45. Eden and Adelaide Phillpotts.

46. *The Times*, 12 September 1928, p. 12.

47. Eden and Adelaide Phillpotts.

48. *Sunday Times*, 7 November 1926, p. 6.

49. Eden and Adelaide Phillpotts.

50. *Sunday Times*, 7 November 1926, p. 6.

51. Eden and Adelaide Phillpotts.

Chapter Four

1. V.M. Kirchon and A.V. Ouspensky, *Red Rust*, translated by F. Vernon and V. Vernon (New York: Rialto Service Bureau, 1929), pp. 16–17. All quotations are taken from this published version, though there is an unpublished manuscript of the play in the Lord Chamberlain's Collection

of Licensed Plays, under the title *Rust*. There are some differences between the two texts.

2. The play was originally presented as *Annajanska, The Wild Grand Duchess* at the Coliseum Theatre, London, on 21 January 1918, as part of a variety bill.

3. A letter which Shaw sent to Boris Lebedeff in November 1920 expresses a view which is by no means dissimilar to the idea expressed in these lines: I have been declaring for years past that Socialism without compulsory labour and ruthless penalization of idleness and exploitation is nothing but a confusion of Socialism with Liberalism.' See Dan H. Laurence, ed., *Bernard Shaw: Collected Letters 1911–1925* (London: Reinhardt, 1985), p. 700. For all quotations from the text see *Annajanska, The Bolshevik Empress*, in G.B. Shaw, *Collected Plays, Volume V* (London: Bodley Head, 1972).

4. *Joan of the Sword*, subtitled 'A modern romantic play', by G. Carlton Wallace, was first licensed for performance at the Theatre Royal, Norwich, on 16 June 1919.

5. From the unpublished manuscript of *Joan of the Sword*, by G. Carlton Wallace, in the Lord Chamberlain's Collection of Licensed Plays.

6. The Liverpool Playhouse reopened under the new direction of Nigel Playfair on 12 September 1921. *The Terror* was a 'curtain raiser', and Mrs Campbell described it as 'very effective', producing 'six and seven calls every night'. It ran for only two weeks, she said, because 'I could not spare more time from my writing'. See Mrs Patrick Campbell, *My Life and Some Letters* (London: Hutchinson, 1922).

7. See the Readers Report in the Lord Chamberlain's Correspondence File: *The Terror*.

8. From the unpublished manuscript of *The Terror*, in the Lord Chamberlain's Collection of Licensed Plays.

9. *The Times* had led a campaign for armed British intervention, and in August 1918 British soldiers had landed in Vladivostock with the declared intention of protecting Russia from the Germans; in fact, the troops remained after the armistice to lend continuing support to Kolchak and the White Armies against the bolsheviks, and withdrew only in November 1919, after a year of farcical military mistakes. See, for example, Phillip Knightley, *The First Casualty* (London: Deutsch, 1975), pp. 138–9. *The Silver Lining*, by Major C.T. Davis, was presented at a matinée in March 1921, along with *The King's Favourite* and *The Dream of a Winter Evening*, both by John Pollock.

10. From the unpublished manuscript of *The Silver Lining*, in the Lord Chamberlain's Collection of Licensed Plays.

11. *The Beating on the Door* opened at St James's Theatre in 1922.

12. All quotations from the unpublished manuscript of *The Beating on the Door* in the Lord Chamberlain's Collection of Licensed Plays.

13. *Observer*, 12 November 1922, p. 11.

14. *Sunday Times*, 12 November 1922, p. 6.

15. *The Forcing House* ran at the Little Theatre from 9 February until 20 March 1926.

16. Zangwill's introduction to the published text criticises the 'decay of seriousness in all the arts', and demands the right for the theatre to engage in serious debate. He claims that part of a writer's duty is to give equal weight to conflicting arguments, and as his manifesto, he adopts a statement by the nineteenth-century French writer and philosopher Renan: 'the other side of every thought ought to be indicated in it, so that the reader may seize at one glance the two opposite sides of which the truth is composed.' See Israel Zangwill, 'Introduction' to *The Forcing House* (London: William Heinemann, 1922). The introduction is in the form of a letter addressed to Maurice Maeterlinck.

17. Israel Zangwill, *Hands Off Russia* (London: Workers' Socialist Federation, 1919), pp. 3–7.

18. Zangwill, 'Introduction' to *The Forcing House*. He says he has chosen not to use the word 'Bolshevism' in the play because it is a word 'which people put into their mouths to steal away their brains'.

19. All quotations from Israel Zangwill, *The Forcing House* (London: William Heinemann, 1922).

20. Zangwill, 'Introduction' to *The Forcing House*.

21. *Saturday Review*, 2 December 1922, p. 839.

22. Mr R. Storry Deans, a Tory MP for Sheffield, booked the entire theatre for the evening of February 19th; some two hundred MPs of all parties attended at his invitation.

23. *Such Men are Dangerous* by Ashley Dukes was performed at the Duke of York's between 19 September 1928 and 5 January 1929, following a provincial tour. *Paul I* was adapted by John Alford and James Dale from a text by Dmitry Merezhkovsky, and performed at the Court Theatre between 4 October and 11 November 1927.

24. Ashley Dukes, *Such Men are Dangerous*, in *Famous Plays of Today—1929* (London: Gollancz, 1929).

25. From the unpublished manuscript of *Paul I*, in the Lord Chamberlain's Collection of Licensed Plays.

26. *The Grand Duchess*, adapted by Harry Graham, from the French of Alfred Savoir, was licensed for its first performance at the Globe Theatre, on 13 January 1925.

27. From the unpublished manuscript of *The Grand Duchess*, in the Lord Chamberlain's Collection of Licensed Plays.

28. There are actually two versions of *The Volga Boatman* in the Lord

Chamberlain's Collection of Licensed Plays. There is hardly an identical line in the two versions, but they tell the same story. The first version was anonymously written, and originally licensed to be performed twice nightly at Mexborough Hippodrome, from 29 September 1927. The second was credited to Shiela [sic] Walsh, and was licensed for twice-nightly performances at the Palace Theatre, Carshalton from 14 February 1929. It was subtitled 'A Tale of the Russian Revolution'.

29. From the unpublished manuscript of *The Volga Boatman* (1927 version), in the Lord Chamberlain's Collection of Licensed Plays.

30. See the Lord Chamberlain's Correspondence Files: *The Volga Boatman*.

31. *Red Nights of the Tcheka*, subtitled 'A Melodrama of the Russian Revolution' was translated by Gray from the French of André de Lorde and Henri Bauche. It was licensed for the Festival Theatre, Cambridge, May 1927. The speech which was excised contains the following lines:

'Your Tzars did things as bad . . . firing parties. Wholesale deportations to Siberia, to the mines . . . Thousands of men and women whom they condemned to die of hunger . . . of cold, of misery . . . And your cowardly, greedy middle-class; your nobility, rotten with vice and drink . . . It is because of them we made the revolution!'

See the unpublished manuscript of *Red Nights of the Tcheka*, in the Lord Chamberlain's Collection of Licensed Plays. This speech has been crossed out by the censor.

32. See the Lord Chamberlain's Correspondence Files: *Red Nights of the Tcheka*.

33. All quotations from the unpublished manuscript of *Red Nights of the Tcheka*.

34. See Wilfred Wellock, 'Soviet Russia Today', *Socialist Review*, January 1928, pp. 23–30. Also, Dorothy Buxton, *The Challenge of Bolshevism* (London: G. Allen and Unwin, 1928). Buxton claimed that the Soviet Union was morally superior to the West, since it concentrated on 'the ideal of life' rather than 'the ideal of wealth'. Strachey was editor of *Socialist Review*.

35. *The Times*, 12 April 1928, reviewing *The Cherry Orchard*.

36. *Stage*, 25 April 1929, p. 10.

37. *The Times*, 23 April 1929, p. 14; *Saturday Review*, 27 April 1929, p. 572.

38. Not that the supposedly anti-German quality had prevented the Berlin production mentioned above, but the British censors were notoriously worried about upsetting other governments. One of the more extreme examples had been the withdrawal of the licence for *The Mikado* during a visit to London by the Japanese Crown Prince in 1907.

39. From the unpublished English translation of *Rasputin*, in the Lord Chamberlain's Collection of Unlicensed Plays.

40. See the Lord Chamberlain's Correspondence Files: *Rasputin*.
41. The play was an adaptation by Virginia and Frank Vernon from the Russian of V.M. Kirchon and A.V. Ouspensky, and was first performed at the Little Theatre on 28 February 1929.
42. *Nation and Athenaeum*, 16 March 1929, p. 840.
43. The first quotation is from *The Times*, 1 March 1929, p. 14. Darlington's comments come in *The Daily Telegraph*.
44. *Nation and Athenaeum*, 16 March 1929, p. 840; *Observer*, 3 March 1929, p. 15.
45. *Observer*, 3 March 1929, p. 15.
46. All quotations from V.M. Kirchon and A.V. Ouspensky, *Red Rust*, translated by F. Vernon and V. Vernon (New York: Rialto Service Bureau, 1929). There is also an unpublished manuscript of the play in the Lord Chamberlain's Collection of Licensed Plays, under the title *Rust*. There are some differences between the two texts.
47. All quotations are taken from the anonymous, unpublished and undated translation of Grubinski's account entitled *Crime and Punishment*, stored in the archives at the Polish Library, London. This describes his trial and imprisonment in the Soviet Union. Grubinski's death sentence was apparently commuted to imprisonment and he was released when Germany declared war on Russia.
48. *Peace, War and Revolution* was performed at the Royalty Theatre on 17 February 1929 by the International Theatre Society, which had been formed in the early twenties 'to present the plays of all the nations who had a dramatic literature, preferably the lesser known, to the London Public', and thus to foster international friendship. (See the society's official leaflet, printed in Anna Irene Miller, *The Independent Theatre in Europe: 1887 to the Present* (New York: R. Long and R.R. Smith, 1931). In this case, several reviews commented on the play suffering from 'insufficient rehearsal'.
49. Grubinski, *Crime and Punishment*.
50. From the anonymous and unpublished translation of *Lenin* by Waclaw Grubinski in the archives of the Polish Library in London. It is not clear whether this is the exact text used in the London performance.
51. Hubert Griffith's play was performed without a licence at the Arts Theatre in June 1929 under the direction of Komisarjevsky. It featured John Gielgud as Trotsky, and Robert Farquharson as Lenin. The circumstances surrounding the refusal of the licence are discussed in Chapter Two.
52. All quotations from Hubert Griffith, *Red Sunday* (London: Cayme Press, 1929).
53. *The Times*, 28 June 1929, p. 14.
54. *Era*, 3 July 1929, p. 1.
55. St John Ervine in the *Observer*, 30 June 1929, p. 15.

56. James Agate in the *Sunday Times*, 30 June 1929, p. 6.
57. Zangwill, 'Introduction' to *The Forcing House*.
58. *The Times*, 18 November 1931, p. 10. It was reviewing *The Red Light*, to be discussed in Chapter Five.

Chapter Five

1. From *Crossroads*, a play by an anonymous writer, performed at Croydon in May 1936. The script is in the Lord Chamberlain's Collection of Licensed Plays.
2. *The Times*, 18 July 1995, p. 19.
3. Montagu Slater, 'The Purpose of a Left Review', *Left Review*, I, no. 9, June 1935, pp. 359–65. See also Neal Wood, *Communism and British Intellectuals* (London: Victor Gollancz, 1959), who cites the following examples of left-wing cultural journals published during the decade: *New Verse, Storm, Cambridge Left, The Wanderer, New Atlantis, New Albion, New Britain, New Europe, The Week, Plan, Controversy.*
4. Montagu Slater, 'Writers' International', *Left Review*, I, no. 4, January 1935, pp. 125–9.
5. Originally one of a series of radio talks, later published in book form as: Frank Birch, *This Freedom of Ours* (Cambridge: Cambridge University Press, 1937).
6. Cited in Ronald Blythe, *The Age of Illusion: England in the Twenties and Thirties, 1919–1940* (London: Hamish Hamilton, 1963), p. 110.
7. John Beverley Nichols, 'Introduction' to *Failures* (London: Jonathon Cape, 1933). *When the Crash Comes* was staged by the Birmingham Repertory Company in March 1933.
8. All quotations from John Beverley Nichols, *When the Crash Comes*, collected in *Failures*.
9. F.L. Lucas, 'Introduction' to *The Bear Dances* (London: Cassell, 1933). The first production was by Leon Lion at the Garrick Theatre in November 1932, and the play was subsequently performed at the People's Theatre in Newcastle.
10. All quotations from Lucas, *The Bear Dances*.
11. Lucas, 'Introduction' to *The Bear Dances*.
12. *The People's Court* was first performed in April 1933 at the Embassy Theatre, and was then taken up by the Rebel Players, the branch of the Workers' Theatre Movement which developed directly into Unity Theatre. Unity revived the play in 1941.
13. Hubert Griffith, *The People's Court* (London: Rich and Cowan, 1933).
14. Griffith, 'Author's Note' to *The People's Court*. Elsewhere, Griffith confirms the accuracy of the source, concluding that 'the story sounds like a fairy-tale—or at least like material for a propagandist one-act play to

convert the Infidel to Bolshevism; but it happens to be authentic'. Hubert Griffith, *Seeing Soviet Russia* (London: John Lane, 1932), pp. 89–92.

15. *What Might Happen* is discussed in Chapter Three. *The Red Light* was performed at the New Theatre in November 1931.

16. From the Reader's Report for the Lord Chamberlain by G.S. Street, November 1931. See the Lord Chamberlain's Correspondence Files: *The Red Light*.

17. Referred to in reviews of the production.

18. The script for *The Red Light* was never published. All quotations are from the manuscript of the play submitted to the Lord Chamberlain.

19. *The Times*, 18 November 1931, p. 10.

20. See the Lord Chamberlain's Correspondence Files: *The Red Light*.

21. *Sunday Times*, 22 November 1931, p. 4.

22. See, for example, the notice in *Left Review* inviting submissions to a playwriting competition: 'The drama of a socialist theatre necessarily evolves new themes which may lend themselves to presentation in the old form but more probably will develop new theatrical forms for themselves'. *Left Review*, I, no. 7, April 1935.

23. Ewan MacColl, in the 'Introduction' to Howard Goorney and Ewan MacColl (eds), *Agit-Prop to Theatre Workshop* (Manchester: Manchester University Press, 1986), p. xxvi.

24. Montagu Slater, 'Writers' International', *Left Review*, I, no. 4, January 1935, pp. 125–8.

25. See Terence Gray, *Dance-Drama: Experiments in the Art of the Theatre* (Cambridge: W. Heffer, 1926), p. 3.

26. From Tom Thomas's private papers, cited in Raphael Samuel, Ewan MacColl and Stuart Cosgrove, *Theatres of the Left 1880—1935* (London: Routledge and Kegan Paul, 1985), pp. 33–4.

27. Tom Thomas 'A propertyless theatre for the propertyless class', in Samuel *et al.* p. 95.

28. The manifesto was printed in the programme for Left Theatre's production of Montague Slater's *Stay Down Miner*, performed in May 1936.

29. Ralph Wright's review of Left Theatre's production of Gorki's story *The Mother*, adapted by Barbara Nixon. See *Left Review*, II, no. 3, December 1935, pp. 143–4.

30. *News Chronicle*, 13 May 1938, p. 8.

31. Goorney and MacColl, p. xxvii.

32. Robert Jardine, *Left Review*, III, no. 15, April 1938, pp. 222–3.

33. John Allen, 'The Socialist Theatre', *Left Review*, III, no. 7, August 1937, pp. 419–22.

34. *Daily Worker*, 25 November 1937, p. 5.

35. See Ness Edwards, *The Workers' Theatre* (Cardiff: Cymric Federation Press, 1930), p. 71.

36. Allen.
37. Unity Theatre Society, *Rules*, 1938, p. 2.
38. Allen.
39. Unity's original production of this play, written by Herbert Hodge and Buckley Roberts, two London taxi drivers, opened in London in 1937. The play was frequently revived and performed by other branches of Unity and left-wing theatres.
40. Herbert Hodge (Roger Gullan) and Buckley Roberts, *Where's that Bomb?* (London: Lawrence and Wishart, 1937).
41. The sound of a toilet flushing was not allowed, and 'toilet paper' had to be changed to 'shaving paper'. See the Lord Chamberlain's Correspondence Files: *Where's that Bomb?*
42. See St John Ervine, *The Theatre in My Time* (London: Rich and Cowan, 1933), p. 135. (The other danger was that it might become 'womanised'.)
43. Ervine, pp. 157–9.
44. Slater was reviewing the published scenario of the film *The Private Life of Henry VIII*, in *Left Review*, I, no. 4, January 1935, p. 144.
45. Barbara Nixon, 'Translator's Note' to Sergei Tretiakov, *Roar China* (London: Martin Lawrence, 1931), pp. 1–4.
46. Tretiakov, *Roar China*.
47. *Bees on the Boat Deck* opened at the Lyric in May 1936.
48. All quotations from *Bees on the Boat Deck*. Collected in J.B. Priestley, *The Plays of J.B. Priestley: Volume II* (London: Heinemann, 1949).
49. *Trial of a Judge* was performed by Group Theatre—at Unity Theatre—in March 1938.
50. Stephen Spender, *Trial of a Judge* (London: Faber and Faber, 1938).
51. *Geneva* was produced at the Malvern Festival Theatre in August 1938 and then ran for 237 performances in London at the Saville Theatre and St James's Theatre from November 1938.
52. G.B. Shaw, *Geneva* (London: Constable, 1939).
53. See, for example, David Smith, in *Socialist Propaganda in the Twentieth-Century British Novel* (London: Macmillan, 1978).
54. *Horizon*, Issue 1, January 1940, p. 5.
55. Harry Kemp, Laura Riding et al., *The Left Heresy in Literature and Life* (London: Methuen, 1939).
56. Neal Wood queries whether the control had ever in fact existed: 'Was communism during the thirties a grave threat to British intellectual life? . . . Were the nineteen-thirties . . . a 'red decade'? Upon the basis of all evidence, the answer is a conclusive no.' (Wood, p. 73). Similarly, Ronald Blyth argues that 'The communist flirtation ran little risk of developing to the point of consummation. The intellectual Left and the small solid Red heart of the C.P.G.B. were not made for each other, and they knew it . . .' Blythe, p. 119.

57. *Tsar Lénine* was first produced in Paris by Charles Dullin in 1930. Partly because of censorship, it was June 1937 before it received a British production at the Westminster Theatre.
58. Quotations are taken from the translation by Roy Newlands, as submitted to the Lord Chamberlain by the Festival Theatre in 1933. See the Lord Chamberlain's Collection of Unlicensed Plays: *Tsar Lenin*. It is possible that the text used in the 1937 first production may have been a different translation from this.
59. All quotations from Françoise Porché, 'Examen de "Tsar Lénine"'. Published as an introduction to *Tsar Lénine* (Paris: Flammarion, 1932).
60. Ivor Brown writing in the *Observer*, 4 July 1937.
61. *Tovarich* opened at the Lyric Theatre in April 1935.
62. See Robert E. Sherwood, 'Foreword' to Jacques Deval, *Tovarich* (London: S. French, 1938).
63. See the Lord Chamberlain's Correspondence Files: *Tovarich*.
64. Sherwood.
65. H.R. Lenormand, 'Propaganda in the Theatre', reprinted in *Drama*, December 1938.

Chapter Six

1. From Louis MacNeice's *Salute to the U.S.S.R.*, broadcast on BBC radio, April 1942. Quotation taken from the unpublished manuscript.
2. In a speech broadcast on the night of the German invasion of the Soviet Union, Churchill explained his changed position: 'The Nazi regime . . . is indistinguishable from the worst features of communism . . . No one has been a more consistent opponent of communism than I have for the last twenty-five years. I will unsay no word that I have spoken about it . . . The past with its crimes, its follies and its tragedies flashes away . . . I see the ten thousand villages of Russia . . . where maidens laugh and children play . . . The cause of any Russian fighting for his hearth and home is the cause of free men and free peoples in every quarter of the globe.' See Angus Calder, *The People's War: Britain 1939–45* (London: Jonathan Cape, 1969), p. 260.
3. Unity performed the play privately under club conditions. It ran with two alternating casts for over eighty performances, and received widespread national reviews. The circumstances of the production are detailed in Colin Chambers, *The Story of Unity Theatre* (London: Lawrence and Wishart, 1989), pp. 204–9.
4. See the Lord Chamberlain's Correspondence Files: *The Star Turns Red*.
5. See Sean O'Casey, *The Letters of Sean O'Casey, 1910–1941, Volume I* (London: Macmillan, 1975), p. 817.
6. Jim Larkin, the Dublin trade union leader, was a hero and personal friend

of O'Casey. As early as 1922 O'Casey had planned to write a play about Larkin under the title of *The Red Star*. See his letter to Lennox Robinson in Sean O'Casey, *The Letters of Sean O'Casey*, pp. 104–5.

7. The published script specifies the music of Glazounov, but Allan Bush wrote the music for Unity.

8. O'Casey, *The Letters of Sean O'Casey*, p. 775.

9. All quotations from *The Star Turns Red*, as published in Sean O'Casey, *Collected Plays*, vol. VII (London: Macmillan, 1949).

10. See, for example, C. Desmond Greaves, *Sean O'Casey: Politics and Art* (London: Lawrence and Wishart, 1979), pp. 145–6.

11. Shaw's postcard, dated 22 April 1940, is cited in Eileen O'Casey, *Sean* (London: Macmillan, 1971), p. 177.

12. Stephen Spender, 'A Morality Play with No Morals' in *The New Statesman and Nation*, 16 March 1940, pp. 363–4.

13. The author and exact performance details of *Launcelot's Dream* are not known. It was probably first produced in 1940/41 by Teeside Unity Theatre.

14. From the unpublished manuscript of *Launcelot's Dream*.

15. *Our Time*, I, no. 6, August 1941, p. 10.

16. Quoted in *Our Time*, I, no. 10, January 1942, p. 27.

17. *The Spectre that Haunts Europe* was submitted to the Lord Chamberlain from Manchester on 12 September 1941, author(s) unknown.

18. The original 'Yes, my Darling Daughter' was recorded in September 1940, and—appropriately perhaps—was adapted from an old Yiddish folk song.

19. Quotations from the unpublished script of *The Spectre that Haunts Europe*, in the Lord Chamberlain's Collection of Unlicensed Plays.

20. From the Readers Report by H.C. Game in the Lord Chamberlain's Correspondence Files: *The Spectre that Haunts Europe*.

21. *The Times*, 1 July 1940.

22. Written in the winter of 1940–41, *House of Regrets* opened at the Arts Theatre in October 1942.

23. Quotations from Peter Ustinov, *House of Regrets* (London: Jonathon Cape, 1943).

24. See Ian McLaine, *Ministry of Morale: Home Front Morale and the Ministry of Information in World War II* (London: G. Allen and Unwin, 1979), pp. 194–5.

25. Home Intelligence Report from March 1942. See McLaine, pp. 149–50.

26. Cited in Paul Addison, *The Road to 1945* (London: Cape, 1977), p. 135.

27. R.H. Parker, Director of the Home Publicity Division, July 1941. Cited in McLaine, p. 199.

28. Werth, a Russian journalist working for British newspapers, proposed this angle of attack. See Addison, p. 198.

29. 'Communism under Stalin has produced the most valiant fighting army in

Europe. Communism under Stalin has provided us with examples of patriotism equal to the finest in the annals of history. Communism under Stalin has produced the best generals in this war.' Beaverbrooks's speech in New York is quoted in George Bilainkin, *Maisky* (London: G. Allen Unwin, 1944). Lord Mottistone's praise is quoted in Ivan Maisky, *Memoirs of a Soviet Ambassador* (London: Hutchinson, 1967), pp. 259–60.

30. See McLaine, pp. 196–7.
31. See Calder, p. 348.
32. *Our Time*, II, no. 9, February 1943, p. 13.
33. *Our Time*, I, no. 11, February 1942, pp. 23–4.
34. *Radio Times*, 29 May 1942, p. 4.
35. Unpublished manuscript by Louis MacNeice, *Alexander Nevsky*.
36. For discussion of this see Barbara Coulton, *Louis MacNeice in the BBC* (London: Faber, 1980), p. 56.
37. Unpublished manuscript by Louis MacNeice, *Salute to the U.S.S.R.*
38. Unpublished manuscript by Louis MacNeice, *Spirit of Russia*.
39. *Four Soviet War Plays* (London: Hutchinson, 1944).
40. *According to Plan*, by Geoffrey Parsons. It was performed as part of an evening of short plays called *This Our World*, which also included a revival of Hubert Griffith's *The People's Court*. It was published with *Erma Kremer of Ebenstadt* by the Russia Today Society in 1941, under the collective title *The Theatre is Our Weapon*. A slightly different version of *According to Plan* appears in manuscript form in the Lord Chamberlain's Collections.
41. P. Yaltsev, *The Ocean*, in Herbert Marshall (ed.), *Soviet One-Act Plays* (London: Pilot Press, 1944), pp. 29–30.
42. Originally called *Face to Face*, *Comrade Detective*, was translated, designed and produced by Herbert Marshall on the suggestion of the wife of the Soviet Ambassador. It was staged by Unity in December 1944.
43. Quotations from the unpublished manuscript of Comrade Detective by the brothers Tour and L. Sheynin, in the Lord Chamberlain's Collection of Licensed Plays.
44. *The Russians* ran at the Playhouse in London between June and August 1943. The script was published in *Four Soviet War Plays*.
45. *The Times*, 12 June 1943.
46. *Observer*, 20 June 1943, p. 2.
47. 'Programme Note' for *The Russians*.
48. *An Agreement of the Peoples* was staged to mark the first anniversary of the Anglo–Soviet Alliance in June 1942. An adaptation of it, *Over to You*, was licensed for performance in Bristol a year later.
49. Quotations from the version of the text published in *Our Time* 2, July 1942, p. 8.
50. The script of *Alliance for Victory* was issued by the 'National Council for British–Soviet Unity', and was licensed for performance in Thomas

Shanks Public Park, Johnstone on 9 June 1943. Quotations are from the unpublished manuscript in the Lord Chamberlain's Collections of Licensed Plays.

51. See the Lord Chamberlain's Correspondence Files: *Alliance for Victory*.
52. All documents referred to in relation to this performance are in the unpublished Cabinet Papers Foreign Office File 371—1943: Soviet Union File No. 186. Reference 36973. This is stored in the Public Records Office. The file includes the script for the performance by Louis MacNeice.
53. *The Times*, 22 February 1943, p. 2.
54. *The Times*, 22 February 1943.
55. Unpublished Cabinet Papers Foreign Office File 371—1943.
56. Stephen Spender, *Life and the Poet* (London: Secker and Warburg, 1942), p. 18.
57. Searchlight Books. For discussion of this see Robert Hewison, *Under Seige: Literary Life in London 1939–1945* (London: Weidenfeld and Nicolson, 1977), p. 42.
58. André Van Gyseghem, 'Introduction' to *The Theatre is Our Weapon* (London: Russia Today Society, 1941), p. 2.

Afterword

1. From Louis MacNeice, *Salute to all Fools*, in the collection of MacNeice's radio plays, *'The Dark Tower' and Other Radio Plays* (London: Faber and Faber, 1947).
2. *Salute to All Fools* was broadcast on 1 April 1946.
3. Robert Bolt, 'Introduction' to *State of Revolution* (London: Heinemann Educational, 1977). The play was first performed at the National Theatre in 1977.
4. Howard Brenton, 'Preface' to *Plays: Two* (London: Metheun, 1989), p. xi.
5. Brenton, *Thirteenth Night* in *Plays: Two*, p. 153.
6. The sketch is entitled 'Their Theatre and Ours'. Quotations from the text published in Raphael Samuel, Ewan MacColl and Stuart Cosgrove, *Theatres of the Left 1880–1935 (London: Routledge and Kegan Paul, 1985)*.
7. Victor L. Allen, *The Russians Are Coming: The Politics of Anti-Sovietism* (Shipley: Moor Press, 1987), pp. 13–14.

Appendix
Biographies and Production Details

Clemence Dane (1888?–1965)

Clemence Dane, who changed her name from Winifred Ashton, had a brief career as an actress before the First World War, and then taught in a girls' school before beginning her long career as a writer. She had written three novels, including *Regiment of Women*, by the time her first play was performed in March 1921. This was the highly successful *A Bill of Divorcement*, a play about the lives of a mother and daughter, which enjoyed a long run at St Martin's Theatre, where it was directed by Basil Dean. In November 1921 Dane's *Will Shakespeare*, a biography written in verse, opened at the Shaftesbury, and although none of them quite matched the success of *A Bill of Divorcement*, she went on to write a number of other plays, as well as musicals, radio plays and a television drama about Elizabeth I. Dane also wrote novels, several of which were set within theatrical circles, worked on film scripts, and made further appearances on stage. Among the actors who performed in her work were Ivor Novello, Vivien Leigh, Sybil Thorndike, Lewis Casson and Douglas Fairbanks Junior, and several of these were personal friends. Clemence Dane was awarded a CBE in 1953.

The Terror was produced in September 1921 in Liverpool, for a two-week run as a curtain-raiser on the reopening of Liverpool Playhouse under Nigel Playfair. Mrs Patrick Campbell played the main part, which Dane had written especially for her. The script was never published.

John Davison (Dates unknown)

Few biographical details are known about Davison. At the time of writing his first play, *Shadows of Strife*, he was a young engineer from Rotherham. The play was performed at Sheffield in March 1928 and Birmingham in November 1929, before coming to the Arts Theatre

Club in London in December 1929. It was presented by the Arts Theatre in conjunction with Sir Barry Jackson of the Birmingham Repertory Theatre, and in his introduction to the published text, Jackson described Davison as 'an author of acute and vigorous observation', stressing the playwright's working-class background as a guarantee of the authenticity of his portrayal of a family suffering and arguing the during the General Strike:

> Mr Davison's daily toil amidst machinery has confined his wanderings and knowledge of the world to meagre limits, and his time for studying and writing to his leisure evenings . . . He forms one more instance of the mysterious power of intuitive ability.

Davison went on to write several plays during the 1930s, including a chronicle of the life of the Brontë family and a version of *Wuthering Heights*, which was staged at the Little Theatre in 1937. Reviewing this, *The Times* wrote that 'Mr Davison's contention with his intractable material, though little short of heroic, is ill-rewarded in the result'.

André de Lorde (1871–1942)

De Lorde relished his nickname of 'The Prince of Terror', being one of the main exponents of the Grand Guignol movement which developed in French theatre at the end of the nineteenth century with the aim of shocking and horrifying audiences. He wrote or co-wrote over seventy short plays, most of them involving scenes of suspense and torture or violent deaths. These included *L'Horrible Expérience*, *Figures de Cire* and *L'Obsession*, and de Lorde claimed Edgar Allen Poe as his mentor. In *The Old Woman*, a girl is seen having her eyes picked out by three mad old women; in *La Dernière Torture*, a man is shown strangling his infant son.

Les Nuits Rouges de la Tcheka was one of several plays which de Lorde co-wrote with Henri Bauche, and Terence Gray translated and adapted it for the Festival Theatre in Cambridge in 1927 as part of an evening of three plays. The Lord Chamberlain dismissed it as 'an ordinary piece of lurid melodrama' and a local newspaper called it a 'a rather hysterical specimen of writing . . . unworthy of the company's efforts'. Grand Guignol was never so successful in Britain as in Paris, though De Lorde's *The Hand of Death* was staged at the Little Theatre in 1920, and in 1932 he contributed three plays to a season at the Duke of York's, where the plays were performed continuously from 2.00 p.m. till midnight.

Jacques Deval (1890–1972)

The son of a well-known Parisian theatre director, Deval studied medicine before he began writing for the stage. *Une Faible Femme*, written in 1918 and performed in Paris in 1920, was the the first of more than twenty plays to be written over the next half century, several of them being widely performed in other countries. Four of Deval's plays were staged in London during the 1930s, and another in 1949; none, however, had anything like the international success of the rather sentimental and romantic comedy *Tovarich*, written in 1933, which ran at the Lyric for over 400 performances in 1935–6 with Cedric Hardwicke and Eugenie Leontovitch in the main parts, and which was successful in numerous productions throughout Europe and in America. The playwright's *St Etienne* had already been produced in London in 1931, and after the success of *Tovarich*, Noel Coward's production of *Mademoiselle* opened in September 1936 to high expectations; however, its story of a woman who hates men but wants a baby was not well received by the theatrical establishment. *Behold the Bride* ran for fifty performances in 1939, but most critics found it shallow, describing it as 'sentimental claptrap' and 'unwhisperable nonsense'. Deval continued to be more popular and successful in France, though some of his darker plays and criticisms of the bourgeoisie were less widely appreciated. In its obituary, *Le Monde* summed up his stage writing as follows:

> Toujours spirituel, ce théâtre mêle la tendresse et l'humour, l'ironie et, parfois, la férocité

Deval also worked in French and American cinema, writing scripts in Hollywood for eleven films, including, inevitably, an adaptation of *Tovarich* which was released in 1937. He also wrote several novels, one of which received a prize in 1964, and two volumes of essays published in 1935 and 1970.

Ashley Dukes (1885–1959)

Ashley Dukes was a playwright, a director, a manager and a critic who had a long career in the theatre. The son of a clergyman, he was first attracted by the serious work of the Court Theatre seasons and the so-called 'highbrow' plays of writers such as Shaw, Ibsen and Granville-Barker, but he quickly became dissatisfied with the 'commonplace' staging and naturalistic approach, preferring the European tradition he discovered in Maeterlinck, Hauptmann and D'Annunzio. Dukes resigned from his post as a science lecturer at London University, and in 1907 went to live in Germany. By 1909 he was back in London as a theatre critic, and his own first play was produced by the Stage Society in 1910. He continued to champion foreign playwrights, and he translated and adapted many plays from German, French and Italian, thus helping to bring them to English audiences for the first time. Amongst the playwrights whose work he made accessible to English audiences were Kaiser, Guitry and Ernst Toller, who was a personal friend. In 1933 he opened the Mercury Theatre in London, providing a venue for playwrights such as Auden, Isherwood, Eliot and Duncan, and also, under the direction of his wife, Marie Rambert, for ballet. He wrote regularly about theatre, publishing several books and editing *Theatre Arts Monthly*, an international publication. In 1926 and 1927 he was the British delegate to the International Congress of Critics, and in 1937 he was appointed Professor of Drama of the Royal Society of Literature. Dukes's most successful original play was *The Man With a Load of Mischief* (1924).

Hubert Griffith (1896–1953)

After serving in the Air Force during the First World War, Griffith became a theatre critic with the *Daily Chronicle* in 1922, and sub-sequently wrote for other newspapers, including the *Observer*, the *Manchester Guardian* and the *Evening Standard*. In 1927 he published a book about the future of Shakespeare, and during the thirties he wrote several travel books, including *Seeing Soviet Russia* and *Playtime in Russia*. His earliest play was *Tunnel Trench* in 1924, based on his own experiences during the First World War, and over the next ten years he wrote several original plays, including *Red Sunday* and *The People's Court*. He also translated and adapted several plays into English, including *Distant Point* from the Russian of Alexander Afinogenev, which was staged at the Gate Theatre in 1937, by Unity Theatre in 1940, and at the Embassy Theatre in 1941.

Griffith was generally and broadly sympathetic to the Left and the Soviet Union. During the Second World War, Griffith not only served as a Flight-Lieutenant in the RAF, but also lectured on Russia at Air Force stations, produced two books about life in Russia, and was London editor for *Britanskii Sóyuznik* (The British Ally) and for the *British Weekly Illustrated*, which was published in Russian in the Soviet Union. Best known as a theatre critic, Griffith's Introduction to the published version of *Red Sunday* remains one of the most powerful indictments of the power of the Lord Chamberlain, and a stinging and bitter attack on theatre censorship.

Waclaw Grubinski (1883–1973)

A novelist, playwright and critic, Grubinski was born into an intellectual family in Warsaw, and studied philosophy, literature and political science before becoming a columnist and critic for a daily newspaper. In 1928 he was appointed as editor of a monthly journal, *Teatr*, and in 1931 became the chairman of an organisation representing Polish playwrights. He received an award from the Academy for Polish Literature in 1939, but was subsequently arrested for writing anti-Soviet literature and sentenced to death. According to his own account, Grubinski was interrogated about his 1921 play, *Lenin*, but told the court that his subject had been 'the psychology of revolution' rather than 'the ideology which caused it', and that it was a non-political work in which the choice of the Soviet Union as an example had been arbitrary. The sentence was reduced to imprisonment, and in 1942 Grubinski was released; he travelled widely before settling in England in 1943, where he continued to write. In 1948, for example, he contributed an essay to a collection published in London by the Polish Writers Association on the relationship between literature and politics, and he was to receive several awards and honours for his services to literature and to Poland. Grubinski is remembered primarily as a critic and as a writer of paradoxical short stories, in which his style has been compared to that of Oscar Wilde and Anatole France.

Grubinski's play *Lenin* was actually part of a trilogy entitled *Peace, War and Revolution*, first performed in Warsaw in 1921, and presented in London at the Royalty Theatre in 1929 by the International Theatre Society; this was a group which had been formed in the early twenties 'to present the plays of all the nations who had a dramatic literature, preferably the lesser known, to the London Public'. The first play of the trilogy consisted of a conversation between Diogenes and Alexander, contrasting the man of action and the philosopher, and the second is set in Troy and satirises man's urge for war. *Lenin* was the final part. The *Saturday Review* commented that the trilogy 'was so much under-rehearsed that judgment is difficult', and Donald Wolfit, who played Lenin, also remembered it in his autobiography as 'a muddled satire and under-rehearsed'. Incidentally, there was no truth in the rumour printed in some newspapers at the time that 'Grubinski' was a *nom de plume* adopted by George Bernard Shaw, though Shaw did attend the London performance.

Herbert Hodge (1901–1962)

After leaving school at fourteen, Herbert Hodge worked on ships, in mines, and as a harvester in the United States before becoming a London taxi driver. He stood as a candidate for Mosley's New Party in the 1931 General Election, but left when its fascist character became clearer, joining the committee of Unity Theatre after seeing a performance of Clifford Odets's *Waiting for Lefty* there in 1936. He immediately co-wrote *Where's that Bomb?* with another taxi driver, and this 'political cartoon' was first staged at London's Unity theatre in November 1936. This became one of Unity's most popular and successful plays, being widely performed by regional branches, with Merseyside billing it as 'the most robust farce since the days of Ben Jonson', and reviews suggesting that the authors were destined to become 'the Freddy Lonsdale and Noel Coward of the working class'. The play's original director, John Allen, called it 'a magnificent proletarian guffaw at the propaganda of the capitalist class' and contrasted it with the style of political theatre being developed by W.H. Auden and the Group Theatre:

> I can think of no two writers whose work is more dissimilar than these two. Auden's is introverted and twisted, Hodge's extravert and robust, Auden's exclusive, a thing of class, Hodge's popular, a thing of the people.

The following year, Hodge wrote a less successful political satire, *Cannibal Carnival*, and he subsequently contributed to the Unity Collective of writers which produced the first Living Newspaper in Britain, documenting the busmen's strike. Hodge later worked for BBC Radio, and also published books about his experiences as a taxi driver in London and in New York.

Henry Ernest Hutchinson (1885–1921)

Born into the Lancashire cotton trade, Hutchinson had his first play, *Votes for Children*, produced at the Little Theatre in London in 1912. During the First World War he was invalided home from the Front, but subsequently served in the War Office. *The Right to Strike* ran for eighty-three controversial performances at the Garrick, Lyric and

Queen's Theatres between September and December 1920, becoming, according to its producer, Leon Lion, 'the talk of the political *salons* and the London clubs' before it was rather prematurely withdrawn. Lion suggests that the play's appeal was too limited to the 'intelligentsia' for it to be a box-office success, though it also toured nationally and internationally, with *The Times* noting in its obituary for Hutchinson that it had 'had a great success on the continent, except in Rome, where it was coldly received last July'.

Hutchinson died in his mid thirties, apparently of a heart attack, following an operation. A version of *The Right to Strike* was published as a novel in 1921, closely based on the play and dedicated to Lion, who commented that 'but for Ernest Hutchinson's untimely death I feel certain we should have had other notable and even better plays from his pen'. *The Times* records that at the time of his death Hutchinson was engaged in making minor amendments to another full-length play which had already been accepted by a London management, but his only other performed work appears to have been two scenes which he contributed to a musical revue, *Puss! Puss!*, for the Vaudeville Theatre in May 1921.

Elsie Janis (1889–1956)

Born in Ohio, Janis was touring America in musical comedies as a dancer, a singer and a mimic by the time she was a teenager. She was already well known when she came to London in 1914 to appear in *The Passing Show*, which ran for nearly 400 performances amid great acclaim. This was followed by other musicals, and in 1918 she went to France to perform to the allied troops, becoming immensely popular as 'the nightingale overseas', before returning to London to appear in *Hullo, America!* at the Palace. Janis therefore had a very high and popular reputation in London when she appeared in 1920 in *It's All Wrong*, for which she was also the author and part-composer, and which was also her first venture in management. Janis performed in two other London shows during the twenties, and subsequently appeared in a number of films as well as writing songs and an autobiography. In *Famous Actors on the American Stage*, Janis is described as 'a star who loved to play the role of a star' and who spent huge amounts of money on constructing her image and on living a life of luxury.

It's All Wrong, subtitled 'A Musical Complaint', opened at the Queen's Theatre in December 1920, with Stanley Lupino, Arthur Margetson and Janis among the performers, and ran for 112 performances. The

Princess Royal and Princess Maud were present at the first performance, and received Janis in their box.

Vladimir Kirchon (1902–1938)

Kirchon began writing plays in 1920, and his most significant works were *Bread* in 1930, which dealt with the liquidation of the Kulaks, *The Rails are Humming* in 1927, about industrialisation in the Soviet Union, and *The Miraculous Alloy* in 1934, a social comedy. In Soviet theatre of the 1920s and 30s, the most distinctive feature of his approach to writing was the continuing commitment to individual and psychological characterisation within the ideological contexts to which plays were increasingly expected to restrict themselves. He was also opposed to the tendency to oversimplify both social issues and aesthetic styles. During Stalin's purges of the thirties, Kirchon was arrested and denounced as a Trotskyite; his plays were banned, and he was executed at the age of 36.

Red Rust was a translation of Kirchon's first successful play, *Konstantin Terekhin*, which he co-wrote with Andrei Ouspensky in 1926. It was presented in an adaptation from the Russian by Virginia and Frank Vernon in London at the Little Theatre in February 1929, with Ion Swinley and John Gielgud in the two main parts, and by the Theatre Guild in New York in December of the same year with a cast which included Lee Strasberg. In London it was billed as the first Soviet play to reach the London stage.

Leon Lion (1879–1947)

Lion was primarily an actor-manager and producer, though he also co-wrote a number of plays. Having toured in Shakepeare productions with Forbes-Robertson at the turn of the century, he soon became a successful and well-known performer, and began his managerial career in 1918 at the New Theatre, going on to produce some seventy plays over the next twenty years. He also appeared in a number of films. In 1928, Lion was invited to represent Britain at an International Festival in Paris, and was made a Chevalier of the Legion of Honour. In 1920 he had produced Ernest Hutchinson's *The Right to Strike*, in which he also appeared as the socialist agitator, Montague, and in 1932 he produced *The Bear Dances*, by F.L. Lucas. However, he was particularly known for his work on the plays of John Galsworthy, to which he remained committed even when they were out of fashion. In its obituary, *The Times* described Lion as 'one of those actor-managers who are prepared on occasion to risk and lose money in putting on plays of undoubted merit which may not produce good box-office business'. His managerial career had in fact ended with a financially disastrous presentation of a cycle of Galsworthy's plays.

F.L. Lucas (1894–1967)

Lucas was a distinguished scholar, critic and writer across a range of fields, and was also widely known as a literary and anti-fascist campaigner in the thirties. From a classical background, he taught English literature at King's College, Cambridge, and published essays, criticism, poetry, novels, short stories, travel writing about Greece and translations of classical texts. He also edited selections of Greek poetry and drama.

Lucas wrote several plays during the thirties, which were more successful at the People's Theatre in Newcastle than in London. *The Bear Dances* was first produced by Leon Lion at the Garrick Theatre in November 1932, and subsequently performed in northern repertory theatres, including that at Newcastle. His 1933 play, *Land's End*, which opened in Newcastle in May 1935, included among its characters a communist who embodies the failings of a presumably typical young left-wing intellectual, who is satirised by Lucas for his arrogance and hypocrisy.

Abused by Ezra Pound for his denunciations of Nazism and fascism, Lucas was on Goebbels's list for post-war extermination; during the Second World War, he worked for the Foreign Office and was subsequently awarded an OBE.

Louis MacNeice (1907–1963)

Born in Ireland, MacNeice graduated with a First from Oxford and became a lecturer at Birmingham University. He emerged as a poet during the thirties, when his name was often linked with those of Auden, Spender and Day Lewis, and in 1936 the Group Theatre staged his translation of Aeschylus's *Agamemnon*, in masks and dinner suits. His *Autumn Journal*, published in 1939, was his most notable collection of verse. During the Second World War, MacNeice wrote and produced a series of feature programmes for BBC Radio, several of which took themes connected with Russia for their starting points. Apart from their celebratory and inspirational narratives, these were often technically and aesthetically innovative, combining words, sound effects and music to dramatic effect, and cutting non-naturalistically across time and space to tell epic and heroic stories. Folk tales and myths provided further source material, and Walton and Britten were among the composers who created scores especially for MacNeice's work. In 1943, he was chosen to write the script for *Salute to the Red Army*, a dramatic pageant presented at the Royal Albert Hall to commemorate the twenty-fifth anniversary of the founding of the Red Army.

MacNeice had probably never been as politically committed as some of his colleagues, and was always suspicious of propagandist art. At the end of the war, two radio plays with an individualistic March Hare as their central character used satirical fantasy to attack what he called 'the pedestrian (and repellent) madness' of those who sought to organise the world and to control 'the poetic (and sympathetic) madness of the Hare'. However, among his radio dramas it is *The Dark Tower*, broadcast in 1946 and inspired by the war, which has done most to assure his reputation.

H.F. Maltby (1880–1963)

Born in South Africa, Maltby was a very successful actor who wrote over fifty light and largely forgotten comedies and farces for the stage between 1905 and 1956. He appeared in over seventy films and contributed to the writing of over a hundred.

What Might Happen, Maltby's 1926 dystopian fantasy in which former aristocrats live in poverty and are oppressed by their ex-servants, was supposedly inspired by the sight of makeshift settlements on the South Downs where people lived in old railway coaches or tramcars or huts made from discarded rubbish. 'We have had plays about the backwoods of Kentucky, the wilds of the Congo, and the jungles of India' wrote Maltby, 'This is one about the unmapped settlements of newer England.' While the politics of the play were deeply and instinctively reactionary, Maltby trusted 'that this play will be taken, not as a serious contribution to the drama, but simply as an effort to amuse'. It was performed at the Savoy Theatre for fifty-two performances in 1926 with a strong cast, but Maltby later accused Mrs Patrick Campbell of sabotaging what would otherwise have been a great success: 'she just sulked, lost all interest in the production, made no attempt to learn her lines and deliberately went out to wreck the whole show'. The play met with greater commercial success in America.

In 1931, *The Red Light* represented a much more bitter attack on those who sought a more equal society, but critically the play was a complete failure. It was withdrawn after only seventeen performances, and though it was completely rewritten and revived the following year for a further twelve performances, Maltby makes no reference to it in *Ring Up The Curtain*, his extensive reminiscences which were published in 1950.

Dmitry Merezhkovsky (1865–1941)

Merezhkovsky was a writer and a religious philosopher, whose work included poetry, novels, essays and translations as well as original plays. During the 1890s he championed the work of the French symbolists in Russia, and he became an important figure in the development of Russian modernism. From 1900 onwards he became deeply involved in and committed to a new and mystical form of Christianity, and believed that the 1905 revolution in Russia heralded the coming of the Kingdom of Heaven. After the 1917 revolution he emigrated to Poland and then France, along with his wife, who had published a volume of anti-Soviet poetry. Merezhkovsky became the best-known Russian writer living in Western Europe, and he was a significant and influential member of the exiled intellectual community. He remained a bitter opponent of the communists and the revolution.

Paul I was adapted into English by John Alford and James Dale, and performed at the Court Theatre in October and November 1927.

Allan Monkhouse (1858–1936)

Monkhouse was a dramatist, a novelist and a critic, who contributed for over thirty years to the *Manchester Guardian* and whose success as a playwright was greater in Lancashire than in London. Indeed, he was one of the group of writers associated with A.E. Horniman's management of the Gaiety in Manchester and the development of repertory theatre before the First World War, becoming, along with Harold Brighouse and Stanley Houghton, part of the so-called 'Manchester school of dramatists'. For the *Manchester Guardian*, Monkhouse wrote about the cotton trade and golf as well as about literature and theatre, and also contributed to leader columns. His anti-war play, *The Conquering Hero*, was his most successful play in London, being performed at the Aldwych, Queen's and St Martin's Theatres for sixty performances in 1924. *First Blood* was performed in Stockport and Leeds before running in London at the Gate Theatre Salon for thirteen performances in December 1926, where it was produced and designed by Peter Godfrey.

Monkhouse was a liberal, a humanist, and a Quaker, and the intense seriousness of his writing was sometimes considered too austere and demanding to achieve popularity, while his refusal either to oversimplify or to overstate may have encouraged the neglect of his plays and novels. In the words of the newspaper for which he became literary editor, his 'quality of mind made it almost hopeless that he should become a favourite of the larger public'.

Beverley Nicholls (1898–1983)

Nichols was a journalist, a composer of music for revues and a popular writer, whose work was never quite serious enough to earn him the literary recognition which had seemed inevitable in the early stages of his career. His first novel was written before he was eighteen and published shortly after he started at Oxford University, and he quickly became a well-known celebrity within society, producing further novels and an autobiography by the time he was twenty-five. During the thirties, he was a pacifist and a vigorous campaigner against the arms trade. A prolific, witty and versatile writer of novels and essays as well as several plays, Nichols was best known for the books he wrote about his favourite hobbies of gardening and cats, and for his newspaper gossip column. Some regretted that so much apparent literary talent should be devoted to such relatively slight topics.

In 1933, Nichols published four plays under the collective title of *Failures*—a rather negative title considering that some of them had not yet been produced. *When the Crash Comes* was performed at Birmingham Repertory Theatre, in March 1933; in his introduction to the collection he had written about the play as follows:

> I am perhaps being unduly pessimistic in suggesting that this play is already foredoomed. However, I am so certain that it will fail to attract, that I am willing to take the risk. If, by some miracle, it should turn out to be a success, it will make no difference to my opinion of it.

Sean O'Casey (1880–1964)

Born a Protestant, O'Casey grew up in extreme poverty after the death of his father, and soon became directly involved in political and strike activity. Having been dismissed from his job as a railway worker for union activity in 1911, he contributed to labour journals, then helped to form the Irish Citizen Army in 1914. He became its secretary, and moved from supporting nationalism to advocating socialism. O'Casey began writing plays during the twenties, and was associated with

Dublin's Abbey Theatre, where *The Shadow of a Gunman*, *Juno and the Paycock*, and *The Plough and the Stars* all had their first performances between 1923 and 1926. The last of this trilogy provoked riots in Dublin, and O'Casey moved to England in 1926, where he married and spent the rest of his life. Two years later the Abbey rejected his anti-war play *The Silver Tassie*; it won critical acclaim in London in 1929, but his experimental mixture of realism, fantasy, symbolism and poetry was not always critically well received or commercially successful. Altogether he wrote over twenty plays, several of which are still regularly revived, and he was described by *The Times* in its obituary as 'a writer of acknowledged genius'. O'Casey also worked as a theatre critic, attacking the triviality of much of the London stage and championing the work of avant-garde playwrights from abroad who challenged conventional theatrical forms. He also published poetry, essays and a six-volume autobiography.

O'Casey was sympathetic to communism from the early twenties, and was an admirer and friend of the Dublin trade union leader Jim Larkin. *The Star Turns Red* was staged privately by Unity in March 1940, running for over eighty performances. Unity were aware of the limitations of their production:

> We are under no illusion that we amateurs can do full justice to the quality of this magnificent play, but we have done everything that hard work, enthusiasm, and sincerity can do.

The playwright had specified that Unity should not attempt Irish accents—('there are 32 counties in Ireland, and each has a different accent, so there is no such thing as "an Irish accent" ')—and also retained rights over casting and other decisions. Critical responses were and have remained varied, primarily due to the play's committed and explicit politics. James Agate hailed the first production as a 'masterpiece', but in the 1960s *The Times* described it as 'a piece of communist propaganda . . . best forgotten'. The play was last revived at the Abbey Theatre in 1978.

Austin Page (Dates unknown)

Little is known of Page's life. His first play to be performed was *Pigeon Post*, a spy story set in a château occupied by the French army close to the German frontier, which opened at the Garrick in 1918 and ran for over 400 performances. *The Beating on the Door* was his next play, performed at St James's Theatre in November 1922. Page had clashed with the Lord Chamberlain over *Pigeon Post*, but the Lord Chamberlain's report found *The Beating on the Door* to be 'well written' and without 'any possible political objection'. However, the play ran for only fifteen performances, with a cast which included Arthur Wontner, Franklyn Dyall, Mary Jerrold and Doris Lloyd. The performance was punctuated between Acts by a Russian choir singing traditional, national folk-songs, leading *The Times* to comment that 'the wonder is how a people with such music in their souls can ever have become Bolshevists'.

Page's other performed plays were *The Devil in Bronze* (1929), an implausible melodrama set amongst lighthouses and smugglers in Alaska and northern Canada, and *Hocus Pocus* (1932), an adaptation of a short story by Susan Ertz. *Pigeon Post* was revived in London in 1940, when *The Times* commented positively that 'This spy play does not pretend to take itself seriously, and so it is as much at home in this war as in the last'.

Eden Phillpotts (1862–1960)

Phillpotts was a remarkably prolific writer, best known for his many Dartmoor novels, his crime and thriller stories, and his plays about Devon village life. Having abandoned his plans to be an actor or an artist, he began writing fiction in the 1880s, and between 1904 and 1913 alone, his output included twenty-nine novels, three volumes of poetry and four volumes of plays. His early dramas were adaptations of his own novels, and in 1912 *The Secret Woman* was refused a licence for public performance. His first commercially successful play was *The Farmer's Wife*, described as a comedy of 'innocent and rollicking Devon humours', which opened in 1917 and ran for three years and 1,300 performances at the Court from 1924 until 1927. It thus overlapped with *Yellow Sands*, which he co-wrote with his daughter Adelaide, which opened in November 1926 and closed in February 1928, after 612 performances. The original cast included Cedric Hardwicke, Ralph Richardson, Susan Richmond, and Frank Vosper as the Bolshevik. Though rather old-fashioned even when they were written, both these plays were revived in new productions in 1928, and *Yellow Sands* was subsequently made into a feature film.

No other of Phillpotts's plays ever enjoyed as much success as these two had done, but he continued to write new stage material and adaptations, novels, short stories and poetry, most of it fairly light and easy entertainment, and much of it set in Devon; he wrote two other plays with his daughter (who herself wrote more than twenty novels), a volume of reminiscences, and contributed to BBC radio.

François Porché (1877–1944)

Porché was a French poet, playwright and literary critic. His first volume of poetry was published in 1904, and his symbolist style has been linked with that of both Victor Hugo and Baudelaire. He also wrote biographies of Baudelaire and of Verlaine, as well as critical essays about contemporary French poetry, and his poetic style was carried over into a number of plays, several of which were written in verse; these included *Les Butors et la Finette* (1918) and *La Vierge au Grand Coeur* (1925). Porché married a well-known actress, and held a senior administrative position in the Comédie-Française in Paris.

Tsar Lénine was staged in Paris at the Théâtre de l'Atelier in October 1931 under the direction of Charles Dullin, one of the most important and experimental French directors of the twenties and thirties, who also played the title role. The first British performance should have been at the Cambridge Festival Theatre in May 1933, but Terence Gray refused to make the changes which the Lord Chamberlain demanded in return for a licence. The first British production was therefore at Westminster Theatre in June 1937 by the Incorporated Stage Society, in a version by Ossia Trilling and Emanuel Wax, directed by Guy Glover, with Basil Sydney as Lenin. The only other one of Porché's plays to be staged in Britain had also been at the Westminster in the previous year; this was *Peace*, an adaptation of a play by Aristophanes. Although both plays had only the briefest of runs, they were both widely reviewed, and each was also followed by a public discussion led, in the case of *Tsar Lenin*, by Elmer Rice, and in that of *Peace* by Michael St Denis.

Porché's lengthy introduction to the published French text of *Tsar Lénine* is a fascinating essay about the changing possibilities of theatrical form, and especially its relationship to film.

J.B. Priestley (1894–1984)

Born in Bradford, Priestley was an accessible and popular dramatist, novelist, critic and essayist; though not infrequently criticised for being 'middlebrow' and old-fashioned in form, several of his plays continue to be widely performed, especially by repertory companies and amateurs. His first play in 1931 was a version of his own successful novel, *The Good Companions*, and he wrote a string of quasi-philosphical plays in the thirties, a number of which touched on theories concerning the nature of time; these included *Dangerous Corner* (1932), *Time and the Conways*, and *I Have Been Here Before* (both 1937). In the late thirties his own company, the London Mask Theatre, performed his more experimental dramas, including *Johnson over Jordan* (1939) which employed expressionistic techniques. Priestley also wrote comedies satirising middle-class life, such as *When We Are Married* (1938), and his best known non-theatrical work was *English Journey* (1934), which described the everyday landscapes and lives he witnessed in travelling through the country. During the Second World War, Priestley became a regular and popular radio broadcaster, often evoking a nostalgic patriotism through his portrait of the ordinary but seemingly quintessential aspects of the English way of life. *The Times* remembered in its obituary that Priestley's Sunday evening broadcasts 'in the dark days of 1940' made him 'second only to Winston Churchill as the spokesman of England's determination and faith in herself'.

In all, Priestley wrote some forty-nine plays, of which the best-known and most often performed is *An Inspector Calls* (1946), in which he marries his interest in the nature of time with a narrative about injustice in society and exploitation of the poor by the rich. *Bees on the Boat Deck* was performed at the Lyric Theatre in May 1936, with Ralph Richardson and Laurence Olivier, and was one of his less commercially successful plays.

George Bernard Shaw (1856–1950)

Shaw's vast output of published work spans nearly sixty years of serious writing. Though best known for his dramas, he also wrote copious numbers of critical essays and other prose work, some of which appeared as extended prefaces to his plays. At the end of the nineteenth and in the early twentieth century he wrote a series of stage works which attempted to introduce serious analysis and intellectual and political debate to a largely frivolous theatre; these included *Arms and the Man* (1894), *The Devil's Disciple* (1897) and *Major Barbara* and *Man and Superman* (both 1905). Between 1904 and 1907 his plays were crucial to the success of the Court Theatre under the management of Vedrenne and Granville-Barker, and he was one of the early champions in Britain of Ibsen, whose plays were dismissed by most critics and by the censor. After the success of *Pygmalion* in 1914 Shaw was to write a further thirty plays, including *Heartbreak House* (first performed in 1920), *Back to Methuselah* (1922) and *Saint Joan* (1923). Throughout his career, he clashed frequently with the Establishment, including the Lord

Chamberlain, (for example over *Mrs Warren's Profession* and *The Shewing-Up of Blanco Posnet*), and he was caustic in his attacks on the state of British theatre (and on much else). Almost all of his plays were in some sense political, and though they have often been accused of lacking action and of presenting a series of rhetorical debates, it has also been said that their strength lies in the fact that Shaw gives the best arguments to those characters with whom he most disagrees. Shaw often identified himself as a socialist, and in 1933 he went on a tour of the Soviet Union which left him naïvely supportive of Stalin. He continued writing up until his death, and never lost his ability to provoke controversy.

Annajanska, The Bolshevik Empress, was originally presented as *Annajanska, The Wild Grand Duchess*, at the Coliseum Theatre, London, 21 January 1918, with Lillah McCarthy in the main role. It claimed to be 'from the Russian of Gregory Biessipoff', and was part of a variety bill, being the ninth of twelve items in a programme which included Herculean Gymnasts, Dainty Doris (Comedienne), Neil Kenyon (Studies in Scottish Humour), Elastic Eccentric Dancers, performing dogs and horses, and Vesta Tilley. In its review, *The Times* commented that 'there is hardly room and verge enough for intellect within the limits of a music-hall "sketch"'.

Geneva was first staged at the Festival Theatre, Malvern, in August 1938, and then ran in London at the Saville Theatre and subsequently at St James's Theatre for a total of 237 performances from 23 November 1938 onwards.

Konstantin Simonov (1915–1979)

Simonov was a Soviet playwight, poet and short-story writer, who not only survived Stalinism but gained many awards and even government posts for his patriotic, ideologically reliable and anti-capitalist writing. He published his first collection of poems in 1938 and his first play in 1940, and during the war against Germany worked as a journalist, sending inspirational propaganda from the Front in the form of essays and stories glorifying the heroism of the Soviet army. His novel about the siege of Stalingrad won an award from Stalin in 1946, as did a collection of poems in 1949. His post-war writing followed predictable and required themes, with *Alien Shadow* (1949) showing how a Soviet scientific discovery which could save humanity from a fatal disease is used by the Americans as a weapon of destruction. Simonov remained in the Communist Party, and in the 1960s he published more memories of the Second World War, including a novel about the threat of the Soviet secret police. In all, he received six Stalin prizes, a Lenin prize and a Hero of Socialist Labour. He was not only secretary of the Union of Soviet Writers, but also a Deputy of the Supreme Soviet. His novels were widely read in the Soviet Union, and some of his patriotic poems became a part of popular culture during the war. He wrote ten plays.

The Russian People was written in 1941/42, and celebrates the heroic determination of a group of ordinary Russians trying to hold their village against the Nazis. Nothing can destroy their commitment and their wish for freedom. *The Russians*, an English adaptation from a translation by Gerald Shelley, was produced by Tyrone Guthrie for the Old Vic Company at the Playhouse in London between June and August 1943. *The Times* claimed that the leading Nazi was 'surely the unpleasantest character ever to tread the London stage'.

Montagu Slater (1902–1956)

Montagu Slater was born in Cumberland, and after going to Oxford on a scholarship, worked as a journalist in Liverpool and London while writing poetry. In 1931 he published his first novel and became a freelance writer, increasingly turning to dramatic writing. During the thirties he produced stage-plays (notably *Stay Down Miner* and *Easter 1916*), puppet plays and large pageants for the Communist Party and the Co-operative movement. One of these, *Towards Tomorrow*, was presented at Wembley Stadium in 1938. In the mid thirties Slater was a founding editor of (and frequent contributor to) *Left Review*, and worked with both the professional Left Theatre and the non-professional Unity Theatre, contributing as part of the collective which devised Living Newspaper scripts.

During the war, Slater was rejected from active service because of ill health. He helped found the communist cultural journal *Our Time* and became involved with the Films Division of the Ministry of Information, but is best known for having written most of the libretto for the opera *Peter Grimes*. In 1946 Slater tried but failed to help establish a new theatre movement to be funded by the trade union movement. He went on to publish novels which explored the boundaries between fiction and factual documentation, and though he continued to write stage plays, which were rarely performed or published, he became increasingly interested in film and television, winning a British Film Academy award for the documentary he made about the Ibo of Nigeria during the 1950s.

Though his work was rarely explicit propaganda, Slater's long-standing commitment to the Communist Party, which he had joined in the late 1920s, may well have hindered his career opportunities. He died in 1956, leaving sketches for many projects uncompleted. His spectacular pageant to mark the first anniversary of the Anglo–Soviet Alliance, *An Agreement of the Peoples*, was staged in June 1942, and an adaptation of it, *Over to You*, was performed in Bristol a year later.

Stephen Spender (1909–1995)

Spender is best known as a poet, though in the later part of his life he spent more of his time as a lecturer and an academic. He came to prominence as a writer during the thirties as one of the group of left-wing poets which dominated British verse, having made contact with Auden, Isherwood, MacNeice and Day Lewis while at Oxford University, and achieving recognition through an anthology published in 1932. Like Isherwood, he spent time in Germany, where he witnessed the developing threat of the fascists, and his growing political commitment led him in *The Destructive Element* (1935) and *Forward from Liberalism (*1936) to argue that the artist must become directly involved with radical politics:

> If we hope to go on existing, if we want a dog's chance of a right to breathe, to go on being able to write, it seems that we have got to make some choice outside the private entanglements of our private lives.

When the Spanish Civil War began, Spender went to Spain to help the Republicans by writing propaganda, and in 1939 he published *Poems for Spain*. At this time he was a member of the Communist Party, but the allegiance did not last long and he soon recanted. In *Life and the Poet*, published in 1942, Spender suggested that during the thirties, 'our trust in the power of some possible political enlightenment encouraged us to make statements, declaim slogans, lend our names to propaganda, when we should have been asking questions'. He was one of the founders of the literary magazine *Horizon*, helping to edit it from 1939 till 1941, and in 1949 he contributed an essay to the famous Gollancz collection marking the widespread intellectual abandonment of the communist ideal, *The God That Failed*. He continued to explore the relationship between literature and politics, becoming involved in the international struggle against censorship through the journal *Index on Censorship*. He was knighted in 1983.

Spender wrote eight stage works, though a number of these were translations and adaptations, including Sophocles's *Oedipus* trilogy, Wedekind's *Lulu*, Büchner's *Danton's Death*, and Schiller's *Mary Stuart*. *Trial of a Judge* was his first play, performed by the Group Theatre in March 1938, in a production by Rupert Doone, with a set designed by John Piper, and with Godfrey Kenton as the Judge. Both style and content were attacked by the Left, who criticised it as an irrelevant lament for the decline of the liberal middle classes, and for retreating into 'symbolism and mysticism'. The *Daily Worker* accused Spender of having 'lifted himself to Olympian heights above our problems' and was especially disparaging about the fact that the play was in verse.

Aleksei Nikolayevich Tolstoy (1883–1945)

Tolstoy was an aristocrat by birth and a relative of Leo Tolstoy; he was a novelist, a poet and a playwright who at the time of his death was a member of the Supreme Soviet of the USSR, and who has since been described as 'the most authoritative apologist for the Stalin regime'. A war correspondent during the First World War, Tolstoy had already published several novels before the 1917 revolution, as well as articles for *The Times*. He was at first violently opposed to the 1917 revolution, joining the anti-bolshevik White Army under General Denikin, and working in the propaganda section, and between 1918 and 1921 he lived in exile in Paris. He returned to the Soviet Union, and wrote several science fiction and other novels, before his portrait of Peter the Great won the Stalin prize in 1941. His 1924 play *The Revolt of the Machines* was based on Karel Capek's *R.U.R.* It is primarily for his novels that Tolstoy is remembered, but he also wrote a number of historical dramas, accommodating himself to the official ideology. During the Second World War, he headed a special commission investigating Nazi atrocities in Russia, and at the time of his death he was still writing the final part of his trilogy of novels about Peter the Great.

The Empress's Plot (1925), which he co-wrote with Pavel Shchegoleff, was presented in Berlin by Piscator in 1927, and in London by the Stage Society as *Rasputin* in April 1929, adapted from the Russian by Clifford Bax. The cast included Robert Atkins (who also produced the play) as Rasputin. The *Observer* called it 'a play without insight . . . made out of externals', and St John Ervine described it as 'like most

Russian conversation: too long and in places too trivial'. The Lord Chamberlain refused to license the play for public performance because it contained 'too much political talk'.

Sergei Tretiakov (1892–1937)

Graduating from Moscow University in 1916, Tretiakov has been described as one of the earliest post-revolutionary authors to apply a Marxist aesthetic to his playwriting, which was committed not only to revealing but also to changing reality. 'The problem for the playwright', he wrote, 'is to lift the playgoer out of his equilibrium so that he will not leave serene, but ready for action.' A colleague of Mayakovsky on left-wing journals during the twenties, and of Eisenstein and Meyerhold in the theatre, Tretiakov's own plays often combined statistics and propaganda with spectacular performance styles derived more from circus or the fairground than from a Stanislavskian theatre tradition, and were instrumental in the development of agit-prop, with its grotesque caricatures and declamatory style. This style became a significant influence on the development of political theatre, and especially the Workers' Theatre Movement, in much of Europe (including Britain) and in America during the twenties.

Tretiakov's first play was a rewriting of an Ostrovsky text, to which he introduced clowns, acrobats and film, and this was followed by a mass spectacle, *Earth Rampant*, performed in 1923 on the fifth anniversary of the founding of the Red Army, and in the open air to a single audience of 25,000 people at a Moscow Congress the following year. *Roar China*, his best-known play, was written in 1926 and was based on an actual incident which had occurred while Tretiakov was living and working in China during 1924. The first production was directed by Meyerhold, and it was subsequently staged in much of Europe (including Germany, where it was directed by Reinhardt) and America. In style, it was much less obviously challenging to the conventions of established and mainstream theatre than his other plays, though the English translator, Barbara Nixon, pointed out its focus on history rather than on individuals, and its conscious role as propaganda:

> The Russian artist does not make his film or play, and then add the propaganda to suit the public taste. The propagandist idea forms not only the background to, but the essential structure of, his work. In the West we have grown accustomed to artists racking their brains to find a new way of saying the old things—but in Russia . . . there

is everything to say; and this abundance of matter has quite naturally evolved a new method of expression.

In England, *Roar China* was refused a licence in the translation by Barbara Nixon and F. Polianovska which was to have been staged by Herbert Marshall and Terence Gray at the Cambridge Festival Theatre in the spring of 1931. The only British performance was directed by F. Sladin-Smith for the Unnamed Society in Manchester, in November 1931. The text was published in 1931 in a version slightly altered from that submitted for licensing.

Tretiakov's last play, *I Want a Baby* (1926), never received permission for production in the Soviet Union, but it was adapted by Brecht into German. Three of Brecht's own early plays were subsequently translated into Russian by Tretiakov, and Brecht acknowledged Tretiakov's influence on the development of his own epic theatrical techniques, famously referring to him as 'my teacher'. After falling into official disfavour, Tretiakov was arrested by the Soviet authorities and accused of spying, and executed in either 1937 or 1939.

Peter Ustinov (1921–   )

Ustinov is a writer, director, producer and, above all, a performer, who is well known especially for his talent as an impersonator. Though more recently popular on television and in one-man shows for his ability to make audiences laugh through anecdotes and mimicry, he has in the past played major tragic roles, such as King Lear. His acting debut was in Chekhov's *Wood Demon* in 1938, and one of the earliest stage plays he directed was a translation of a Soviet play by Valantin Kataev, *Squaring the Circle*, in its first British production in 1941. *House of Regrets* was his first full-length work as a playwright, and it was performed at the Arts Theatre in October 1942, directed by Alec Clunes and starring Max Adrian. Ustinov has written over twenty stage plays which were regularly performed in mainstream theatres in London and elsewhere, especially during the fifties. He has also written a number of screenplays. His best known play is probably *Romanoff and Juliet* (1956), which he himself turned into a filmscript in 1961. Ustinov has won numerous awards, many of them as a stage and film actor, but also for his work for UNICEF. He was knighted in 1990.

Israel Zangwill (1864–1926)

Born in London, Zangwill wrote plays, novels and philosophical essays and was an active political campaigner, especially on Jewish issues. His first significant piece of writing was *Children of the Ghetto*, a novel published in 1892, which proved to be the first of several explorations of Jewish history, society and culture. He began writing serious drama in 1908 with *The Melting Pot*—a phrase he is often credited with having coined—which celebrated the overcoming of racial and nationalistic differences among immigrants to the United States. *The War God*, staged by Sir Herbert Tree in London in 1911, placed Bismarck and Tolstoy on the stage to argue the merits of pacifism and militarism in blank verse. Zangwill believed passionately in a serious, intellectual theatre, and his other plays included an exploration of the nature of religion, which was banned by the Lord Chamberlain. In political life, Zangwill devoted considerable energies to supporting the struggle to create an area for Jewish settlement, to help the victims of anti-Semitism establish a new existence.

The Forcing House ran at the Little Theatre from 9 February until 20 March 1926, though the text had been published in 1922. In his Introduction, which takes the form of a letter addressed to Maurice Maeterlinck, Zangwill specifically demands the right for the theatre to engage in serious debate, and criticises the 'decay of seriousness in all the arts', which he blames on managers and writers rather than the public. Part of a writer's commitment, insists Zangwill, is to give equal weight to arguments on all sides of the issues being addressed. Unsurprisingly, his writing had a reputation for making considerable demands on its audiences, with the *Sunday Times* referring to the 'mental indigestion' caused by *The Forcing House*, and warning that 'some of the smaller heads in the audience may well be unequal to the challenge'. In its obituary *The Times* suggested that Zangwill's weaknesses as a playwright were 'over-emphasis, rhetoric, and preaching', and also commented that 'as dramatist and politician, his sensitiveness to criticism was excessive and his passion for self-vindication not easily controllable'.

Select Bibliography

Published Playscripts

Afinogenev, Alexander, *Distant Point*, translated and adapted by Hubert Griffith (London: Pushkin Press, 1941).

Davison, John, *Shadows of Strife* (London: J.M. Dent and Sons, 1929).

Dukes, Ashley, *Such Men are Dangerous*, in *Famous Plays of Today* (London: Gollancz, 1929).

Galitzky, Y., *The Cave*, in *Our Time*, 2 (June 1942), 1–9.

Gorki, Maxim, *And the Others*, adapted by Gibson-Cowan (London: Unity Theatre Edition, 1941).

Griffith, Hubert, *Red Sunday* (London: Cayme Press, 1929).

Griffith, Hubert, *The People's Court* (London: Rich and Cowan, 1934).

Hodge, Herbert, and Roberts, Buckland, *Where's that Bomb?* (London: Lawrence and Wishart, 1937).

Kirchon, Vladimir M., and Ouspensky, A.V., *Red Rust* (New York: Rialto Service Bureau, 1929).

Korneichuk, Alexander, *Guerillas Of The Ukranian Steppes*, in *Four Soviet War Plays* (London: Hutchinson, 1944).

Korneichuk, Alexander, *The Front*, in *Four Soviet War Plays* (London: Hutchinson, 1944).

Leonov, Leonid, *Invasion* in *Four Soviet War Plays*, (London: Hutchinson, 1944).

Lucas, Frank L., *The Bear Dances* (London: Cassell, 1934).

Lucas, Frank L., *Land's End*, in F.L. Lucas, *Four Plays* (Cambridge: Cambridge University Press, 1935).

MacNeice, F. Louis, *Salute to all Fools*, in Louis MacNeice, *'The Dark Tower' and Other Radio Scripts* (London: Faber and Faber, 1947).

MacNeice, F. Louis, *The March Hare Resigns*, in Louis MacNeice, *'The Dark Tower' and Other Radio Scripts* (London: Faber and Faber, 1947).

Maltby, H.F., *What Might Happen: A Piece of Extravagance in Three Acts* (London: The Stage Play Publishing Bureau, 1927).

Marshall, Herbert, ed., *Soviet One Act Plays* (London: Pilot Press, 1944).

Monkhouse, Allan *First Blood* (London: Benn, 1924).

Nichols, John Beverley, *When the Crash Comes*, in John Beverley Nichols, *Failures* (London: Jonathan Cape, 1933).

Nikitin, Leo, *Fort Eleven*, in *Our Time*, 2 (August, 1942), 1–7.

O'Casey, Sean, *The Star Turns Red* (London: Macmillan, 1940).

Parsons, Geoffrey, *According to Plan*, in *'The Theatre is Our Weapon . . .': Two One-Act Plays* (London: Russia Today Society, 1941).

Phillpotts, Eden, and Phillpotts, Adelaide, *Yellow Sands* (London: Duckworth, 1926).

Pogodin, Nikolai, *Aristocrats*, in *Four Soviet Plays*, edited by Ben Blake (London: Lawrence and Wishart, 1937).

Porché, François, *Tsar Lénine* (Paris: Flammarion, 1932).

Priestley, J.B., *Bees on the Boat Deck* (London: William Heinemann, 1936).

Shaw, George B., *Annajanska, The Bolshevik Empress*, in Shaw, *'Heartbreak House', 'Great Catherine', and Playlets of the War* (London: Constable, 1919).

Shaw, George B., *Geneva* (London: Constable, 1939).

Simonov, Konstantin *The Russians*, in *Four Soviet War Plays* (London: Hutchinson, 1944).

Slater, Montagu, *An Agreement Of The People*, in *Our Time*, 2 (July 1942), 1–11.

Spender, Stephen, *Trial of a Judge* (London: Faber and Faber, 1938).

Tretiakov, Sergei M., *Roar China*, translated by Barbara Nixon and F. Polianovska (London: Martin Lawrence, 1931).

Ustinov, Peter, *House of Regrets* (London: Jonathan Cape, 1943).

Willis, Ted, [John Bishop] *Erna Kremer of Ebenstadt*, in *'The Theatre is Our Weapon . . .': Two One-Act Plays* (London: Russia Today Society, 1941).

Zangwill, Israel, *The Forcing House* (London: William Heinemann, 1922).

Unpublished Playscripts

N.B. With the exception of the scripts written for radio by Louis MacNeice which are in the BBC Written Archives Centre, or where otherwise stated, all of the following may be consulted in the Lord

Chamberlain's Collections of Licensed and Unlicensed Plays in the Manuscripts section of the British Library.

Allen, John, *Harlequinade*, 1935.

Anonymous, *Crossroads*, 1936.

Anonymous, *Launcelot's Dream*, undated, script shown to me privately.

Anonymous, *Red, Bright and New*, 1943.

Anonymous, *Strike Me Red*, 1940.

Anonymous, *The Volga Boatman*, 1927.

Anonymous, *Utopias Ltd.*, 1936.

Banks, G.G., *The Spectre that Haunts Europe*, 1941.

Barrie, James, *The Truth about the Russian Ballet*, 1926.

Brody, Miksa, and Martos, Franz, *Sybil*, English version by Harry Graham, 1920.

Brooke, A. Edward, *The Bolshevik*, 1919.

Dane, Clemence, *The Terror*, 1921.

Davis, Major C.T., *The Silver Lining*, 1921.

DeGray, Geo. A., *The Russian Monk*, 1918.

de Lorde, André, and Bauche, Henri, *Red Nights of the Tcheka*, 1927.

Grahame, R., *The Bolshevik Peril: A short drama for today*, 1919.

Grubinski, Waclaw, *Lenin*, translated by Florian Sobieniowski and E.A. Pearson, 1921. (Translation 1929?). The script is in the Polish Library, London.

Hutchinson, H. Ernest, *The Right to Strike*, 1920.

Hutchinson, Robert, *Reparation*, 1918.

Janis, Elsie, *It's All Wrong*, 1920.

Lengyel, Melchior, and Biro, Ludwig, *The Czarina*, 1925.

McLeod, Alison, Tuckett, Joan, and Carpenter, Miles, *Over to You*, 1943.

MacNeice, Louis, *Alexander Nevsky*, 1941.

MacNeice, Louis, *Salute to the New Year*, 1941.

MacNeice, Louis, *Salute to the Red Army*, 1943. In the unpublished Cabinet Papers Foreign Office File 371—1943: Soviet Union File No. 186. Reference 36973, in the Public Records Office, Kew.

MacNeice, Louis, *Salute to the U.S.S.R.*, 1942.

MacNeice, Louis, *Sunbeams in his Hat*, 1944.

MacNeice, Louis, *The Spirit of Russia*, 1943.

MacNeice, Louis, *We are Advancing*, 1943.

Maltby, H.F., *The Red Light*, 1931.

Merezkovsky, Dmitry, *Paul I*, translated and adapted by John Alford and James Dale, 1927.

National Council for British–Soviet Unity, *Alliance for Victory*, 1943.

Page, Austin, *The Beating on the Door*, 1922.

Parsons, Geoffrey, and Mitchell, Robert, *Babes in the Wood*, 1938.

Podmore, C.T., *Labour on Top*, 1926.

Porché, François, *Tsar Lenin*, Translated by Ossia Trilling and Emanuel Wax, 1933.

Ross, Alexander Carton, *Russian Roundabout*, 1937.

Savoir, Alfred, *The Grand Duchess*, translated and adapted by Harry Graham, 1925.

Sheynin, Tour, and Sheynin, L., *Comrade Detective*, 1944.

Tolstoy, A.N., and Shchegoleff, P.E., *Rasputin*, translated by Clifford Bax, 1929.

Unity Theatre Collective, *Crisis*, 1938.

Wallace, G. Carlton, *Joan of the Sword*, 1919.

Walsh, Shiela, *The Volga Boatman* (2nd version), 1929.

Secondary Material
The following books and articles are amongst those of particular value and/or relevance:

Addison, Paul, *The Road to 1945* (London: Cape, 1977).

Allen, Victor L., *The Russians Are Coming: The Politics of Anti-Sovietism* (Shipley: Moor Press, 1987).

Arnot, R. Page, *The Impact of the Russian Revolution in Britain* (London: Lawrence and Wishart, 1967).

Bell, Thomas, *The British Communist Party: A Short History* (London: Lawrence and Wishart, 1937).

Bilainkin, George, *Maisky* (London: G. Allen and Unwin, 1944).

Birch, Francis L., *This Freedom of Ours* (Cambridge: Cambridge University Press, 1937).

Blythe, Ronald, *The Age of Illusion: England in the Twenties and Thirties, 1919–1940* (London: Hamish Hamilton, 1963).

Branson, Noreen, and Heinemann, Margot, *Britain in the Nineteen Thirties* (London: Weidenfeld and Nicolson, 1971).

Brewster, Dorothy, *East–West Passage* (London: G. Allen and Unwin, 1954).

Briggs, Asa, *The History of Broadcasting in the United Kingdom; Volume III: The War of Words* (London: Oxford University Press, 1970).

Buxton, Dorothy, *The Challenge Of Bolshevism* (London: G. Allen and Unwin, 1928).

Calder, Angus, *The People's War: Britain 1939–45* (London: Jonathan Cape, 1969).

Campbell, Mrs Patrick, *My Life and Some Letters* (London: Hutchinson, 1922).

Carter, Huntley, *The New Spirit in the European Theatre 1914–1924* (London: Benn, 1925).

Challinor, Raymond, *The Origins of British Bolshevism* (London: Croom Helm, 1977).

Chambers, Colin, *The Story of Unity Theatre* (London: Lawrence and Wishart, 1989).

Chothia, Jean, *English Drama of the Early Modern Period 1890–1940* (London: Longman, 1996).

Clark, Jon; Heinemann, Margot; Margolies, David; Snee, Carol, eds, *Culture and Crisis in Britain in the Thirties* (London: Lawrence and Wishart, 1979).

Coulton, Barbara, *Louis MacNeice in the BBC* (London: Faber, 1980).

Cross, Anthony G., *The Russian Theme in English Literature* (Oxford: Oxford University Press, 1985).

Cunningham, Valentine, *British Writers of the Thirties* (Oxford: Oxford University Press, 1988).

Curran, James, and Seaton, Jean, *Power without Responsibility: The Press and Broadcasting in Britain* (London: Fontana, 1981).

Davies, Andrew, 'A theatre for a People's Army?: The story of the ABCA Play Unit', *Red Letters*, 13, 1982.

Davies, Andrew, *Other Theatres: The Development of Alternative and Experimental Theatre in Britain* (Basingstoke: Macmillan Education, 1987).

Dawson, Jerry, *Left Theatre: Merseyside Unity Theatre* (Liverpool: Merseyside Writers, 1985).

Dean, Basil, *The Theatre at War* (London: Harrap, 1956).

Dewar, Hugo, *Communist Politics in Britain* (London: Pluto Press, 1976).

Edwards, Ness, *The Workers' Theatre* (Cardiff: Cymric Federation Press, 1930).

Ervine, St John, *The Theatre in My Time* (London: Rich and Cowan, 1933).

Ettlinger, Amrei, and Gladstone, Joan, *Russian Literature, Theatre and Art: A Bibliography of Works in English Published 1900–1945* (London: Hutchinson, 1947).

Gloversmith, Frank, ed., *Class, Culture and Social Change: A New View of the 1930s* (Brighton: Harvester Press, 1980).

Gollancz, Victor, ed., *The Betrayal of the Left* (London: Victor Gollancz, 1941).

Goorney, Howard, and MacColl, Ewan, eds, *Agit-Prop to Theatre Workshop* (Manchester: Manchester University Press, 1986).

Graubard, Stephen Richards, *British Labour and the Russian Revolution 1917–1924* (London: Oxford University Press, 1956).

Graves, Robert, and Hodge, Allan, *The Long Weekend: A Social History of Great Britain 1918–1939* (London: Four Square Books, 1961).

Grierson, Philip, *Books on Soviet Russia, 1917–1942: A Bibliography and a Guide to Reading* (London: Methuen, 1943).

Griffith, Hubert, *Playtime in Russia* (London: Methuen, 1935).

Griffith, Hubert, *Seeing Soviet Russia* (London: John Lane, 1932).

Harrisson, Tom, 'Public opinion about Russia', *Political Quarterly*, 12 (no. 4, 1941).

Hewison, Robert, *Under Siege: Literary Life in London 1939–1945* (London: Weidenfeld and Nicolson, 1977).

Hogenkamp, Bert, *Deadly Parallels: Film and the Left in Britain 1929–39* (London: Lawrence and Wishart, 1986).

Hoskins, Katharine Bail, *Today the Struggle: Literature and Politics in England during the Spanish Civil War* (Austin and London: University of Texas Press, 1969).

Hynes, Samuel, *The Auden Generation—Literature and Politics in England in the 1930s* (London: Bodley Head, 1976).

Jackson, T.A., *Solo Trumpet. Some Memories of Socialist Agitation and Propaganda* (London: Lawrence and Wishart, 1953).

Johnston, John, *The Lord Chamberlain's Blue Pencil* (London: Methuen, 1990).

Kemp, Harry, et al., *The Left Heresy in Literature and Life* (London: Methuen, 1939).

Kendall, Walter, *The Revolutionary Movement in Britain 1900–1921: The Origins of British Communism* (London: Weidenfeld and Nicolson, 1969).

Klugmann, James, *History of the Communist Party of Great Britain* (London: Lawrence and Wishart, 1968).

Knightley, Phillip, *The First Casualty* (London: Deutsch, 1975).

Knowles, Dorothy, *The Censor, The Drama and The Film, 1900–1934* (London: G. Allen and Unwin, 1934).

Leach, Robert, *Revolutionary Theatre* (London: Routledge, 1994).

Lion, Leon M., *The Surprise of My Life* (London: Hutchinson, 1948).

Loveman, Jack, 'Workers' Theatre: Personal recollections of political theatre in Greenwich during the 1920s and 1930s', *Red Letters*, 13, 1982.

Lucas, John, ed., *The 1930s: A Challenge to Orthodoxy* (Sussex: Harvester Press, 1978).

Lyons, Eugene, *Assignment in Utopia* (London: G.G. Harrap, 1938).

Macfarlane, L.J., *The British Communist Party. Its Origin and Development until 1929* (London: MacGibbon and Kee, 1966).

Macintyre, Stuart, *A Proletarian Science: Marxism in Britain 1917–1933* (Cambridge: Cambridge University Press, 1980).

McLaine, Ian, *Ministry of Morale: Home Front Morale and the Ministry of Information in World War II* (London: G. Allen and Unwin, 1979).

Maisky, Ivan, *Memoirs of a Soviet Ambassador: The War 1939–1943* (London: Hutchinson, 1967).

Maltby, H.F., *Ring Up The Curtain* (London: Hutchinson & Co., 1950).

Marshall, Norman, *The Other Theatre* (London: John Lehmann, 1947).

Miller, Anna Irene, *The Independent Theatre in Europe: 1887 to the Present* (New York: R. Long and R.R. Smith, 1931).

Mowat, Charles Loch, *Britain Between the Wars, 1918–1940* (London: Methuen, 1955).

Nicholson, Steve, 'Montagu Slater and theatre of the thirties' in Patrick Quinn (ed.) *Re-Charting the Thirties* (London: Associated University Presses, 1996).

Nicholson, Steve, ' "Irritating tricks": Aesthetic experimentation and political theatre' in Keith Williams and Steven Matthews (eds), *Rewriting the Thirties: Modernism and After* (London: Longman, 1997).

Nicoll, Allardyce, *English Drama 1900–1930: The Beginnings of the Modern Period* (Cambridge: Cambridge University Press, 1973).

Northedge, F.S., and Wells, Audrey, *Britain and Soviet Communism: The Impact of a Revolution* (London: Macmillan, 1982).

O'Casey, Sean, *The Letters of Sean O'Casey, 1910–1941, Volume I* (London: Macmillan, 1975).

O'Reilly, Kenneth, '*The Times* of London and the Bolshevik revolution', *Journalism Quarterly* (1979, Part 56), 69–76.

Rabey, David Ian, *British and Irish Political Drama in the Twentieth Century* (Basingstoke: Macmillan, 1986).

Rain, G.E., and Luboff, E., *Bolshevik Russia* (London: Nisbit, 1920).

Rees, G., 'Politics on the London stage', *Penguin New Writing*, Spring 1939, edited by J. Lehmann (London: Penguin, 1939).

Rickword, Edgell, *Nothing is Lost: Anne Lindsay 1914–1954* (London: Communist Party Writers Group, 1954).

Samuel, Raphael; MacColl, Ewan; Cosgrove, Stuart, *Theatres of the Left 1880–1935* (London: Routledge and Kegan Paul, 1985).

Sayers, Michael, and Khan, Albert E., *The Great Conspiracy against Russia* (New York: Boni and Gaer, 1946).

Schillinger, Elisabeth H., 'British and U.S. newspaper coverage of the Bolshevik revolution', *Journalism Quarterly* (Spring 1966).

Seldes, George, *World Panorama 1918–1933* (London: Hamish Hamilton, 1933).

Shaw, G.B., *The Prefaces* (London: Constable, 1934).

Sidnell, Michael, *Dances of Death: The Group Theatre of London in the Thirties* (London: Faber, 1984).

Smith, David, *Socialist Propaganda in the Twentieth-Century British Novel* (London: Macmillan, 1978).

Spender, Stephen, *Life and the Poet* (London: Secker and Warburg, 1942).

Stourac, Richard, and McCreery, Kathleen, *Theatre as a Weapon: Workers' Theatre in the Soviet Union, Germany and Britain, 1917–1934* (London: Routledge and Kegan Paul, 1986).

Symons, Julian, *The Thirties: A Dream Revolved* (London: Cresset Press, 1960).

Taylor, A.J.P., *English History 1914–1945* (Oxford: Clarendon Press, 1965).

Times, The, *The History of The Times; Volume 4: The 150th Anniversary and Beyond, 1912–1948* (London: Published at the Office of The Times, 1952).

Toynbee, Arnold J., ed., *The Impact of the Russian Revolution 1917–1967: The Influence of Bolshevism on the World Outside Russia* (London: Oxford University Press, 1967).

Trewin, John Courtenay, *The Turbulent Thirties—A Further Decade of the Theatre* (London: Macdonald, 1960).

Van Gyseghem, André, *Theatre in Soviet Russia* (London: Faber and Faber, 1943).

Veitch, Norman, *The People's: Being a History of the People's Theatre*

Newcastle Upon Tyne 1911–1939 (Gateshead: Northumberland Press, 1950).

Wearing, J.P., *The London Stage 1920–1929: a Calendar of Plays and Players* (London The Scarecrow Press Inc., 1984).

Wearing, J.P., *The London Stage 1930–1939: a Calendar of Plays and Players* (London: The Scarecrow Press Inc., 1990).

Wearing, J.P., *The London Stage 1940–1949: a Calendar of Plays and Players* (London: The Scarecrow Press Inc., 1991).

Wood, Neal, *Communism and British Intellectuals* (London: Victor Gollancz, 1959).

Woodfield, James, *English Theatre in Transition, 1881–1914* (Beckenham: Croom Helm, 1984).

Zangwill, Israel, *Hands off Russia* (London: Workers' Socialist Federation, 1919).

The following have been among the most useful publications for theatre reviews, articles about the theatre, and contemporary historical analysis:

The Times, Daily Worker, Manchester Guardian, Our Time, Left Review, Stage Year Book, the festival theatre review. New Statesman and Nation, Stage, Saturday Review, Era, Observer, Illustrated London News, Nation and Athenaeum, Night and Day.

The following two archives have both been used extensively:

The Theatre Museum (Covent Garden) for Production Files.

The Manuscript Department of the British Library for the Lord Chamberlain's Correspondence Files and for scripts of unpublished plays.

The following unpublished dissertations are also relevant:

Florance, John, 'Theatrical Censorship in Britain 1901–1968', Ph.D. dissertation, University of Wales, 1980.

Jones, Len, 'The British Workers' Theatre 1917–1935', Ph.D. dissertation, University of Leipzig, 1964.

Saville, Ian, 'Ideas, Forms and Developments in the British Workers' Theatre, 1929–1935', Ph.D. dissertation, The City University, 1990.

Travis, Ron, 'The Unity Theatre of Great Britain 1936–1946', dissertation, University of Southern Illinois, 1968.

Watson, Don, 'British Socialist Theatre 1930–1979: Class, Politics and Dramatic Form', Ph.D. dissertation, University of Hull, 1985.

Index